North Carolina High School Algebra I

A Comprehensive Review and Step-by-Step Guide to Mastering Algebra 1

By

Reza Nazari

Published by: **Effortless Math Education**

for Online Math Practice Visit www.EffortlessMath.com

Welcome to
North Carolina High School Algebra I Prep 2024

Thank you for choosing Effortless Math for your High School Algebra I preparation and congratulations on making the decision to take the High School Algebra I course! It's a remarkable move you are taking, one that shouldn't be diminished in any capacity.

That's why you need to use every tool possible to ensure you succeed on the test with the highest possible score, and this extensive study guide is one such tool.

North Carolina High School Algebra I is designed to be comprehensive and cover all the topics that are typically covered in a High School Algebra I course. It provides clear explanations and examples of the concepts and includes practice problems and quizzes to test your understanding of the material. The textbook also provides step-by-step solutions to the problems, so you can check your work and understand how to solve similar problems on your own.

Additionally, this textbook is written in a user-friendly way, making it easy to follow and understand even if you have struggled with math in the past. It also includes a variety of visual aids such as diagrams, graphs, and charts to help you better understand the concepts.

North Carolina High School Algebra I is flexible and can be used to supplement a traditional classroom setting, or as a standalone resource for self-study. With the help of this comprehensive textbook, you will have the necessary foundation to master the material and succeed in the High School Algebra I course.

Effortless Math's High School Algebra I Online Center

Effortless Math Online High School Algebra I Center offers a complete study program, including the following:

✓ Step-by-step instructions on how to prepare for the Algebra I test

✓ Numerous Algebra I worksheets to help you measure your math skills

✓ Video lessons for all High School Algebra I topics

✓ Full-length Algebra I practice tests

✓ And much more…

No Registration Required.

Visit **EffortlessMath.com/Algebra1** to find your online Algebra I resources.

North Carolina Algebra I Review

In North Carolina, students take the Common Core State Standards (CCSS) exams, which are standardized assessments designed to evaluate their proficiency in English Language Arts (ELA) and Mathematics. These exams are based on the CCSS, a unified set of educational benchmarks aimed at ensuring all students across the United States receive a consistent and high-quality education from kindergarten through 12th grade.

The Common Core tests, also known as assessments or exams, are intended to evaluate students' progress towards meeting the standards and to provide valuable feedback to teachers, schools, and districts about areas for improvement. The tests are typically administered annually and are used to measure student achievement, identify areas where students may be struggling, and help inform instruction.

There are two primary consortia of states that have developed Common Core-aligned assessments: the Smarter Balanced Assessment Consortium (SBAC) and the Partnership for Assessment of Readiness for College and Careers (PARCC). Each consortium has created its own unique assessments that are designed to measure students' understanding of the Common Core State Standards in both ELA and Mathematics.

While the Common Core tests have been widely adopted across the United States, they have also faced criticism from some educators, parents, and policymakers who argue that the assessments place too much emphasis on standardized testing and may not accurately reflect the full range of students' abilities and learning needs. Some states have chosen to develop their own assessments or have opted out of using the Common Core-aligned tests altogether.

Number and Quantity	
The Real Number System	**N. RN**

Extend the properties of exponents to rational exponents.

MGSE9 − 12. N. RN. 2 Rewrite expressions involving radicals (i.e., simplify and/or use the operations of addition, subtraction, and multiplication, with radicals within expressions limited to square roots).

Use properties of rational and irrational numbers.

MGSE9 − 12. N. RN. 3 Explain why the sum or product of rational numbers is rational; why the sum of a rational number and an irrational number is irrational; and why the product of a nonzero rational number and an irrational number is irrational.

Quantities	**N. Q.**

Reason quantitatively and use units to solve problems.

MGSE9 − 12. N. Q. 1 Use units of measure (linear, area, capacity, rates, and time) as a way to understand problems:

 a. Identify, use, and record appropriate units of measure within context, within data displays, and on graphs;
 b. Convert units and rates using dimensional analysis (English-to-English and Metric-to-Metric without conversion factor provided and between English and Metric with conversion factor);
 c. Use units within multi-step problems and formulas; interpret units of input and resulting units of output.

MGSE9 − 12. N. Q. 2 Define appropriate quantities for the purpose of descriptive modeling. Given a situation, context, or problem, students will determine, identify, and use appropriate quantities for representing the situation.

MGSE9 − 12. N. Q. 3 Choose a level of accuracy appropriate to limitations on measurement when reporting quantities.

Algebra	
Seeing Structure in Expressions	**A. SSE**

Interpret the structure of expressions.

MGSE9 − 12. A. SSE. 1 Interpret expressions that represent a quantity in terms of its context.

 MGSE9 − 12. A. SSE. 1a Interpret parts of an expression, such as terms, factors, and coefficients, in context.

 MGSE9 − 12. A. SSE. 1b Given situations which utilize formulas or expressions with multiple terms and/or factors, interpret the meaning (in context) of individual terms or factors.

MGSE9 − 12. A. SSE. 2 Use the structure of an expression to rewrite it in different equivalent forms.

Write expressions in equivalent forms to solve problems.

MGSE9 − 12. A. SSE. 3 Choose and produce an equivalent form of an expression to reveal and explain properties of the quantity represented by the expression.

> **MGSE9 − 12. A. SSE. 3a** Factor any quadratic expression to reveal the zeros of the function defined by the expression.

> **MGSE9 − 12. A. SSE. 3b** Complete the square in a quadratic expression to reveal the maximum and minimum value of the function defined by the expression.

Arithmetic with Polynomials and Rational Expressions   **A. APR**

Perform arithmetic operations on polynomials.

MGSE9 − 12. A. APR. 1 Add, subtract, and multiply polynomials; understand that polynomials form a system analogous to the integers in that they are closed under these operations.

Creating Equations   **A. CED**

Create equations that describe numbers or relationships.

MGSE9 − 12. A. CED. 1 Create equations and inequalities in one variable and use them to solve problems. Include equations arising from linear, quadratic, and exponential functions (integer inputs only).

MGSE9 − 12. A. CED. 2 Create linear, quadratic, and exponential equations in two or more variables to represent relationships between quantities; graph equations on coordinate axes with labels and scales. (The phrase "in two or more variables" refers to formulas like the compound interest formula, in which $A = P(1 + r/n)^{nt}$ has multiple variables.)

MGSE9 − 12. A. CED. 3 Represent constraints by equations or inequalities, and by systems of equations and/or inequalities, and interpret data points as possible (i.e. a solution) or not possible (i.e. a non-solution) under the established constraints.

MGSE9 − 12. A. CED. 4 Rearrange formulas to highlight a quantity of interest, using the same reasoning as in solving equations.

Reasoning with Equations and Inequalities   **A. REI**

Understand solving equations as a process of reasoning and explain the reasoning.

MGSE9 − 12. A. REI. 1 Using algebraic properties and the properties of real numbers, justify the steps of a simple, one-solution equation. Students should justify their own steps, or if given two or more steps of an equation, explain the progression from one step to the next using properties.

Solve equations and inequalities in one variable.

MGSE9 − 12. A. REI. 3 Solve linear equations and inequalities in one variable, including equations with coefficients represented by letters. For example, given ax + 3 = 7, solve for x.

MGSE9 − 12. A. REI. 4 Solve quadratic equations in one variable.

MGSE9 − 12. A. REI. 4a Use the method of completing the square to transform any quadratic equation in x into an equation of the form $(x - p)^2 = q$ that has the same solutions. Derive the quadratic formula from $ax^2 + bx + c = 0$.

MGSE9 − 12. A. REI. 4b Solve quadratic equations by inspection (e.g., for $x^2 = 49$), taking square roots, factoring, completing the square, and the quadratic formula, as appropriate to the initial form of the equation (limit to real number solutions).

Solve systems of equations.

MGSE9 − 12. A. REI. 5 Show and explain why the elimination method works to solve a system of two-variable equations.

MGSE9 − 12. A. REI. 6 Solve systems of linear equations exactly and approximately (e.g., with graphs), focusing on pairs of linear equations in two variables.

Represent and solve equations and inequalities graphically.

MGSE9 − 12. A. REI. 10 Understand that the graph of an equation in two variables is the set of all its solutions plotted in the coordinate plane.

MGSE9 − 12. A. REI. 11 Using graphs, tables, or successive approximations, show that the solution to the equation $f(x) = g(x)$ is the x-value where the y-values of $f(x)$ and $g(x)$ are the same.

MGSE9 − 12. A. REI. 12 Graph the solution set to a linear inequality in two variables.

Functions

Interpreting Functions   **F. IF**

Understand the concept of a function and use function notation.

MGSE9 − 12. F. IF. 1 Understand that a function from one set (the input, called the domain) to another set (the output, called the range) assigns to each element of the domain exactly one element of the range, i.e., each input value maps to exactly one output value. If f is a function, and x is the input (an element of the domain), then $f(x)$ is the output (an element of the range). Graphically, the graph is $y = f(x)$.

MGSE9 − 12. F. IF. 2 Use function notation, evaluate functions for inputs in their domains, and interpret statements that use function notation in terms of a context.

MGSE9 − 12. F. IF. 3 Recognize that sequences are functions, sometimes defined recursively, whose domain is a subset of the integers. (Generally, the scope of high school math defines this subset as the set of natural numbers 1, 2, 3, 4, …) By graphing or calculating terms, students should be able to show how the recursive sequence $a_1 = 7, a_n = a_n - 1 + 2$; the sequence $s_n = 2(n - 1) + 7$; and the function $f(x) = 2x + 5$ (when x is a natural number) all define the same sequence.

Interpret functions that arise in applications in terms of the context.

MGSE9 − 12. F. IF. 4 Using tables, graphs, and verbal descriptions, interpret the key characteristics of a function which models the relationship between two quantities. Sketch a graph showing key features including intercepts; interval where the function is increasing, decreasing, positive, or negative; relative maximums and minimums; symmetries; end behavior; and periodicity.

MGSE9 − 12. F. IF. 5 Relate the domain of a function to its graph and, where applicable, to the quantitative relationship it describes.

MGSE9 − 12. F. IF. 6 Calculate and interpret the average rate of change of a function (presented symbolically or as a table) over a specified interval. Estimate the rate of change from a graph.

Analyze functions using different representations.

MGSE9 − 12. F. IF. 7 Graph functions expressed algebraically and show key features of the graph both by hand and by using technology.

> **MGSE9 − 12. F. IF. 7a** Graph linear and quadratic functions and show intercepts, maxima, and minima (as determined by the function or by context).

> **MGSE9 − 12. F. IF. 7e** Graph exponential and logarithmic functions, showing intercepts and end behavior.

MGSE9 − 12. F. IF. 8 Write a function defined by an expression in different but equivalent forms to reveal and explain different properties of the function.

> **MGSE9 − 12. F. IF. 8a** Use the process of factoring and completing the square in a quadratic function to show zeros, extreme values, and symmetry of the graph, and interpret these in terms of a context.

MGSE9 − 12. F. IF. 9 Compare properties of two functions each represented in a different way (algebraically, graphically, numerically in tables, or by verbal descriptions).

Building Functions   **F − BF**

Build a function that models a relationship between two quantities.

MGSE9 − 12. F. BF. 1 Write a function that describes a relationship between two quantities.

> **MGSE9 − 12. F. BF. 1a** Determine an explicit expression and the recursive process (steps for calculation) from context.

MGSE9 − 12. F. BF. 2 Write arithmetic and geometric sequences both recursively and explicitly, use them to model situations, and translate between the two forms. Connect arithmetic sequences to linear functions and geometric sequences to exponential functions.

Build new functions from existing functions.

MGSE9 − 12. F. BF. 3 Identify the effect on the graph of replacing $f(x)$ by $f(x) + k, k\, f(x), f(kx)$, and $f(x + k)$ for specific values of k (both positive and negative); find the value of k given the graphs. Experiment with cases and illustrate an explanation of the effects on the graph using technology. Include recognizing even and odd functions from their graphs and algebraic expressions for them.

Linear, Quadratic, and Exponential Models	F. LE

Construct and compare linear, quadratic, and exponential models and solve problems.

MGSE9 − 12. F. LE. 1 Distinguish between situations that can be modeled with linear functions and with exponential functions.

> **MGSE9 − 12. F. LE. 1a** Show that linear functions grow by equal differences over equal intervals and that exponential functions grow by equal factors over equal intervals. (This can be shown by algebraic proof, with a table showing differences, or by calculating average rates of change over equal intervals).

> **MGSE9 − 12. F. LE. 1b**. Recognize situations in which one quantity changes at a constant rate per unit interval relative to another.

> **MGSE9 − 12. F. LE. 1c** Recognize situations in which a quantity grows or decays by a constant percent rate per unit interval relative to another.

MGSE9 − 12. F. LE. 2 Construct linear and exponential functions, including arithmetic and geometric sequences, given a graph, a description of a relationship, or two input-output pairs (include reading these from a table).

MGSE9 − 12. F. LE. 3 Observe using graphs and tables that a quantity increasing exponentially eventually exceeds a quantity increasing linearly, quadratically, or (more generally) as a polynomial function.

Interpret expressions for functions in terms of the situation they model.

MGSE9 − 12. F. LE. 5 Interpret the parameters in a linear ($f(x) = mx + b$) and exponential ($f(x) = a \cdot d^x$) function in terms of a context. (In the functions above, "m" and "b" are the parameters of the linear function, and "a" and "d" are the parameters of the exponential function.) In context, students should describe what these parameters mean in terms of change and starting value.

Statistics and Probability	
Interpreting Categorical and Quantitative Data	S. ID

Summarize, represent, and interpret data on a single count or measurement variable.

MGSE9 − 12. S. ID. 1 Represent data with plots on the real number line (dot plots, histograms, and box plots).

*MGSE*9 − 12. *S. ID.* 2 Use statistics appropriate to the shape of the data distribution to compare center (median, mean) and spread (interquartile range, mean absolute deviation) of two or more different data sets.

MGSE9 – 12. S. ID. 3 Interpret differences in shape, center, and spread in the context of the data sets, accounting for possible effects of extreme data points (outliers).

Summarize, represent, and interpret data on two categorical and quantitative variables.

MGSE9 – 12. S. ID. 5 Summarize categorical data for two categories in two-way frequency tables. Interpret relative frequencies in the context of the data (including joint, marginal, and conditional relative frequencies). Recognize possible associations and trends in the data.

MGSE9 – 12. S. ID. 6 Represent data on two quantitative variables on a scatter plot and describe how the variables are related.

> **MGSE9 – 12. S. ID. 6a** Decide which type of function is most appropriate by observing graphed data, charted data, or by analysis of context to generate a viable (rough) function of best fit. Use this function to solve problems in context. Emphasize linear, quadratic and exponential models.

> **MGSE9 – 12. S. ID. 6c** Using given or collected bivariate data, fit a linear function for a scatter plot that suggests a linear association.

Interpret linear models.

MGSE9 – 12. S. ID. 7 Interpret the slope (rate of change) and the intercept (constant term) of a linear model in the context of the data.

MGSE9 – 12. S. ID. 8 Compute (using technology) and interpret the correlation coefficient "r" of a linear fit. (For instance, by looking at a scatterplot, students should be able to tell if the correlation coefficient is positive or negative and give a reasonable estimate of the "r" value.) After calculating the line of best fit using technology, students should be able to describe how strong the goodness of fit of the regression is, using "r".

MGSE9 – 12. S. ID. 9 Distinguish between correlation and causation.

Contents

Chapter: **Inequalities and System of Equations** 97

Chapter: **Quadratic** 131

CHAPTER

1 Integers and Order of Operations

Math topics that you'll learn in this chapter:

- ☑ Adding and Subtracting Integers
- ☑ Multiplying and Dividing Integers
- ☑ Translate a Phrase into an Algebraic Statement
- ☑ Order of Operations
- ☑ Integers and Absolute Value
- ☑ Percent Problems
- ☑ Percent of Increase and Decrease
- ☑ Discount, Tax, and Tip
- ☑ Simple Interest
- ☑ The Distributive Property

Adding and Subtracting Integers

Integers are a set of numbers that include zero, counting numbers, and the negative versions of counting numbers. They can be represented on a number line as $\{\dots, -3, -2, -1, 0, 1, 2, 3, \dots\}$.

To add a positive integer, move to the right on the number line, which will result in a larger number.

To add a negative integer, move to the left on the number line, which will result in a smaller number. To subtract an integer, add its opposite.

Number line

Adding integers: When adding integers, the signs of the numbers being added determine the overall sign of the result.

- If both numbers have the same sign (both positive or both negative), add their absolute values and give the result the same sign as the numbers being added.

- If the numbers have different signs (one positive and one negative), subtract the absolute value of the smaller number from the absolute value of the larger number and give the result the same sign as the larger number.

Let's review some examples of adding integers:

- $2 + 3 = 5$ (Both numbers are positive)

- $-4 + (-2) = -6$ (Both numbers are negative)

- $5 + (-3) = 2$ (5 is positive and -3 is negative, so we subtract the absolute value of -3 from 5 and the result is positive)

Subtracting integers: When subtracting integers, it is the same as adding the opposite of the number being subtracted. To subtract a positive number, add its opposite (negative) To subtract a negative number, add its opposite (positive)

Let's review some examples of subtracting integers:

- $5 - 2 = 3$ (Same as $5 + (-2)$)

- $-2 - (-5) = 3$ (Same as $-2 + 5$)

- $7 - (-3) = 10$ (Same as $7 + 3$)

Consider another example: Solve. $6 + (3 - 12) =$

First, subtract the numbers in brackets, $3 - 12 = -9$.

Then: $6 + (-9) = \rightarrow$ change addition into subtraction: $6 - 9 = -3$.

Let's do another example together: Solve. $(-4) - (-7) =$

Keep the first number and convert the sign of the second number to its opposite.

Change subtraction into addition.

Then: $(-4) + 7 = 3$.

✎ Find each sum or difference.

1) $9 + (-4) =$

2) $(-2 + 6) - (1 - 5) =$

3) $-7 + 9 =$

4) $4 + (-4 - 2) =$

5) $(-4 + 2) - 8 =$

6) $(-14) - (-19) =$

7) $2 + (-3 + 2) - 1 =$

8) $3 - (-11 - 3) =$

9) $(-7 + 9) - 39 =$

10) $(8 - 19) - (-4 + 12) =$

bit.ly/3aKx5vl

Find more at

Multiplying and Dividing Integers

When multiplying and dividing integers, the signs of the numbers being multiplied determine the overall sign of the result.

- If both numbers are positive, the result will be positive.
- If both numbers are negative, the result will be positive.
- If one number is positive and the other is negative, the result will be negative.

Use the following rules for multiplying and dividing integers:

- $(negative) \times (negative) = positive$
- $(negative) \div (negative) = positive$
- $(negative) \times (positive) = negative$
- $(negative) \div (positive) = negative$
- $(positive) \times (positive) = positive$
- $(positive) \div (negative) = negative$

Multiplying integers: When multiplying integers, the signs of the numbers being multiplied determine the overall sign of the result.

- If both numbers are positive, the result will be positive.
- If both numbers are negative, the result will be positive.
- If one number is positive and the other is negative, the result will be negative.

Let's review some examples of multiplying integers:

- $2 \times 3 = 6$ (Both numbers are positive)
- $-2 \times (-5) = 10$ (Both numbers are negative)
- $2 \times (-5) = -10$ (One number is positive, the other is negative)

Dividing integers: When dividing integers, the signs of the numbers being divided determine the overall sign of the result.

- If both numbers are positive, the result will be positive.
- If both numbers are negative, the result will be positive.
- If the dividend (the number being divided) is positive and the divisor (the number doing the dividing) is negative, the result will be negative.
- If the dividend is negative and the divisor is positive, the result will be negative.

Dividing integers:

- $\frac{8}{4} = 2$ (Both numbers are positive)
- $\frac{-8}{-4} = 2$ (Both numbers are negative)
- $\frac{8}{-4} = -2$ (The dividend is positive; the divisor is negative)
- $\frac{-8}{4} = -2$ (The dividend is negative; the divisor is positive)

It's important to note that when dividing integers if the result is not a whole number, it will be expressed as a fraction or decimal. It's also important to pay attention to the rules of the algebra and not mix the signs and operations.

✎ Solve.

11) $(3 - 9) \div (-3) =$

12) $-25 \times (-3 + 1) =$

13) $(-4) \times 3 \times (-2) =$

14) $(-49) \div (-7) =$

15) $2 \times (-5) =$

16) $(-5) \times 6 =$

17) $(-63) \div (15 - 6) =$

18) $(-32) \times (-1) \div (-4) =$

19) $(-15) \div (-17 + 12) =$

20) $(-64) \div (-16 + 8) =$

Translate a Phrase into an Algebraic Statement

An algebraic statement is a mathematical sentence that uses variables and operations (such as $+$, $-$, $\times$, $\div$) to express a relationship or equality. To translate a phrase into an algebraic statement, you can identify the variables and operations in the phrase and write them out using mathematical symbols.

Let's review some examples:

- The phrase "the product of *a* number and 3 is 12" can be translated into the algebraic statement:

$$a \times 3 = 12$$

  Where "*a*" is the variable representing the number, and "$\times$" represents multiplication, and "$=$" represents equality.

- The phrase "the sum of *a* number and 4 is equal to 10" can be translated into the algebraic statement:

$$a + 4 = 10$$

- Where "*a*" is the variable representing the number, and "$+$" represents addition, and "$=$" represents equality.

In general, phrases like "the difference between two numbers" can be translated into an algebraic statement using the subtraction operator "$-$" and "the quotient of two numbers" can be translated into an algebraic statement using the division operator "$\div$".

Translating keywords and phrases into algebraic expressions:

- Addition: plus, more than, the sum of, etc.

- Subtraction: minus, less than, decreased, etc.

- Multiplication: times, product, multiplied, etc.

- Division: quotient, divided, ratio, etc.

bit.ly/3suDB1V

Find more at

To better understand the issue, let's translate some expressions into algebraic expressions:

8 more than a number is 45.

More than mean plus a number $+x$.

Then: $8 + x = 45$.

17 times the sum of 3 and x.

The sum of 3 and x: $3 + x$. Times means multiplication. Then: $17 \times (3 + x) = 17(3 + x)$.

Three more than a number is 19.

"More than" means plus. "a number" is x.

Then: $3 + x = 19$.

16 times the sum of 5 and x.

The sum of 5 and x: $5 + x$. Times means multiplication.

Then: $16 \times (5 + x) = 16(5 + x)$.

Seven more than a number is 28.

"More than" means plus. "a number" is x.

Then: $7 + x = 28$.

25 times the sum of 1 and x.

The sum of 1 and x: $1 + x$. Times means multiplication.

Then: $25 \times (1 + x) = 25(1 + x)$.

✎ Write an algebraic expression for each phrase.

21) -3 divided by a is 18.

22) The difference between 10 and x is 9.

23) The cube of 4.

24) The square of b is 25.

25) -5 more than a number is 7.

26) The sum of x and 1 times 5 is 25.

Order of Operations

The order of operations is a set of rules that dictate the order in which mathematical operations should be performed. This ensures that all mathematical expressions are evaluated consistently and correctly. The acronym PEMDAS is often used to help remember the order of operations:

P: Parentheses

E: Exponents (i.e. powers and square roots, etc.)

MD: Multiplication and Division (from left to right)

AS: Addition and Subtraction (from left to right)

When working with an algebraic equation, it's important to remember to follow the order of operations to simplify the equation correctly. Parentheses must be simplified first, followed by exponents, then any multiplication and division, and finally any addition and subtraction.

For example: $3 + 4 \times 5 = 3 + 20 = 23$.

If one doesn't follow the order of operations, the result would be incorrect:

$$7 \times 5 = 35$$

It's also important to remember that when there are multiple operations of the same level of precedence, you should work from left to right.

For example: $4 \times 5 \div 2 + 3 = 20 \div 2 + 3 = 10 + 3 = 13$.

It's important to follow the order of operations to ensure that mathematical expressions are evaluated consistently and correctly.

Let's review an example:

Calculate. $(2 + 3) \times (4 - 7) + 5$

1. First, we simplify anything inside of parentheses. So, we have: $(2 + 3) = 5$ and $(4 - 7) = -3$.

2. Next, we simplify any exponents, but there are none in this case.

3. Then, we simplify any multiplication and division, working from left to right. We have: $5 \times (-3) = -15$.

4. Finally, we simplify any addition and subtraction, working from left to right. We have: $-15 + 5 = -10$.

So, the final simplified expression is -10.

Another example:

Calculate. $-5[(5 \times 8) \div (10 \times 2)] =$

First, calculate within parentheses:

$-5[(40) \div (10 \times 2)] = -5[(40) \div (20)] = -5[2]$.

Multiply -5 and 2. Then: $-5[2] = -10$.

Another example for better understanding:

Solve. $(63 \div 9) + (-15 + 12) =$

First, calculate within parentheses:

$(63 \div 9) + (-15 + 12) = (7) + (-3)$.

Then: $(7) - (3) = 4$.

✎ Evaluate each expression.

27) $(7 - 3) - (28 \div 7) =$

28) $[(2 \times 3) + (1 - 3)] \times (-1) =$

29) $(-3) \times 2 + 5 =$

30) $(-11 + 6) + (2 \times 4) =$

31) $(-9) + (4 \times 3) =$

32) $(-2 + 11) - (15 \div 5) =$

33) $[(63 \div 9) + 17] \div 3 - 18 =$

34) $-2(15 - 4) - (-24) =$

bit.ly/37LBw7X

Find more at

Integers and Absolute Value

Absolute value is the distance a number is from zero on the number line, regardless of its sign. It is represented by two vertical lines (| |) surrounding the number. For example, the absolute value of −5 is 5 and the absolute value of 5 is also 5. Absolute value can be thought of as the magnitude of a number, regardless of its sign.

The absolute value of any real number is always non-negative, so $|a| \geq 0$.

$|-5| = 5$ (The absolute value of −5 is 5) $|5| = 5$ (the absolute value of 5 is also 5)

$|-8| = 8$ (the absolute value of −8 is 8) $|0| = 0$ (the absolute value of 0 is 0).

You can use absolute value to find the distance between two numbers on a number line, regardless of their order. For example, $|3 - 6| = |-3| = 3$, which is the distance between the numbers 3 and 6 on the number line.

Let's review some examples:

1. Calculate. $|14 - 2| \times 5 =$

First, solve $|14 - 2|$: $\rightarrow |14 - 2| = |12|$, the absolute value of 12 is 12, $|12| = 12$.

Then: $12 \times 5 = 60$.

2. Solve. $\frac{|-24|}{4} \times |5 - 7| =$

First, find $|-24| \rightarrow$ the absolute value of −24 is 24. Then: $|-24| = 24$,

$\frac{24}{4} \times |5 - 7| =$.

Now, calculate $|5 - 7|$, $\rightarrow |5 - 7| = |-2|$, the absolute value of −2 is 2: $|-2| = 2$.

Then: $\frac{24}{4} \times 2 = 6 \times 2 = 12$.

3. Solve. $|8 - 2| \times \frac{|-4 \times 7|}{2} =$

First, calculate $|8 - 2|$, $\rightarrow$ $|8 - 2| = |6|$, the absolute value of 6 is 6, $|6| = 6$. Then:

$6 \times \frac{|-4 \times 7|}{2}$.

Now calculate $|-4 \times 7|$, $\rightarrow$ $|-4 \times 7| = |-28|$, the absolute value of -28 is 28,

$|-28| = 28$. Then: $6 \times \frac{28}{2} = 6 \times 14 = 84$.

4. Solve. $\frac{|-36|}{4} - |20 - 44| =$

First, find $|-36| \rightarrow$ the absolute value of -36 is 36. Then:

$|-36| = 36$, $\frac{36}{4} - |20 - 44| =$.

Now, calculate $|20 - 44|$, $\rightarrow$ $|20 - 44| = |-24|$, the absolute value of -24 is 24:

$|-24| = 24$. Then: $\frac{36}{4} - 24 = 9 - 24 = -15$.

5. Solve. $|12 - 9| \times \frac{|-32 \div 8|}{4} =$

First, calculate $|12 - 9|$, $\rightarrow$ $|12 - 9| = |3|$, the absolute value of 3 is 3, $|3| = 3$.

Then: $3 \times \frac{|-32 \div 8|}{4}$.

Now calculate $|-32 \div 8|$, $\rightarrow$ $|-32 \div 8| = |-4|$, the absolute value of -4 is 4, $|-4| =$

4. Then: $3 \times \frac{4}{4} = 3 \times 1 = 3$.

✎ Find the answers.

35) $\frac{|3 \times (-10)|}{5} \div \frac{|-21|}{7} =$

36) $|2 - 8| - |-11| =$

37) $|-4| - |8 + 1| =$

38) $-3 + |8 - 2| - |-3 + 2| =$

39) $\frac{|-21|}{7} + |-3 + 4| =$

40) $|-2 - 3| + |1 + 4| =$

41) $-|-11 - 3| + |7| =$

42) $|-5 + 9| \times |-2| =$

Percent Problems

Percent problems involve using the concept of percent, which is a way of expressing a number as a fraction of 100. In percent problems, you may need to use the following concepts:

- Percentage: A number expressed as a fraction of 100, represented by the symbol "%". For example, 50% represents $\frac{50}{100}$ or 0.5.

- Percent of: The concept of finding what percentage one number is of another. For example, "50% of 80" means "$\frac{50}{100}$ of 80" or "0.5×80".

- Increase/Decrease by a certain percentage: The concept of finding the change in value when a number is increased or decreased by a certain percentage. For example, if the price of a product is increased by 10%, the new price is 110% of the original price.

- Finding the original amount: The concept of finding the original amount before a percentage increase or decrease. For example, if the price of a product is increased by 10% from \$100, the new price is \$110. To find the original price, you need to divide the new price by 1.1 (110% in decimal form).

Let's review some examples:

What is 50% of 80?

50% of 80 can be found by multiplying $\frac{50}{100}$ by 80. So, 50% of 80 $= 0.5 \times 80 = 40$

If a product is on sale for 20% off, and the original price is \$100, how much will it cost?

To find the sale price, we need to subtract 20% of the original price from the original price. 20% of \$100 $= \frac{20}{100} \times \$100 = \$20$. So, the sale price $=$ \$100 $-$ \$20 $=$ \$80

If you invest $1000 and earn a 5% interest rate, how much money will you have after one year?

To find the amount of money after one year, we need to add 5% of the initial investment to the initial investment. 5% of $1000 $= \frac{5}{100} \times \$1000 = \$50$. So, the total amount of money after one year $= \$1000 + \$50 = \$1050$

If a test score is 80% and you need to get at least 90% to pass, what percent must you score on the remaining questions to pass?

To find the percentage you need to score on the remaining questions to pass, we need to subtract the current percentage score from the passing percentage. 90% − 80% = 10%. So, you need to score at least 10% on the remaining questions to pass the test.

What is 30% of 90?

In this problem, we have the percent (30%) and the base (90) and we are looking for the "part".

Use this formula: *Part = Percent × Base*.

Then: $Part = 30\% \times 90 = \frac{30}{100} \times 90 = 0.30 \times 90 = 27$.

The answer: 30% of 90 is 27.

✎ Solve each problem.

43) What is 19% of 100?

44) 38 is what percent of 150?

45) 22 is 45% of what number?

46) What is 8% of 280?

47) 14 is 35% of what number?

48) 49 is what percent of 300?

Percent of Increase and Decrease

Percent of increase and decrease refers to the concept of finding the change in value when a number is increased or decreased by a certain percentage.

Percent of increase is calculated by finding the ratio of the increase to the original value, and then multiplying that ratio by 100 to express it as a percentage. The formula is: $\frac{(New\ value\ -\ Original\ value)}{Original\ value} \times 100 = $ Percent of increase

Percent of decrease is calculated by finding the ratio of the decrease to the original value, and then multiplying that ratio by 100 to express it as a percentage. The formula is: $\frac{(Original\ value - New\ value)}{Original\ value} \times 100 = $ Percent of decrease

For example,

- If the price of a product is increased from \$100 to \$120, the percent of increase can be calculated as $\frac{(120\ -\ 100)}{100} \times 100 = 20\%$

- If the price of a product is decreased from \$100 to \$80, the percent of decrease can be calculated as $\frac{(100-80)}{100} \times 100 = 20\%$

Let's review some examples:

The price of a product was increased from \$50 to \$60. What is the percentage of increase?

The percent of increase can be calculated as $\frac{(60-50)}{50} \times 100 = 20\%$. The price of the product increased by 20%.

The population of a city decreased from 100,000 to 80,000. What is the percentage of decrease?

The percent of the decrease can be calculated as $\frac{(100,000 - 80,000)}{100,0000} \times 100 = 20\%$. The population of the city decreased by 20%.

Worker's salary was decreased from $40,000 to $35,000. What is the percent of the decrease?

The percent of the decrease can be calculated as $\frac{(40,000 - 35,000)}{40,0000} \times 100 = 12.5\%$. The worker's salary decreased by 12.5%.

The price of a table decreased from $200 to $150. What is the percent of the decrease?

Use this formula:

$Percent\ of\ change = \frac{new\ number - original\ number}{original\ number} \times 100$.

Then: $\frac{150 - 200}{200} \times 100 = \frac{-50}{200} \times 100 = -25$.

The percentage decrease is 25. (The negative sign means a percentage decrease.)

Therefore, the price of the table decreased by 25%.

✎ Solve each problem.

49) Find 720 decreased by 20%.

50) James puts $1,800 in a bank account. He takes it out 7 years later. It's now worth $2430. Find the percentage increase.

51) Find 810 increased by 15%.

52) A chemical solution contains 37% alcohol. If there is 111 ml of alcohol, what is the volume of the solution?

Discount, Tax, and Tip

Discount:

To solve Discount problems:

1. Express the discount percentage as a decimal by dividing it by 100.

2. Multiply the decimal value by the original price to find the amount of the discount.

3. Subtract the discount amount from the original price to find the final or selling price.

Let's review some examples of discount problems:

If an item is priced at $100 and has a 20% discount, the discount amount is $(\frac{20}{100}) \times 100 = \$20$. The final price is $\$100 - \$20 = \$80$

An item is priced at $200 and has a 25% discount.

To find the discount amount, we would calculate $(\frac{25}{100}) \times \$200 = \$50$. The final price of the item would be $\$200 - \$50 = \$150$.

With a 30% discount, Ella saved $60 on a dress. What was the original price of the dress? Let x be the original price of the dress. Then: 30% of $x = 60$.

Write an equation and solve for x:

$0.30 \times x = 60 \rightarrow x = \frac{60}{0.30} = 200$. The original price of the dress was $200.

Tax:

To solve Tax problems:

1. Express the tax rate as a decimal by dividing it by 100.

2. Multiply the decimal value by the taxable amount to find the amount of tax owed.

Let's review some examples of tax problems:

If the taxable amount is $1000 and the tax rate is 10%, the amount of tax owed

is $(\frac{10}{100}) \times 1000 = \$100$

A person has an income of $50,000 and the tax rate is 20%.

To find the amount of tax owed, we would calculate $(\frac{20}{100}) \times \$50,000 = \$10,000$.

Tip:

To solve Tip problems:

1. Express the tip percentage as a decimal by dividing it by 100.

2. Multiply the decimal value by the final price (or selling price) to find the

    amount of the tip.

Let's review some examples of tax problems:

If the final price of an item is $50 and the tip rate is 15%, the amount of tip is

$(\frac{15}{100}) \times 50 = \$7.50$

A restaurant bill comes out to $100 and the customer wants to leave a 20% tip.

To find the tip amount, we would calculate $(\frac{20}{100}) \times \$100 = \$20$

Nicole and her friends went out to eat at a restaurant. If their bill was $60.00

and they gave their server a 15% tip, how much did they pay altogether?

First, find the tip. To find the tip, multiply the rate by the bill amount.

Tip $= 60 \times 0.15 = 9$. The final price is: $60 + $9 = $69.

✍ Find the selling price of each item.

53) The original price of a phone: $850. Tax: 9.5%, Selling price: $_____

54) Sara orders a $18 lunch. The tax rate is 9% and she wants to leave a

    10% tip. What will be her total cost? $ _____

55) If your cell phone bill was $93.85 and there is a 6% late fee, how much

    will your bill be? $ _____

Simple Interest

Simple interest is a method of calculating the interest on a loan or investment where the interest is based only on the original principal or the initial amount invested. The formula for calculating simple interest is:

$$\text{Simple Interest} = \frac{\text{Principal} \times \text{Interest Rate} \times \text{Time}}{100}$$

Where:

- Principal is the initial amount of the loan or investment
- Interest Rate is the percentage of the interest that is charged on the principal
- Time is the length of the loan or investment, usually measured in years

For example, if you invest $1,000 at a 5% interest rate for 1 year, the simple interest would be: $\frac{(1,000 \times 5 \times 1)}{100} = \$50$

It's important to note that simple interest does not take into account the effect of compounding, which can significantly affect the total interest earned over time.

Simple interest is commonly used for short-term loans or investments, such as personal loans, car loans, and savings accounts.

Let's review some examples:

You invest $5,000 at an interest rate of 4% for 2 years. How much interest will you earn?

The simple interest can be calculated as $\frac{(5,000 \times 4 \times 2)}{100} = \$400$. You will earn $400 in interest.

A company borrows $25,000 at an interest rate of 6% for 3 years. How much interest will they pay?

The simple interest can be calculated as $\frac{(25,000\times6\times3)}{100} = \$4,500$. The company will pay $4,500 in interest.

You deposit $1000 in a savings account with an interest rate of 2% per year. How much interest will you earn after 3 years?

The simple interest can be calculated as $\frac{(1000\times2\times3)}{100} = \$60$. You will earn $60 in interest after 3 years.

Find simple interest for $1,600 at 6% for 6 years.

Use Interest formula:

$I = prt$ ($P = \$1,600$, $r = 6\% = \frac{6}{100} = 0.06$ and $t = 6$).

Then: $I = 1,600 \times 0.06 \times 6 = \$576$.

✍ Determine the simple interest for the following loans.

56) $1300 at 7% for 11 years. $_____

57) $800 at 12% for 3 years. $_____

✍ Solve.

58) A new car, valued at $20,000, depreciates at 8% per year. What is the value of the car one year after purchase? $_____

59) Jake puts $12,000 into an investment yielding 2.5% annual simple interest; he leaves the money in for seven years. How much interest does Jake get at the end of those seven years? $ _____

The Distributive Property

The distributive property is a rule in mathematics that allows you to simplify expressions by distributing a term outside of parentheses to each term inside the parentheses. The distributive property is often used to simplify expressions that include both multiplication and addition or subtraction.

The distributive property can be applied in the following ways:

- $a(b + c) = ab + ac$
- $a(b - c) = ab - ac$

Here, "a" is a constant or a variable, and "b" and "c" are also variables or constants. The distributive property states that you can multiply "a" by "b" and "c" individually and then add or subtract them to get the same result as multiplying "a" by the expression inside the parentheses.

For example, consider the expression $4(3 + 2)$. If we use the distributive property, we can simplify it to $4(3) + 4(2) = 12 + 8 = 20$. Instead of multiplying the entire expression inside the parentheses, we can split it into two separate terms and multiply each term individually.

Let's review this concept with an example:

Simplify the expression $3x(2y + 4)$

Using the distributive property, we can simplify the expression by distributing the $3x$ to each term inside the parentheses:

$$3x(2y + 4) = 3x(2y) + 3x(4) = 6xy + 12x$$

So, the simplified expression is $6xy + 12x$.

The distributive property is a fundamental concept in algebra and is used in many different areas of mathematics, including factoring polynomials, solving equations, and simplifying complex expressions.

Keep in mind that the distributive property is a property of arithmetic, and it applies to both real and complex numbers. It is a fundamental property that is widely used in mathematical operations, and it is a key concept to understand when working with algebraic expressions.

Another example: Simply. $(6)(4x - 5) - 8x$

First, simplify $(6)(4x - 5)$ using the distributive property.

Then: $(6)(4x - 5) = 24x - 30$.

Now combine like terms: $(6)(4x - 5) - 8x = 24x - 30 - 8x$.

In this expression, $24x$ and $-8x$ are "like" terms and we can combine them.

$24x - 8x = 16x$. Then: $24x - 30 - 8x = 16x - 30$.

One more example:

Simply. $(-3)(3x - 5) + 4x$

First, simplify $(-3)(3x - 5)$ using distributive property.

Then: $(-3)(3x - 5) = -9x + 15$.

Now combine like terms: $(-3)(3x - 5) + 4x = -9x + 15 + 4x$.

In this expression, $-9x$ and $4x$ are "like" terms and we can combine them. $-9x + 4x = -5x$. Then: $-9x + 15 + 4x = -5x + 15$.

✎ Use the distributive property to simplify each expression.

60) $4(x + 3) =$ _____

61) $-2(3x - 1) =$ _____

62) $(4 - x)2 =$ _____

63) $(-4)(2x + 1) =$ _____

64) $(-4x - 8)(-2) =$ _____

65) $-(-7 + 5x) =$ _____

Chapter 1: Answers

1) 5

2) 8

3) 2

4) −2

5) −10

6) 5

7) 0

8) 17

9) −37

10) −19

11) 2

12) 50

13) 24

14) 7

15) −10

16) −30

17) −7

18) −8

19) 3

20) 8

21) $-\dfrac{3}{a} = 18$

22) $10 - x = 9$

23) 4^3

24) $b^2 = 25$

25) $-5 + x = 7$

26) $(x + 1) \times 5 = 25$

27) 0

28) −4

29) −1

30) 3

31) 3

32) 6

33) −10

34) 2

35) 2

36) −5

37) −5

38) 2

39) 4

40) 10

41) −7

42) 8

43) 19

44) 25.3

45) 48.9

46) 22.4

47) 40

48) 16.3

49) 576

50) 35%

51) 931.5

52) 300 ml

53) $930.75

54) $21.42

Effortless Math Education

55) $99.48

56) $1,001

57) $288

58) 18,400

59) $2,100

60) $4x + 12$

61) $-6x + 2$

62) $-2x + 8$

63) $-8x - 4$

64) $8x + 16$

65) $-5x + 7$

Effortless
Math
Education

CHAPTER

2 Exponents and Variables

Math topics that you'll learn in this chapter:

- ☑ Multiplication Property of Exponents
- ☑ Division Property of Exponents
- ☑ Powers of Products and Quotients
- ☑ Zero and Negative Exponents
- ☑ Match Exponential Functions and Graphs I
- ☑ Write Exponential Functions: Word Problems
- ☑ Scientific Notation
- ☑ Addition and Subtraction in Scientific Notation

25

Multiplication Property of Exponents

The Multiplication Property of Exponents is a mathematical rule that applies to expressions with the same base raised to different exponents. When you multiply two such expressions, you can simplify the product by adding the exponents. The property can be stated as follows:

For any real numbers a, m, and n: $a^m a^n = a^{m+n}$.

Here, "a" is the base, and "m" and "n" are the exponents. This property holds for both positive and negative exponents, as well as for fractions.

Here are some examples to illustrate the Multiplication Property of Exponents:

Evaluate. $(2^3)(2^4) =$

Use the Multiplication Property of Exponents. We can add the exponents:

$(2^3)(2^4) = 2^{3+4} = 2^7 = 128$.

Evaluate. $5^2 \times 5^{-3} =$

Again, add the exponents: $5^2 \times 5^{-3} = 5^{2+(-3)} = 5^{-1} = \frac{1}{5}$.

Simplify. $3^{\frac{1}{2}} \times 3^{\frac{1}{3}} =$

Add the exponents: $3^{\frac{1}{2}} \times 3^{\frac{1}{3}} = 3^{\left(\frac{1}{2}\right)+\left(\frac{1}{3}\right)} = 3^{\frac{5}{6}}$.

The Multiplication Property of Exponents is useful in simplifying expressions involving exponential terms with the same base, making it easier to perform calculations and solve problems.

Let's dive deeper into the Multiplication Property of Exponents and look at more examples, including ones with variables and multiple terms.

1. Variables as bases:

When you have variables as bases, the Multiplication Property of Exponents still holds. If you have the same base (variable) with different exponents, you can add the exponents when multiplying the expressions.

Simplify. $x^2 \times x^3 =$

According to the Multiplication Property of Exponents, we can add the exponents: $x^2 \times x^3 = x^{2+3} = x^5$.

Evaluate. $a^4 \times a^{-2} =$

Add the exponents: $a^4 \times a^{-2} = a^{4-2} = a^2$.

2. Multiple terms:

When you have expressions with multiple terms, you can apply the Multiplication Property of Exponents separately for each pair of terms with the same base.

Multiply. $2^3x^2 \times 2^4x^5 =$

Apply the property for the numerical bases (2) and the variable bases (x) separately: $2^3x^2 \times 2^4x^5 = (2^{3+4}) \times (x^{2+5}) = 2^7 \times x^7 = 128x^7$.

Evaluate. $(3^2a^3b) \times (3^4a^{-1}b^2) =$

Apply the property for each pair of terms with the same base:

$(3^2a^3b) \times (3^4a^{-1}b^2) = (3^{2+4}) \times (a^{3+(-1)}) \times (b^{1+2}) = 3^6 \times a^2 \times b^3 = 729a^2b^3$.

The Multiplication Property of Exponents helps simplify expressions and solve problems in various fields of mathematics, including algebra, calculus, and number theory. Remember that this property only applies when the bases are the same.

✎ Find the products.

1) $x^2 \times 4xy^2 =$

2) $3x^2y \times 5x^3y^2 =$

3) $6x^4y^2 \times x^2y^3 =$

4) $7xy^3 \times 2x^2y =$

5) $-5x^5y^5 \times x^3y^2 =$

6) $-8x^3y^2 \times 3x^3y^2 =$

7) $-6x^2y^6 \times 5x^4y^2 =$

8) $-3x^3y^3 \times 2x^3y^2 =$

9) $-6x^5y^3 \times 4x^4y^3 =$

10) $-2x^4y^3 \times 5x^6y^2 =$

11) $-7y^6 \times 3x^6y^3 =$

12) $-9x^4 \times 2x^4y^2 =$

bit.ly/34AWHr1

Find more at

Division Property of Exponents

The Division Property of Exponents is a mathematical rule that applies to expressions with the same base raised to different exponents when they are being divided. When you divide two such expressions, you can simplify the quotient by subtracting the exponent of the denominator from the exponent of the numerator. The property can be stated as follows:

For any real numbers a, m, and n, and $a \neq 0$:

$$\frac{a^m}{a^n} = a^{m-n}$$

Here, "a" is the base, and "m" and "n" are the exponents. This property holds for both positive and negative exponents, as well as for fractions.

Here are some examples to illustrate the Division Property of Exponents:

Simplify. $\frac{2^5}{2^2} =$

According to the Division Property of Exponents, we can subtract the exponents:

$$\frac{2^5}{2^2} = 2^{5-2} = 2^3 = 8.$$

Evaluate. $\frac{7^3}{7^{-2}} =$

Subtract the exponents:

$$\frac{7^3}{7^{-2}} = 7^{3-(-2)} = 7^{3+2} = 7^5 = 16{,}807.$$

Simplify. $\frac{x^6}{x^3} =$

Subtract the exponents: $x^{6-3} = x^3$.

Simplify. $\frac{a^5 b^3}{a^2 b} =$

Subtract the exponents for each pair of terms with the same base:

$$(a^{5-2})(b^{3-1}) = a^3 b^2.$$

The Division Property of Exponents is useful in simplifying expressions involving exponential terms with the same base when dividing, making it easier to perform calculations and solve problems in various areas of mathematics, including algebra and calculus.

In summary, for the division of the exponents use following formulas:

- $\frac{x^a}{x^b} = x^{a-b} \ (x \neq 0)$

- $\frac{x^a}{x^b} = \frac{1}{x^{b-a}} , \ (x \neq 0)$

- $\frac{1}{x^b} = x^{-b}, \ (x \neq 0)$

More examples:

Simplify. $\frac{16x^3y}{2xy^2} =$

First, cancel the common factor: $2 \to \frac{16x^3y}{2xy^2} = \frac{8x^3y}{xy^2}$.

Use Exponent's rules: $\frac{x^a}{x^b} = x^{a-b} \ \to \frac{x^3}{x} = x^{3-1} = x^2$ and $\frac{x^a}{x^b} = \frac{1}{x^{b-a}} \to \frac{y}{y^2} = \frac{1}{y^{2-1}} = \frac{1}{y}$.

Then: $\frac{16x^3y}{2xy^2} = \frac{8x^2}{y}$.

Simplify. $\frac{24x^8}{3x^6} =$

Use Exponent's rules: $\frac{x^a}{x^b} = x^{a-b} \ \to \frac{x^8}{x^6} = x^{8-6} = x^2$.

Then: $\frac{24x^8}{3x^6} = 8x^2$.

✍ Simplify.

13) $\frac{5^3 \times 5^4}{5^9 \times 5} =$

14) $\frac{3^3 \times 3^2}{7^2 \times 7} =$

15) $\frac{15x^5}{5x^3} =$

16) $\frac{16x^3}{4x^5} =$

17) $\frac{72y^2}{8x^3y^6} =$

18) $\frac{10x^3y^4}{50x^2y^3} =$

19) $\frac{13y^2}{52x^4y^4} =$

20) $\frac{50xy^3}{200x^3y^4} =$

21) $\frac{48x^2}{56x^2y^2} =$

22) $\frac{81y^6x}{54x^4y^3} =$

bit.ly/37JAclZ

Find more at

Powers of Products and Quotients

Powers of Products and Quotients are properties that describe how to deal with exponential expressions that involve products (multiplication) or quotients (division) raised to a power. These properties allow you to simplify expressions and perform calculations more easily. We'll discuss each property separately.

1. Power of a Product:

The Power of a Product rule states that when a product is raised to an exponent, you can distribute the exponent to each factor in the product. Mathematically, this can be expressed as:

$$(ab)^n = a^n b^n$$

Here, "a" and "b" are the factors, and "n" is the exponent.

Simplify. $(2 \times 3)^4 =$

According to the Power of a Product rule, distribute the exponent to each factor:

$$(2 \times 3)^4 = 2^4 \times 3^4 = 16 \times 81 = 1296$$

Evaluate. $(xy)^3 =$

Distribute the exponent to each factor: $(xy)^3 = x^3 y^3$.

2. Power of a Quotient:

The Power of a Quotient rule states that when a quotient is raised to an exponent, you can distribute the exponent to both the numerator and the denominator. Mathematically, this can be expressed as:

$$\left(\frac{a}{b}\right)^n = \frac{a^n}{b^n}, \text{ where } b \neq 0$$

Here, "a" is the numerator, "b" is the denominator, and "n" is the exponent.

Simplify. $\left(\frac{4}{2}\right)^3 =$

According to the Power of a Quotient rule, distribute the exponent to the numerator and the denominator: $\left(\frac{4}{3}\right)^3 = \frac{4^3}{3^3} = \frac{64}{8} = 8$.

Evaluate. $\left(\frac{x}{y}\right)^5 =$

Distribute the exponent to the numerator and the denominator: $\frac{x^5}{y^5}$.

These properties are particularly useful when simplifying expressions or solving problems in algebra, calculus, and other areas of mathematics that involve products or quotients raised to powers. In summary:

- For any nonzero numbers a and b and any integer x,

$$(ab)^x = a^x \times b^x \text{ and } \left(\frac{a}{b}\right)^x = \frac{a^x}{b^x}$$

Let's review an example:

Simplify. $(3x^3y^2)^2 =$

Use Exponents rules: $(x^a)^b = x^{a \times b}$.

$$(3x^3y^2)^2 = (3)^2(x^3)^2(y^2)^2 = 9x^{3 \times 2}y^{2 \times 2} = 9x^6y^4.$$

Another example:

Simplify. $\left(\frac{2x^3}{3x^2}\right)^2 =$

First, cancel the common factor:

$$x \rightarrow \left(\frac{2x^3}{3x^2}\right) = \left(\frac{2x}{3}\right)^2.$$

Use Exponents rules: $\left(\frac{a}{b}\right)^c = \frac{a^c}{b^c}$.

Then: $\left(\frac{2x}{3}\right)^2 = \frac{(2x)^2}{(3)^2} = \frac{4x^2}{9}.$

✑ Solve.

23) $(x^3y^3)^2 =$

24) $(3x^3y^4)^3 =$

25) $(4x \times 6xy^3)^2 =$

26) $(5x \times 2y^3)^3 =$

27) $\left(\frac{9x}{x^3}\right)^2 =$

28) $\left(\frac{3y}{18y^2}\right)^2 =$

29) $\left(\frac{3x^2y^3}{24x^4y^2}\right)^3 =$

30) $\left(\frac{26x^5y^3}{52x^3y^5}\right)^2 =$

31) $\left(\frac{18x^7y^4}{72x^5y^2}\right)^2 =$

32) $\left(\frac{12x^6y^4}{48x^5y^3}\right)^2 =$

bit.ly/34CgPJm

Find more at

Zero and Negative Exponents

Zero and negative exponents are mathematical concepts that help simplify expressions involving the powers of numbers.

Zero exponent: The concept of a zero exponent might seem counterintuitive at first, as it's not immediately clear why any non-zero number raised to the power of zero should equal one. However, this rule is consistent with the properties of exponents and can be explained using the following rationale:

Consider the general rule for dividing numbers with the same base but different exponents:

$$\frac{a^m}{a^n} = a^{m-n}$$

Now, let's assume $m = n$: $\frac{a^m}{a^m} = a^{m-m}$.

Since $m - m = 0$, the expression simplifies to: $\frac{a^m}{a^m} = a^0$.

On the left side of the equation, any non-zero number divided by itself is equal to 1: $1 = a^0$.

This is why any non-zero number raised to the power of zero is equal to one.

Negative exponent: Negative exponents indicate that the base should be inverted (reciprocal) and raised to the positive value of the exponent. This can also be understood using the properties of exponents.

Consider the general rule for dividing numbers with the same base but different exponents, as mentioned earlier: $\frac{a^m}{a^n} = a^{m-n}$.

Now, let's assume $m = 0$: $\frac{a^0}{a^n} = a^{0-n}$.

Since $0 - n = -n$, the expression simplifies to: $\frac{a^0}{a^n} = a^{-n}$.

We already know that $a^0 = 1$ for any non-zero number a, so the expression becomes: $\frac{1}{a^n} = a^{-n}$.

This is why a number with a negative exponent is equal to one divided by the same number with a positive exponent.

- Zero-Exponent Rule: $a^0 = 1$, this means that anything raised to the zero power is 1. For example: $(5xy)^0 = 1$. (Number zero is an exception: $0^0 = 0$.)

- A negative exponent simply means that the base is on the wrong side of the fraction line, so you need to flip the base to the other side. For instance, "x^{-2}" (pronounced as "ecks to the minus two") just means "x^2" but underneath, as in $\frac{1}{x^2}$.

More examples:

Evaluate. $\left(\frac{4}{5}\right)^{-2} =$

Use negative exponents rule:

$$\left(\frac{x^a}{x^b}\right)^{-2} = \left(\frac{x^b}{x^a}\right)^2 \rightarrow \left(\frac{4}{5}\right)^{-2} = \left(\frac{5}{4}\right)^2.$$

Then: $\left(\frac{5}{4}\right)^2 = \frac{5^2}{4^2} = \frac{25}{16}.$

Evaluate. $\left(\frac{3}{500}\right)^0 =$

Use zero-exponent Rule: $a^0 = 1$.

Then: $\left(\frac{3}{500}\right)^0 = 1.$

✍ Evaluate each expression.

33) $\left(\frac{1}{4}\right)^{-2} =$

34) $\left(\frac{1}{3}\right)^{-2} =$

35) $\left(\frac{1}{7}\right)^{-3} =$

36) $\left(\frac{2}{5}\right)^{-3} =$

37) $\left(\frac{2}{3}\right)^{-3} =$

38) $\left(\frac{3}{5}\right)^{-4} =$

Match Exponential Functions and Graphs

Exponential functions are mathematical functions that involve a base raised to a variable exponent. They can be represented by the general equation:

$$f(x) = a(b)^x$$

Here, 'a' is the initial value (y−intercept), 'b' is the base, and 'x' is the exponent. The base 'b' must be a positive number different from 1 to be considered an exponential function.

To match exponential functions and their graphs, follow these steps:

1. Identify the initial value (y−intercept): Find the point where the graph intersects the y−axis. This point corresponds to the initial value 'a' in the equation $f(x) = a(b)^x$.

2. Determine if the function represents growth or decay: Examine the graph to see if it increases or decreases as x increases. If the graph increases, the function represents exponential growth, and $b > 1$. If the graph decreases, the function represents exponential decay, and $0 < b < 1$.

3. Estimate the base 'b': To estimate the base 'b', find a point on the graph where x has increased by 1 (e.g., from $x = 0$ to $x = 1$). Then, calculate the ratio between the function's values at these two points. This ratio should be equal to 'b' in the equation $f(x) = a(b)^x$.

4. Write the equation: Using the information gathered from the previous steps, write the equation for the exponential function: $f(x) = a(b)^x$.

5. Match the function to the graph: Compare the equation you've derived with the given graph. Ensure the initial value, growth or decay behavior, and the horizontal asymptote match the graph. If they do, then you've successfully matched the exponential function to its graph.

Let's review an example:

Match each exponential function to its graph.

$$f(x) = \left(\frac{1}{2}\right)^x, \ g(x) = \left(\frac{3}{2}\right)^x, \ h(x) = \left(\frac{1}{3}\right)^x$$

A

B

C

According to the base value of the exponential equation, notice that one of the functions is growing and the other two functions are decaying. So, the function $g(x) = \left(\frac{3}{2}\right)^x$ can be equivalent to graph A. Now, evaluate the two remaining functions at a few inputs to find some points on the graph. Choose a point such as -1 to plug into the equation. Therefore, start with $f(x) = \left(\frac{1}{2}\right)^x$.

$$f(-1) = \left(\frac{1}{2}\right)^{-1} = 2.$$

You can see that the ordered pair $(-1, 2)$ for the function $f(x) = \left(\frac{1}{2}\right)^x$ is equivalent to a point on graph C. In the same way, substitute -1 in $h(x) = \left(\frac{1}{3}\right)^x$. Therefore, $h(-1) = \left(\frac{1}{3}\right)^{-1} = 3$. That is, graph B represented the function $h(x)$.

Match each equation to the correct graph.

39) $f(x) = -4(3)^x, \ f(x) = 2^x + 5, \ f(x) = 3(2)^x + 3$

A

B

C

Write Exponential Functions: Word Problems

Exponential functions are mathematical expressions that model the behavior of quantities that grow or decay at a constant rate. They are particularly useful for modeling real-world phenomena such as population growth, radioactive decay, and compound interest. To solve word problems involving exponential functions, it's important to understand the basic form of an exponential function, how to set up an equation, and then solve for the unknown variable.

The general form of an exponential function is: $y = ab^x$, where:

y is the final amount after some time or number of instances.

a is the initial amount (when $x = 0$).

b is the base or growth factor ($b > 1$ for growth and $0 < b < 1$ for decay).

x is the independent variable, which represents time or number of instances.

Let's go through the process of solving an exponential word problem step by step.

Step 1:   Identify the given information: Carefully read the problem and identify the information provided. Pay attention to the initial amount, the growth or decay factor, and the time or instances involved.

Step 2:   Determine the form of the exponential function: Determine if the problem involves exponential growth or decay. If it's growth, $b > 1$; if it's decay, $0 < b < 1$.

Step 3:   Set up the exponential function: Using the general form $y = ab^x$, plug in the given values and set up the exponential function to model the situation.

Step 4:   Solve the equation: Solve the equation for the unknown variable(s), either by isolating the variable or by using logarithms.

Let's work through an example to illustrate these steps:

A bacteria culture starts with 50 bacteria and doubles in number every 3 hours. How many bacteria will be present after 12 hours?

Step 1:   Identify the given information:

Initial amount (a) = 50 bacteria, Growth factor (b) = 2 (doubles every 3 hours), Time period (x) = 12 hours

Step 2: Determine the form of the exponential function. Since the bacteria culture is growing, we have an exponential growth function.

Step 3: Set up the exponential function The general form of the exponential function is $y = ab^x$. In this case, we have: $y = 50(2)^{\frac{x}{3}}$.

Step 4: Solve the equation. We want to find the number of bacteria after 12 hours, so we need to solve for y when $x = 12$:

$$y = 50(2)^{\frac{12}{3}} \rightarrow y = 50(2)^4 \rightarrow y = 50(16) \rightarrow y = 800.$$

After 12 hours, there will be 800 bacteria in the culture.

Let's another example:

In a laboratory sample, if it starts with 100 bacteria which can double every hour, how many bacteria will there be after 6 hours?

Since it grows at a constant ratio of 2, you have to use the formula of exponential to find the number of bacteria in this sample. Use the formula,

$y = ab^n$, where $a = 100$ is the initial number of bacteria, and b is equal to 2. Substitute the given value in the formula, then: $y = 100(2)^n$.

Now, plug $n = 6$ into the equation. Therefore, $y = 100(2)^6 = 100(64) = 6,400$.

✍ Write each number in scientific notation.

40) As of 2019, the world population is 8.716 billion and growing at a rate of 1.2% per year. Write an equation to model population growth, where $p(t)$ is the population in billions of people and t is the time in years.

41) You decide to buy a used car that costs $20,000. You have heard that the car may depreciate at a rate of 10% per year. At this rate, how much will the car be worth in 6 years?

bit.ly/3HjClGF

Find more at

Scientific Notation

In scientific notation, a number is represented as a decimal multiplied by a power of 10. The decimal, also known as the coefficient, is a number between 1 and 10, and the exponent tells us how many times the decimal must be multiplied by 10 to obtain the original number.

For example, the number 0.00005 can be written in scientific notation as 5×10^{-5}. To convert this to standard form, we move the decimal point 5 places to the left, giving us 0.00005. Similarly, a number like 35,000 can be written in scientific notation as 3.5×10^4. To convert this to standard form, we move the decimal point 4 places to the right, giving us 35,000.

It's important to note that in scientific notation, the decimal point is always placed after the first non-zero digit. This helps to make the numbers more readable and easier to compare. This notation is particularly useful in scientific and technical fields, where large or small numbers are commonly encountered.

Here are a few examples of numbers written in scientific notation and their equivalent in standard form:

$3.2 \times 10^3 = 3200$

$4.5 \times 10^{-7} = 0.00000045$

$6.78 \times 10^5 = 678000$

$2 \times 10^{-9} = 0.000000002$

$9 \times 10^6 = 9000000$

In the first example, the coefficient is 3.2 and the exponent is 3, so we move the decimal point 3 places to the right to get 3200.

In the second example, the coefficient is 4.5 and the exponent is -7, so we move the decimal point 7 places to the left to get 0.00000045.

Similarly, the third example, 6.78×10^5 is 678000, and so on.

It's worth noting that the exponent tells us how many times we have to move the decimal point, if the exponent is positive, we move the decimal point to the right and if the exponent is negative, we move the decimal point to the left.

Let's understand this more with another example:

Write 0.0034 in scientific notation.

First, move the decimal point to the right so you have a number between 1 and 10. That number is 3.4.

Now, determine how many places the decimal moved in step 1 by the power of 10. We moved the decimal point 3 digits to the right. Then: $10^{-3} \rightarrow$ When the decimal moved to the right, the exponent is negative. Then: $0.0034 = 3.4 \times 10^{-3}$.

Another example:

Write 4.8×10^{-4} in standard notation.

The exponent is negative 4. Then, move the decimal point to the left four digits. (Remember $4.8 = 00004.8$.) When the decimal moved to the right, the exponent is negative. Then: $4.8 \times 10^{-4} = 0.00048$.

One more example:

Write 0.00024 in scientific notation.

First, move the decimal point to the right so you have a number between 1 and 10. That number is 2.4. Now, determine how many places the decimal moved in step 1 by the power of 10. We moved the decimal point 4 digits to the right. Then: $10^{-4} \rightarrow$ When the decimal moved to the right, the exponent is negative. Then: $0.00024 = 2.4 \times 10^{-4}$.

✎ Write each number in scientific notation.

42) $0.00412 =$ 44) $66,000 =$

43) $0.000053 =$ 45) $72,000,000 =$

Addition and Subtraction in Scientific Notation

In order to add or subtract numbers written in scientific notation, they must have the same exponent. This is because the exponent represents the power of 10, and adding or subtracting numbers with different exponents would not make sense mathematically.

For example, to add 2.5×10^4 and 3.6×10^4, we first align the exponents, which in this case are both 4. Then we add the coefficients, $2.5 + 3.6 = 6.1$.

Finally, we write the result in scientific notation: 6.1×10^4.

To subtract, the process is similar. We align the exponents and subtract the coefficients.

For example, to subtract 6.1×10^4 and 3.6×10^4, we align the exponents which are both 4, then we subtract the coefficients $6.1 - 3.6 = 2.5$ and write the result in scientific notation 2.5×10^4.

It's important to keep in mind that the coefficient, m, should always be a number between 1 and 10, and if it's not, you'll need to adjust the coefficient and the exponent accordingly.

Let's review another example:

Simplify. $(3.4 \times 10^4) + (2.6 \times 10^5) =$

3.4×10^4 and 2.6×10^5 have different exponents, so we cannot add or subtract them directly.

To add them, we have to rewrite them so that they have the same exponent, for example we can rewrite 3.4×10^4 as 0.34×10^5 so that the exponents match and we can add the coefficient, $0.34 + 2.6 = 2.94$. So, the result would be

$$2.94 \times 10^5$$

Let's another example:

Simplify. $(5.4 \times 10^4) - (2.6 \times 10^3) =$

To subtract 5.4×10^4 and 2.6×10^3, we have to rewrite them so that they have the same exponent.

In this case, we can rewrite 2.6×10^3 as 0.26×10^4, so that the exponents match and we can subtract the coefficient, $5.4 - 0.26 = 5.14$. So, the result would be

$$5.14 \times 10^4$$

More examples:

Simplify. $(0.34 \times 10^2) + (46 \times 10^{-1}) =$

First, write each term to the same exponent:

$0.34 \times 10^2 = 3.4 \times 10$

$4.6 \times 10^{-1} = 0.46 \times 10.$

Next, add the coefficient: $3.4 + 0.46 = 3.86$.

Now, we get: $(0.34 \times 10^2) + (46 \times 10^{-1}) = 3.86 \times 10.$

Simplify. $(10^{-3}) - (4.2 \times 10^{-2}) + (3700 \times 10^{-5}) =$

First, rewrite the term 0.0037×10^{-5} as standard notation:

$3700 \times 10^{-5} = 3.7 \times 10^{-2}$

Then, write other terms to the same exponent with 10^{-2}: $10^{-3} = 0.1 \times 10^{-2}$

Next, we have:

$$(0.1 \times 10^{-2}) - (4.2 \times 10^{-2}) + (3700 \times 10^{-5}) = (0.1 - 4.2 + 3.7) \times 10^{-2}$$
$$= -0.4 \times 10^{-2} = -4 \times 10^{-3}$$

✍ Write the answer in scientific notation.

46) $6 \times 10^4 + 10 \times 10^4 =$ _____

47) $7.2 \times 10^6 - 3.3 \times 10^6 =$ _____

48) $2.23 \times 10^7 + 5.2 \times 10^7 =$ _____

49) $8.3 \times 10^9 - 5.6 \times 10^8 =$ _____

50) $1.4 \times 10^2 + 7.4 \times 10^5 =$ _____

51) $9.6 \times 10^6 - 3 \times 10^4 =$ _____

bit.ly/3v9xCRZ

Find more at

Multiplication and Division in Scientific Notation

Multiplication: When multiplying numbers in scientific notation, we multiply the coefficients and add the exponents.

For example, to multiply $(4.3 \times 10^3) \times (2.6 \times 10^5)$, we first multiply 4.3 and 2.6 to get 11.18, then add the exponents 3 and 5 to get 8. The result is 11.18×10^8. The coefficient, 11.18, in the example provided is greater than 10.

In scientific notation, the coefficient should always be between 1 and 10. When the coefficient is greater than 10, it's called an "overflow" and it needs to be adjusted by moving the decimal point to the left and increasing the exponent by one for each move.

In this case, we move the decimal point to the left once, which would give us 1.118×10^9. This is now in the correct form for scientific notation.

Division: When dividing numbers in scientific notation, we divide the coefficients and subtract the exponents of the denominator from the numerator.

For example, to divide $\frac{4.3 \times 10^3}{2.6 \times 10^5}$, we first divide 4.3 by 2.6 to get 1.65, then subtract the exponent of the denominator (5) from the exponent of the numerator (3) to get -2. The result is 1.65×10^{-2}.

It's important to keep in mind that the exponent tells us how many times we have to move the decimal point, if the exponent is positive, we move the decimal point to the right and if the exponent is negative, we move the decimal point to the left, this is why in multiplication we add the exponents and in division we subtract them.

When dividing numbers in scientific notation, we divide the coefficients and subtract the exponents of the denominator from the numerator. This is because the exponents represent the power of 10, and dividing by a power of 10 is the same as moving the decimal point to the left or right, depending on the sign of the exponent.

Let's another example:

Simplify. $\frac{8 \times 10^3}{2 \times 10^2} =$

In this example, we first divide 8 by 2 to get 4, then subtract the exponent of the denominator (2) from the exponent of the numerator (3) to get 1.

The result is 4×10^1, which is the same as moving the decimal point one place to the right.

$$\frac{8 \times 10^3}{2 \times 10^2} = 4 \times 10^1$$

More examples:

Simplify. $\left(\frac{6 \times 10^{-8}}{3 \times 10^{-6}}\right) =$

In this example, we first divide 6 by 3 to get 2, then subtract the exponent of the denominator (-8) from the exponent of the numerator (-6) to get -2.

The result is 2×10^{-2}, which is the same as moving the decimal point one place to the left.

$$\left(\frac{6 \times 10^{-8}}{3 \times 10^{-6}}\right) = 2 \times 10^{-2}$$

✍ Simplify. Write the answer in scientific notation.

52) $\frac{9 \times 10^8}{3 \times 10^7} =$ _____

53) $(3 \times 10^{-8})(7 \times 10^{10}) =$ _____

54) $(9 \times 10^{-3})(4.2 \times 10^6) =$ _____

55) $\frac{125 \times 10^9}{50 \times 10^{12}} =$ _____

56) $\frac{2.8 \times 10^{12}}{0.4 \times 10^{20}} =$ _____

57) $(5.6 \times 10^{12})(3 \times 10^{-7}) =$ _____

Chapter 2: Answers

1) $4x^3y^2$

2) $15x^5y^3$

3) $6x^6y^5$

4) $14x^3y^4$

5) $-5x^8y^7$

6) $-24x^6y^4$

7) $-30x^6y^8$

8) $-6x^6y^5$

9) $-24x^9y^6$

10) $-10x^{10}y^5$

11) $-21x^6y^9$

12) $-18x^8y^2$

13) $\frac{1}{125}$

14) $\frac{243}{343}$

15) $3x^2$

16) $\frac{4}{x^2}$

17) $\frac{9}{x^3y^4}$

18) $\frac{xy}{5}$

19) $\frac{1}{4x^4y^2}$

20) $\frac{1}{4x^2y}$

21) $\frac{6}{7y^2}$

22) $\frac{3y^3}{2x^3}$

23) x^6y^6

24) $27x^9y^{12}$

25) $576x^4y^6$

26) $1{,}000x^3y^9$

27) $\frac{81}{x^4}$

28) $\frac{1}{36y^2}$

29) $\frac{y^3}{512x^6}$

30) $\frac{x^4}{4y^4}$

31) $\frac{x^4y^4}{16}$

32) $\frac{x^2y^2}{16}$

33) 16

34) 9

35) 343

36) $\frac{125}{8}$

37) $\frac{27}{8}$

38) $\frac{625}{81}$

39) $A: f(x) = 3(2)^x + 3,$

 $B: f(x) = 2^x + 5,$

 $C: f(x) = -4(3)^x$

40) $p(t) = 8.716(1 + 0.012)^t$

41) $A = 20{,}000(1 - 0.1)^6$

42) 4.12×10^{-3}

43) 5.3×10^{-5}

44) 6.6×10^4

45) 7.2×10^7

46) 1.6×10^5

47) 3.9×10^6

48) 7.43×10^7

49) 7.74×10^9

50) 7.4014×10^5

51) 9.57×10^6

52) 3×10^1

53) 2.1×10^3

54) 3.78×10^4

55) 2.5×10^{-3}

56) 7×10^{-8}

57) 1.68×10^6

CHAPTER

3 Expressions and Equations

Math topics that you'll learn in this chapter:

- ☑ Simplifying Variable Expressions
- ☑ Evaluating One Variable
- ☑ Evaluating Two Variables
- ☑ One–Step Equations
- ☑ Multi–Step Equations
- ☑ Rearrange Multi-Variable Equations
- ☑ Graphing Absolute Value Equations

45

Simplifying Variable Expressions

In algebra, a variable is a symbol that represents an unknown value. Variables are often represented by letters such as x, y, z, a, b, c, m, and n. These letters can take on different values, allowing us to express a wide range of mathematical relationships.

An algebraic expression is a mathematical phrase that contains variables, integers, and mathematical operations.

For example, the expression "$3x + 2y$" is an algebraic expression because it contains variables (x and y), integers (3 and 2), and mathematical operations (+).

In algebra, we can simplify expressions by combining "like" terms. Like terms are terms that have the same variable and the same exponent.

For example, the terms "$4x$" and "$2x$" are like terms because they have the same variable (x) and the same exponent (1). We can combine these terms by adding their coefficients (4 and 2) to get "$6x$". This simplifies the expression and makes it easier to work with.

Example of simplifying an expression:

Original expression: $3x^2 + 5x - 2x^2 - 8x + 6 =$

  Step 1: Combine like terms: $3x^2 - 2x^2 = x^2$.

  Step 2: Combine like terms: $5x - 8x = -3x$.

  Step 3: Combine like terms: $x^2 - 3x + 6$.

Simplified expression: $x^2 - 3x + 6$.

This is a basic example of simplifying algebraic expression by combining like terms. Algebraic simplification can be more complex and can include expanding polynomials and factoring expressions.

Let's take a look at another example:

Simplify. $(-2 + 5x^2 + 4x^2 + 7x) =$

The answer is:

$(-2 + 5x^2 + 4x^2 + 7x) = (5x^2 + 4x^2 + 7x - 2) = (9x^2 + 7x - 2)$.

In this expression, I have combined the like terms that have the same variable and exponent ($5x^2$ and $4x^2$) and also combined the coefficients of the like terms of x is ($7x$) and constant term (-2) which results in the final simplified expression of $9x^2 + 7x - 2$.

Another example:

Simplify. $(4x + 2x + 4) =$

In this expression, there are three terms: $4x$, $2x$, and 4.

Two terms are "like" terms: $4x$ and $2x$.

Combine like terms. $4x + 2x = 6x$.

Then: $(4x + 2x + 4) = 6x + 4$.

(Remember you cannot combine variables and numbers.)

Let's solve another example:

Simplify. $-2x^2 - 5x + 4x^2 - 9 =$

Combine "like" terms: $-2x^2 + 4x^2 = 2x^2$.

Then: $-2x^2 - 5x + 4x^2 - 9 = 2x^2 - 5x - 9$.

✎ Simplify each expression.

1) $(3 + 4x - 1) =$

2) $(-5 - 2x + 7) =$

3) $(12x - 5x - 4) =$

4) $(-16x + 24x - 9) =$

5) $(6x + 5 - 15x) =$

6) $2 + 5x - 8x - 6 =$

7) $5x + 10 - 3x - 22 =$

8) $2x^2 - 7x - 3x^2 + 4x + 6 =$

bit.ly/2WFVudQ

Find more at

Evaluating One Variable

Evaluating an algebraic expression with one variable involves substituting a specific value for that variable and then performing the arithmetic operations according to the order of operations.

For example, if we have an expression $2x + 3$ and we want to evaluate it for $x = 4$, we would substitute 4 in for x, getting $2(4) + 3 = 8 + 3 = 11$.

Another example is if we have an expression $5x^2 - 3x + 2$, and we want to evaluate it for $x = -2$, we would substitute -2 in for x, getting

$5(-2)^2 - 3(-2) + 2 = 20 + 6 + 2 = 28$.

Keep in mind that evaluating an algebraic expression with one variable gives a specific numerical value, whereas simplifying an algebraic expression gives an algebraic expression in the simplest form.

Let's take a look at some examples:

Calculate this expression for $x = 3$: $13 + 5x$.

To calculate the expression "$13 + 5x$" when $x = 3$, we need to substitute the value of 3 for the variable x in the expression.

So, $13 + 5x = 13 + 5(3) = 13 + 15 = 28$.

Therefore, for $x = 3$, the expression evaluates to 28.

Another example:

Solve this expression for $x = -4$: $13 - 5x$.

To solve the expression "$13 - 5x$" for "$x = -4$", we need to substitute the value of -4 for the variable x in the expression.

So, $13 - 5x = 13 - 5(-4) = 13 + 20 = 33$.

Therefore, for $x = -4$, the expression evaluates to 33.

bit.ly/3ppujQZ
Find more at

Let's do another example:

Calculate this expression for $x = 2$: $8 + 2x$.

First, substitute 2 for x.

Then: $8 + 2x = 8 + 2(2)$.

Now, use the order of operation to find the answer:

$8 + 2(2) = 8 + 4 = 12$.

Another example:

Evaluate this expression for $x = -1$: $4x - 8$.

First, substitute -1 for x.

Then: $4x - 8 = 4(-1) - 8$.

Now, use the order of operation to find the answer:

$4(-1) - 8 = -4 - 8 = -12$.

To better understand this issue, consider this example:

Find the value of this expression when $x = 4$: $(16 - 5x)$.

First, substitute 4 for x.

Then: $16 - 5x = 16 - 5(4) = 16 - 20 = -4$.

✎ Evaluate each expression using the value given.

9) $x = 2 \rightarrow x + 3 =$

10) $x = -4 \rightarrow 8 + x =$

11) $y = 0 \rightarrow 2y + 3 =$

12) $x = -2 \rightarrow -\frac{1}{2}x =$

13) $a = -7 \rightarrow 2a + 14 =$

14) $x = 6 \rightarrow 5 + 2x =$

15) $x = 1.5 \rightarrow -2x + 1 =$

16) $x = 5 \rightarrow 12 - 3x =$

bit.ly/3ppujQZ

Find more at

Evaluating Two Variables

To evaluate an algebraic expression, we substitute a specific numerical value for each variable in the expression. Then, we perform the arithmetic operations according to the order of operations to find the numerical value of the expression. This process is also known as "plugging in" the values and solving the equation.

For example, if we have an expression $2x + y + 3$ and we want to evaluate it for $x = 4$ and $y = 5$, we would substitute 4 in for x and 5 in for y, getting $2(4) + 5 + 3 = 8 + 5 + 3 = 16$.

Let's review some examples:

Calculate this expression for $a = 4$ and $b = -3$: $(5a - 6b)$.

To calculate the expression "$5a - 6b$" when $a = 4$ and $b = -3$, we need to substitute the values of 4 for the variable a and -3 for the variable b in the expression. So, $5a - 6b = 5(4) - 6(-3) = 20 + 18 = 38$.

Therefore, for $a = 4$ and $b = -3$, the expression evaluates to 38.

Evaluate this expression for $x = -5$ and $y = -3$: $(4x + 2y)$.

To evaluate the expression "$4x + 2y$" for $x = -5$ and $y = -3$, we need to substitute the values of -5 for the variable x and -3 for the variable y in the expression. So, $4x + 2y = 4(-5) + 2(-3) = -20 - 6 = -26$.

Therefore, for $x = -5$ and $y = -3$, the expression evaluates to -26.

Find the value of this expression $3(3a - 6b)$, when $a = -2$ and $b = 5$.

To find the value of the expression "$3(3a - 6b)$" when $a = -2$ and $b = 5$, we need to substitute the values of -2 for the variable a and 5 for the variable b in the expression. So, $3(3a - 6b) = 3(3(-2) - 6(5)) = 3(-6 - 30) = 3(-36) = -108$.

Therefore, for $a = -2$ and $b = 5$, the expression evaluates to -108.

Calculate this expression for $a = 2$ and $b = -1$: $(4a - 3b)$.

First, substitute 2 for a, and -1 for b.

Then: $4a - 3b = 4(2) - 3(-1)$.

Now, use the order of operation to find the answer:

$4(2) - 3(-1) = 8 + 3 = 11$.

Evaluate this expression for $x = -2$ and $y = 2$: $(3x + 6y)$.

Substitute -2 for x, and 2 for y.

Then: $3x + 6y = 3(-2) + 6(2) = -6 + 12 = 6$.

Find the value of this expression $2(6a - 5b)$, when $a = -1$ and $b = 4$.

Substitute -1 for a, and 4 for b.

Then: $2(6a - 5b) = 2(6(-1) - 5(4)) = 2(-6 - 20) = 2(-26) = -52$.

Evaluate this expression. $-7x - 2y$, $x = 4$, $y = -3$.

Substitute 4 for x, and -3 for y and simplify.

Then: $-7x - 2y = -7(4) - 2(-3) = -28 + 6 = -22$.

✍ Evaluate each expression using the values given.

17) $x = -1$ and $y = 3 \rightarrow 2x + y =$

18) $x = 7$ and $y = 2 \rightarrow x - 4y =$

19) $a = -3$ and $b = 3 \rightarrow a + b =$

20) $r = 2$ and $s = 2 \rightarrow -r + 2s - 4 =$

21) $x = -8$ and $y = 4 \rightarrow x - y + 2 =$

22) $x = 1$ and $y = -1 \rightarrow 3x + 4y =$

One–Step Equations

An equation is a statement of equality between two expressions. For example, in the equation "$ax = b$", the expression "ax" is equal to the expression "b". The variable "x" is the unknown value that we want to find.

Solving an equation means determining the value of the variable that makes the equation true. To solve a one-step equation, we need to use the inverse operation of the one being performed on the variable. Inverse operations are operations that undo each other, for example, addition and subtraction, multiplication, and division.

The inverse operations are:

- Addition and subtraction
- Multiplication and division

For example, if we have an equation $x + 3 = 7$, we can solve for x by subtracting 3 from both sides: $x + 3 = 7$.

Then $x + 3 - 3 = 7 - 3 = 4$.

Another example:

If we have an equation $\frac{x}{5} = 6$, we can solve for x by multiplying both sides by 5:

$\frac{x}{5} = 6 \rightarrow x = 30$.

It is important to note that solving an equation means finding the value of the variable that makes the equation true.

Let's review another example:

Solve this equation for x: $3x = 10.5 \rightarrow x = ?$

To solve the equation "$3x = 10.5$" for x, we need to isolate x on one side of the equation. $3x = 10.5$

To do this, we divide both sides of the equation by 3: $x = \frac{10.5}{3} \rightarrow x = 3.5$

Therefore, $x = 3.5$ is the solution of the equation $3x = 10.5$.

Another example:

Solve this equation for x: $4x = 16 \rightarrow x = ?$

Here, the operation is multiplication (Variable x is multiplied by 4.) and its inverse operation is division. To solve this equation, divide both sides of an equation by 4: $4x = 16 \rightarrow \frac{4x}{4} = \frac{16}{4} \rightarrow x = 4$.

Here is another example:

Solve this equation: $x + 8 = 0 \rightarrow x = ?$

In this equation, 8 is added to the variable x. The inverse operation of addition is subtraction. To solve this equation, subtract 8 from both sides of the equation: $x + 8 - 8 = 0 - 8$. Then: $x = -8$.

Let's do another example:

Solve this equation for x: $x - 12 = 0$.

Here, the operation is subtraction and its inverse operation is addition. To solve this equation, add 12 to both sides of the equation: $x - 12 + 12 = 0 + 12 \rightarrow x = 12$.

✍ Solve each equation.

23) $x - 3 = 6$

24) $5 - x = 7$

25) $2 = x + 2$

26) $-5 = 2 + b$

27) $-3 - x = 2$

28) $2x = 12$

29) $x + 5 = 0$

30) $32 = -8x$

31) $0 = 1 - a$

32) $\frac{3}{2}b = 9$

bit.ly/37Jq0tK

Find more at

Multi−Step Equations

To solve a multi-step equation, we need to use a combination of inverse operations and the order of operations. The steps involve:

1. Combining like terms on one side of the equation. This step is important to simplify the equation and help us see the relationship between the variables and constants more clearly.

2. Bringing variables to one side by adding or subtracting. This step is important to isolate the variable on one side of the equation.

3. Simplifying the equation by using the inverse of addition or subtraction. This step is important to eliminate any constant terms and obtain the value of the variable.

4. Simplify further by using the inverse of multiplication or division. This step is important to obtain the value of the variable in the simplest form.

5. Checking the solution by plugging the value of the variable into the original equation. This step is important to confirm that the value found for the variable is a valid solution to the equation.

It is important to note that solving multi-step equations requires logical thinking, patience, and attention to detail, as well as a good understanding of mathematical operations and their inverse operations.

Let's give some examples to better understand the issue:

Solve this equation for x: $2x + 3 = 7x - 4$.

First, we'll bring all the x's to one side of the equation.

$$2x - 7x = -4 - 3 \rightarrow -5x = -7 \rightarrow x = \frac{7}{5}$$

Solve this equation for x: $3x - 2(x + 4) = 2x + 6$.

Find more at

First, we'll use the distributive property to expand $2(x + 4)$:

$3x - 2x - 8 = 2x + 6 \rightarrow x - 8 = 2x + 6$

Next, we'll bring all the x's to one side of the equation.

$-x = 14 \rightarrow x = -14$

Solve this equation for x: $4(x + 2) - 3x = 2x - 8$.

First, we'll use the distributive property to expand $4(x + 2)$:

$4x + 8 - 3x = 2x - 8 \rightarrow x + 8 = 2x - 8$

Next, we'll bring all the x's to one side of the equation.

$-x = -16 \rightarrow x = 16$

Solve this equation for x: $-5x + 4 = 24$.

Subtract 4 from both sides of the equation.

$-5x + 4 = 24 \rightarrow -5x + 4 - 4 = 24 - 4 \rightarrow -5x = 20$.

Divide both sides by -5, then:

$-5x = 20 \rightarrow \frac{-5x}{-5} = \frac{20}{-5} \rightarrow x = -4$.

Now, check the solution:

$x = -4 \rightarrow -5x + 4 = 24 \rightarrow -5(-4) + 4 = 24 \rightarrow 24 = 24$.

The answer $x = -4$ is correct.

✎ Solve each equation.

33) $1 = \frac{1}{2}x - 5$

34) $-(2 - x) = 3$

35) $-3 = -2x + 3$

36) $8 = 2(1 - 3x)$

37) $-\frac{1}{3}(2x - 10) = x$

38) $3(5x - 2) = 9$

39) $1 - (x + 1) = 2x + 3$

40) $3x - 1 = 5$

bit.ly/3nQbSEB

Find more at

Rearrange Multi-Variable Equations

Rearranging a multi-variable equation involves isolating one variable on one side of the equation.

1. Determine the dependent variable: The variable that you want to solve for is called the dependent variable.

2. Isolate the dependent variable on both sides of the equation: To isolate the dependent variable, you need to use the inverse operations to undo the operations that are performed on it. This will leave the dependent variable on one side of the equation, and the other variables on the other side.

3. By undoing the operations on both sides, write the dependent variable on one side and the other variables on the other side of the equation. This step is important to get the equation in a form that we can solve for the dependent variable.

For example, if we have the equation $3x + 2y = 8$, we want to rearrange it to solve for x, we will isolate it on one side:

$$3x + 2y = 8 \rightarrow 3x = 8 - 2y \rightarrow x = \frac{(8 - 2y)}{3}$$

Another example, if we have the equation $x + 2y - 3z = 5$, we want to rearrange it to solve for y, we will isolate it on one side:

$$x + 2y - 3z = 5 \rightarrow 2y = -x + 3z + 5 \rightarrow y = \frac{(-x + 3z + 5)}{2}$$

It is important to note that rearranging an equation is a key step to solving a multi-variable equation, as it allows us to isolate one variable and find its value.

Let's review another example:

Solve this equation for x: $\frac{1}{2}x - t = 5$.

To solve the equation "$\frac{1}{2}x - t = 5$" for x, we need to isolate x on one side of the equation. To do this, we add t to both sides of the equation: $\frac{1}{2}x = 5 + t$

Then we multiply both sides of the equation by 2: $x = 2(5 + t) = 10 + 2t$

Therefore, $x = 10 + 2t$ is the solution of the equation $\frac{1}{2}x - t = 5$.

Another example:

Solve for a in terms of b and c: $-c + b - a = 6$.

To solve the problem, find a. By undoing the operations on both sides, isolate a on one side of the equation. Add a to both sides of the equation. So,

$-c + b - a + a = 6 + a \rightarrow -c + b = a + 6$.

Now, subtract 6 from both sides of the equation, then:

$-c + b - 6 = a + 6 - 6 \rightarrow -c + b - 6 = a$.

In this case, the above equation in terms of a becomes: $a = -c + b - 6$.

Let's do another example:

Solve $V = \frac{1}{3}\pi r^2 h$ for h.

To isolate h on both sides of the equation, just multiply the sides by the expression $\frac{3}{\pi r^2}$. Therefore,

$$\frac{3}{\pi r^2} \times V = \frac{3}{\pi r^2}\left(\frac{1}{3}\pi r^2 h\right) \rightarrow h = \frac{3V}{\pi r^2}$$

✍ Rearrange Multi-Variable Equations.

41) $\frac{1}{2}qp - l = w$ for q.

42) $w + z = \frac{5x}{2y}$ for y.

43) $T = \frac{PV}{nR}$ for P.

44) $d + a = -b - c$ for c.

bit.ly/3XLN6Xz

Find more at

Graphing Absolute Value Equations

The general form of an absolute value function (that is linear) is:

$$y = |mx + b| + c$$

The vertex (the lowest or the highest point) is located at $\left(\frac{-b}{m}, c\right)$.

A vertical line that divides the graph into two equal halves is: $x = -\frac{b}{m}$.

To graph an absolute value equation, you can find the vertex and some other points by substituting some values for x and solving for y. Once you have the vertex and a few other points, you can use them to sketch the graph of the function.

For example, if you have the equation: $y = |2x + 1| + 1$,

the vertex is located at $\left(\frac{-1}{2}, 1\right)$.

To graph the equation, you can substitute $x = -1$, $x = 0$, and $x = 1$ into the equation and solve for y to get 2, 2, and 4, respectively.

These points can be plotted on the coordinate plane and connected to sketch the graph of the function.

It is important to note that the graph of an absolute value function is a V-shaped graph and it is different from a linear function graph which is a straight line.

Let's do an example:

Graph $y = |x + 2|$.

Find the vertex $\left(\frac{-b}{m}, c\right)$.

According to the general form of an absolute value function: $y = |mx + b| + c$.

We have: $x = \frac{-b}{m} \rightarrow x = \frac{-2}{1} = -2$.

The point $(-2,0)$ is the vertex of the graph and represents the center of the table of values. Create the table and plot the ordered pairs.

Now, find the points and graph the equation.

x	$y = |x + 2|$
-4	$|-4 + 2| = 2$
-3	$|-3 + 2| = 1$
-2	$|-2 + 2| = 0$
-1	$|-1 + 2| = 1$

Let's do an example:

Graph $y = |x - 3|$.

Find the vertex $\left(\frac{-b}{m}, c\right)$.

According to the general form of an absolute value function: $y = |mx + b| + c$.

We have: $x = \frac{-b}{m} \rightarrow x = \frac{-(-3)}{1} = 3$.

The point $(3,0)$ is the vertex of the graph and represents the center of the table of values. Create the table and plot the ordered pairs.

Now, find the points and graph the equation.

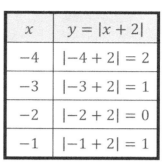

x	$y = |x - 3|$
1	$|1 - 3| = 2$
2	$|2 - 3| = 1$
3	$|3 - 3| = 0$
4	$|4 - 3| = 1$

✑ Graphing absolute value equations.

45) $y = -|x| - 1$

46) $y = -|x - 3|$

Chapter 3: Answers

1) $4x + 2$

2) $-2x + 2$

3) $7x - 4$

4) $8x - 9$

5) $-9x + 5$

6) $-3x - 4$

7) $2x - 12$

8) $-x^2 - 3x + 6$

9) 5

10) 4

11) 3

12) 1

13) 0

14) 17

15) -2

16) -3

17) 1

18) -1

19) 0

20) -2

21) -10

22) -1

23) 9

24) -2

25) 0

26) -7

27) -5

28) 6

29) -5

30) -4

31) 1

32) 6

33) 12

34) 5

35) 3

36) -1

37) 2

38) 1

39) -1

40) 2

41) $q = \frac{2(w+l)}{p}$

42) $y = \frac{5x}{2(w+z)}$

43) $P = \frac{nTR}{V}$

44) $c = -b - a - d$

45) $y = -|x| - 1$

46) $y = -|x - 3|$

CHAPTER

4 Linear Functions

Math topics that you'll learn in this chapter:

- ☑ Finding Slope
- ☑ Writing Linear Equations
- ☑ Graphing Linear Inequalities
- ☑ Finding the Slope, x −intercept, and y −intercept
- ☑ Write an Equation from a Graph
- ☑ Slope-intercept Form and Point-slope Form
- ☑ Write a Point-slope Form Equation from a Graph
- ☑ Find x −and y −intercepts in the Standard Form of Equation
- ☑ Graph an Equation in the Standard Form
- ☑ Equations of Horizontal and Vertical Lines
- ☑ Graph a Horizontal or Vertical Line
- ☑ Graph an Equation in Point-Slope Form
- ☑ Equation of Parallel or Perpendicular Lines
- ☑ Compare Linear Function's Graph and Equations
- ☑ Two-variable Linear Equations Word Problems

63

Finding Slope

The slope of a line is a measure of its steepness and direction on a coordinate plane. A coordinate plane is a two-dimensional surface made up of two perpendicular number lines, the horizontal $x-$axis and the vertical $y-$axis. The point where the two axes intersect is called the origin. An ordered pair (x, y) represents the coordinates of a point on the plane.

A line on a coordinate plane is represented by connecting two points. To determine the slope of a line, we need either the equation of the line or two points on the line.

The slope of a line with two points $A(x_1, y_1)$ and $B(x_2, y_2)$ can be found by using this formula: $\frac{y_2-y_1}{x_2-x_1} = \frac{rise}{run}$, which is the ratio of the rise (the change in y) to the run (the change in x).

The equation of a line is typically written as $y = mx + b$ where m is the slope and b is the $y-$intercept.

Let's review an example:

Find the slope of the line through these two points: $A(3, -6)$ and $B(-2, 2)$.

The slope of a line is the ratio of the change in the $y-$coordinate to the change in the $x-$coordinate between two points on the line. To find the slope of a line through two points, we use the formula: Slope $= \frac{y_2-y_1}{x_2-x_1}$

Given two points $A(3, -6)$ and $B(-2, 2)$. Slope $= \frac{2-(-6)}{-2-3} = \frac{8}{-5} = -1.6$

So, the slope of the line through these two points $A(3, -6)$ and $B(-2, 2)$ is -1.6.

Another example: Find the slope of the line with equation $y = -3x + 8$.

The slope of a line is the coefficient of the x −term in the equation of the line. In the equation $y = -3x + 8$, the coefficient of the x −term is -3. So, the slope of the line is -3.

One more example: Find the slope of the line through these two points: $A(4,0)$ and $B(8,12)$.

The slope of a line is the ratio of the change in the y −coordinate to the change in the x −coordinate between two points on the line. To find the slope of a line through two points, we use the formula: Slope $= \frac{y_2-y_1}{x_2-x_1}$

Given two points $A(4,0)$ and $B(8,12)$. Slope $= \frac{12-0}{8-4} = \frac{12}{4} = 3$

So, the slope of the line through these two points $A(4,0)$ and $B(8,12)$ is 3.

To better explain the problem, I can draw your attention to this example:

Find the slope of the line through these two points: $A(1,-6)$ and $B(3,2)$.

Use the formula: Slope $= \frac{y_2-y_1}{x_2-x_1}$. Let (x_1,y_1) be $A(1,-6)$ and (x_2,y_2) be $B(3,2)$.

(Remember, you can choose any point for (x_1,y_1) and (x_2,y_2)).

Then: Slope $= \frac{y_2-y_1}{x_2-x_1} = \frac{2-(-6)}{3-1} = \frac{8}{2} = 4$.

The slope of the line through these two points is 4.

✍ Find the slope of each line.

1) $y = x - 5$

2) $y = 2x + 6$

3) $y = -5x - 8$

4) Line through $(2,6)$ and $(5,0)$

5) Line through $(8,0)$ and $(-4,3)$

6) Line through $(-2,-4)$ and $(-4,8)$

Writing Linear Equations

The equation of a line in slope-intercept form is $y = mx + b$. This form of the equation is particularly useful because it allows us to quickly identify the slope (m) and the y−intercept (b) of the line.

To write the equation of a line, the first step is to identify the slope. The slope is the ratio of the change in y to the change in x between any two points on the line. It can also be represented by the letter "m" in the equation $y = mx + b$.

The next step is to find the y−intercept. The y−intercept is the point at which the line crosses the y−axis. It can be represented by the letter "b" in the equation $y = mx + b$. To find the y−intercept, we can substitute the slope and the coordinates of a point (x, y) on the line into the equation.

For example, if we know a line has a slope of 3 and the point $(2,5)$ is on the line, we can substitute these values into the equation $y = mx + b$: $y = 3x + b$, and $5 = 3(2) + b \rightarrow 5 = 6 + b \rightarrow b = -1$. So, the equation of the line is $y = 3x - 1$.

It is important to note that the slope-intercept form of the equation of a line is just one of the ways to represent a line, and it can be transformed into other forms such as point-slope form or standard form.

Example: What is the equation of the line that passes through $(2, -4)$ and has a slope of 3?

The equation of a line can be written in the form $y = mx + b$, where m is the slope of the line and b is the y−intercept (The point at which the line crosses the y−axis). To find the equation of a line that passes through a given point and has a given slope, we can use the point-slope form of a line.

The point-slope form of a line is: $y - y_1 = m(x - x_1)$. where (x_1, y_1) is a point on the line and m is the slope of the line. Given point $(2, -4)$ and slope 3, $y - (-4) = 3(x - 2) \rightarrow y = 3x - 6 - 4 \rightarrow y = 3x - 10$. So, the equation of the line that passes through $(2, -4)$ and has a slope of 3 is $y = 3x - 10$.

Another example: What is the equation of the line that passes through (5,2) and has a slope of 4?

The general slope-intercept form of the equation of a line is: $y = mx + b$, where m is the slope and b is the $y-$intercept.

By substitution of the given point and given slope: $y = mx + b \rightarrow 2 = (4)(5) + b$.

So, $b = 2 - 20 = -18$, and the required equation of the line is: $y = 4x - 18$.

One more example: Write the equation of the line through two points $A(6,8)$ and $B(-1,22)$.

First, find the slope: slope $= \frac{y_2 - y_1}{x_2 - x_1} = \frac{22-8}{-1-6} = \frac{14}{-7} = -2 \rightarrow m = -2$.

To find the value of b, use either point and plug in the values of x and y in the equation. The answer will be the same: $y = -2x + b$. Let's check both points.

Then: $(6,8) \rightarrow y = mx + b \rightarrow 8 = -2(6) + b \rightarrow b = 20$.

$(-1,22) \rightarrow y = mx + b \rightarrow 22 = -2(-1) + b \rightarrow b = 20$.

The $y-$intercept of the line is 4. The equation of the line is: $y = -2x + 20$.

✎ Solve.

7) What is the equation of a line with slope 4 and intercept 16?

8) What is the equation of a line with slope 3 and passes through point (1,5)?

9) What is the equation of a line with slope -5 and passes through point $(-2,7)$?

10) The slope of a line is -4 and it passes through point $(-6,2)$. What is the equation of the line?

11) The slope of a line is -3 and it passes through point $(-3,-6)$. What is the equation of the line?

Graphing Linear Inequalities

To graph a linear inequality, we first need to graph the "equals" line. This is the line that separates the solution of the inequality from the non-solution. The equation of this line can be written in slope-intercept form, point-slope form, or standard form.

Once we have the equation of the line, we can graph it on the coordinate plane. The type of inequality symbol used determines the type of line we use to graph the equation. For less than ($<$) and greater than ($>$) signs, we use a dashed line. For less than or equal to ($\leq$) and greater than or equal to ($\geq$) we use a solid line. The next step is to choose a testing point. This can be any point on both sides of the line. We then substitute the values of x and y of that point into the inequality. If the inequality is true, then that part of the line is the solution. If the inequality is not true, then the other part of the line is the solution.

It is important to note that when we graph a linear inequality, we graph the equation of the line, and then shade the half-plane that contains the solution of the inequality, depending on the inequality symbol.

Let's review an example: Sketch the graph of inequality: $y < 2x + 4$.

To sketch the graph of the inequality $y < 2x + 4$, we first need to graph the "equals" line which is $y = 2x + 4$.

1. First, we need to find two points that are on the line $y = 2x + 4$. We can do this by substituting $x = -1$ and $x = 1$ and solving for y.

$$x = -1 \rightarrow y = 2(-1) + 4 = 2$$

$$x = 1 \rightarrow y = 2(1) + 4 = 6$$

So, two points that are on the line are $(-1,2)$ and $(1,6)$.

2. Next, we plot these points on the coordinate plane and draw the line that passes through them.

3. We use a dashed line because the inequality is "less than" and the solution is the area below the line.

4. Shade the region below the line to represent the solution set of the inequality.

5. To check if our graph is correct, we can pick a point in the shaded area, say $(-2, -2)$, and substitute it into the inequality. It should be true, as $-2 < 2 \times (-2) + 4$.

Another example: Sketch the graph of inequality: $y > 3x + 1$.

To draw the graph of $y > 3x + 1$, you first need to graph the line: $y = 3x + 1$.

Since there is a less than (>) sign, draw a dashed line.

The slope is 3 and the y −intercept is 1.

Then, choose a testing point and substitute the value of x and y from that point into the inequality. The easiest point to test is the origin: $(0,0) \to 0 > 3(0) + 1 \to 0 > 1$.

This is incorrect! 0 is not greater than 1. So, this part of the line (on the left side) is the solution of this inequality.

✍ Sketch the graph of each linear inequality.

12) $y > 4x + 2$

13) $y < -2x + 5$

Finding the Slop, x −intercept and y −intercept

When a linear function is graphed, it will always be a straight line. The slope-intercept form of a linear equation is $y = mx + b$, where m is the slope of the line and b is the y −intercept. The slope of a line is a measure of how steep the line is and it is defined as the ratio of the change in the y −coordinate to the change in the x −coordinate between two points on the line. The y −intercept is the point at which the line crosses the y −axis, which means when $x = 0$ the y −coordinate is equal to b. In this form, m and b are constants and x and y are variables. By understanding the slope and y −intercept, we can fully describe the linear function and its characteristics.

In addition to the y −intercept and slope, the x −intercept is also an important aspect of a linear function. The x −intercept is the point at which the line crosses the x −axis, which means when $y = 0$, the x −coordinate is equal to $\frac{-b}{m}$. By finding both x −intercept and y −intercept we can plot the line on the cartesian plane.

Knowing the equation of a line in slope-intercept form allows you to easily graph the line and understand its properties, such as its direction, whether it is increasing or decreasing, and its overall shape.

Let's review an example: Find the slope, x and y intercepts for the following equation. $2x + 8y = 12$

The slope-intercept form of a linear equation is $y = mx + b$, where m is the slope of the line and b is the y −intercept. However, the equation given, $2x + 8y = 12$, is not in that form. To find the slope, x −intercept, and y −intercept, we need to manipulate the equation into that form.

To find the slope, we need to get the equation in the form $y = mx + b$, so we can read off the value of m. To do this, we can divide both sides of the equation by 8: $\frac{2x}{8} + \frac{8y}{8} = \frac{12}{8} \rightarrow \frac{x}{4} + y = \frac{3}{2} \rightarrow y = -\frac{x}{4} + \frac{3}{2}$. So, the slope of the line is $m = -\frac{1}{4}$. To find the y−intercept we need to put $x = 0$ in the equation.

$$2 \times 0 + 8y = 12 \rightarrow 8y = 12 \rightarrow y = \frac{12}{8} \rightarrow y = \frac{3}{2}$$

So, the y−intercept of the line is $(0, \frac{3}{2})$. To find the x−intercept we need to put $y = 0$ in the equation: $2x + 8 \times 0 = 12 \rightarrow 2x = 12 \rightarrow x = 6$.

So, the x−intercept of the line is $(6,0)$. To sum up, the slope of the line is $-\frac{1}{4}$, the y−intercept is $(0, \frac{3}{2})$ and the x−intercept is $(6,0)$.

Another example: Find the slope, x and y intercepts for the following equation.

$$x + 3y = 15$$

To find the x−intercept, arrange the equation $x + 3y = 15$ so that x is isolated:

$$x = -3y + 15$$

Using the point-slope formula, we see that the x−intercept is 15.

To find the y−intercept, rearrange the equation $x + 3y = 15$ so that y is isolated:

$$x + 3y = 15 \rightarrow 3y = -x + 15 \rightarrow y = \frac{-1}{3}x + 5.$$

So, the y−intercept is 5.

To find the slope, use this formula: $y = mx + b \rightarrow y = \frac{-1}{3}x + 5$. The slope is $-\frac{1}{3}$.

✎ Find the slope, x and y intercepts for the following equations.

14) $y = -\frac{1}{3}x - 1$

y−intercept: _____

x−intercept: _____

Slope: _____

15) $y = 5x + 10$

y−intercept: _____

x−intercept: _____

Slope: _____

Write an Equation from a Graph

To write an equation of a line in slope-intercept form, given a graph of that equation, we need to pick two points on the line and use them to find the slope. The slope is the ratio of the change in y to the change in x between any two points on the line. It is also the value of "m" in the equation $y = mx + b$.

Once we have the slope, we can find the coordinates of the y−intercept. The y−intercept is the point at which the line crosses the y−axis. It should be of the form $(0, b)$ where b is the y−coordinate. The b is the value of "b" in the equation $y = mx + b$.

We can now write the equation by substituting the numerical values for m and b we found. The final equation will be of the form $y = mx + b$ where m is the slope and b is the y−intercept.

To check if the equation is correct, we can pick a point on the line (not the y−intercept) and substitute its coordinates (x, y) into the equation. If the equation is true for that point, then the equation is correct.

Let's review an example:

Write the equation of the following line in slope-intercept form.

First, pick two points on the line for example, $(-3, 3)$ and $(6,0)$.

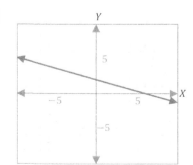

Use these points to calculate the slope:

$$m = \frac{0-3}{6-(-3)} = \frac{-3}{9} = -\frac{1}{3}.$$

Next, find the y−intercept: $(0,2)$. Thus, $b = 2$.

Therefore, the equation of this line is:

$$y = -\frac{1}{3}x + 2.$$

Now, let's check the equation by picking another point on the line. Let's choose point (3,1).

Then: $(3,1) \rightarrow y = -\frac{1}{3}x + 2 \rightarrow 1 = -\frac{1}{3}(3) + 2 \rightarrow 1 = -1 + 2$. This is true!

Another example: Write the equation of the following line in slope-intercept form.

First, pick two points on the line for example, (2,1) and (3,3).

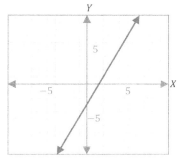

Use these points to calculate the slope: $m = \frac{3-1}{3-2} = \frac{2}{1} = 2$.

Next, find the y−intercept: $(0, -3)$. Thus, $b = -3$.

Therefore, the equation of this line is: $y = 2x - 3$.

Now, let's check the equation by picking another point on the line. Let's choose point $(-2, -7)$.

Then: $(-2, -7) \rightarrow y = 2x - 3 \rightarrow -7 = 2(-2) - 3 \rightarrow -7 = -4 - 3$. This is true!

✍ Write an equation of each of the following lines in slope-intercept from.

16) _____

17) _____

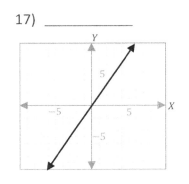

bit.ly/3FDOsw1

Find more at

Slope-intercept Form and Point-slope Form

The slope-intercept form is a way to express the equation of a line. The equation of a line in slope-intercept form is written as $y = mx + b$, where m is the slope of the line and b is the $y-$intercept (the point where the line crosses the $y-$axis). This form is useful because it allows you to easily determine the slope and $y-$intercept of a line from its equation.

The point-slope form is another way to express the equation of a line. The equation of a line in point-slope form is written as $y - y_1 = m(x - x_1)$, where (x_1, y_1) is a point on the line and m is the slope of the line. This form is useful because it allows you to easily find the equation of a line when you know the slope and a point on the line.

Let's review an example:

Find the equation of a line with point $(3,7)$ and slope -4, and write it in slope-intercept and point-slope forms.

Slope-intercept form: $y = -4x + b$. By using the point $(3,7)$ we can find:

$$b = y - mx = 7 + 4 \times 3 = 7 + 12 = 19.$$

So, the equation will be $y = -4x + 19$. Point-slope form: $y - 7 = -4(x - 3)$.

Another example:

Find the equation of a line with point $(2, -2)$ and slope 2, and write it in slope-intercept and point-slope forms.

Slope-intercept form: $y = 2x + b$. By using the point $(2, -2)$ we can find:

$$b = y - mx = -2 - 2 \times 2 = -2 - 4 = -6$$

So, the equation will be $y = 2x - 6$. Point-slope form: $y + 2 = 2(x - 2)$.

One more example:

Find the equation of a line with point $(0,4)$ and slope 3, and write it in slope-intercept and point-slope forms.

Slope-intercept form: $y = 3x + b$. By using the point $(0,4)$ we can find:

$$b = y - mx = 4 - 3 \times 0 = 4$$

So, the equation will be $y = 3x + 4$. Point-slope form: $y - 4 = 3(x - 0)$.

To better explain the problem, I can draw your attention to this example:

Find the equation of a line with point $(4,6)$ and slope 3, and write it in slope-intercept and point-slope forms.

For point-slope form, we have the point and slope: $x_1 = 4$, $y_1 = 6$, $m = 3$. Then:

$$y - y_1 = m(x - x_1) \rightarrow y - 6 = 3(x - 4)$$

The slope-intercept form of a line is: $y = mx + b$.

Since $y = 6$, $x = 4$, $m = 3$, we just need to solve for b.

$$y = mx + b \rightarrow 6 = 3(4) + b \rightarrow b = -6$$

Slope-intercept form: $y = 3x - 6$.

Another example: Find the equation of a line with point $(1,5)$ and slope -3, and write it in slope-intercept and point-slope forms.

For point-slope form, we have the point and slope: $x_1 = 1$, $y_1 = 5$, and $m = -3$.

Then: $y - y_1 = m(x - x_1) \rightarrow y - 5 = -3(x - 1)$.

The slope-intercept form of a line is: $y = mx + b$.

Since $y = 5$, $x = 1$, $m = -3$, we just need to solve for b.

$$y = mx + b \rightarrow 5 = -3(1) + b \rightarrow b = 8$$

Slope-intercept form: $y = -3x + 8$.

✍ Find the equation of each line.

18) Through: $(6, -6)$, slope $= -2$

Point-slope form: _____

Slope-intercept form: _____

19) Through: $(-7,7)$, slope $= 4$

Point-slope form: _____

Slope-intercept form: _____

Write a Point-slope Form Equation from a Graph

The point-slope form equation is used to find the equation of a straight line when given the slope and a point on the line. This form of the equation is only useful when the slope and a point on the line are known. The equation is written as $y - y_1 = m(x - x_1)$, where (x_1, y_1) is a point on the line and m is the slope. The variable (x, y) in the equation represents a random point on the line.

To find the equation of a straight line using the point-slope form, you can follow these steps:

1. Determine the slope, m, of the line using the slope formula: $m = \frac{change\ in\ y}{change\ in\ x}$. Then, find the coordinates (x_1, y_1) of a point on the line.

2. Substitute the slope and point coordinates into the point-slope formula: $y - y_1 = m(x - x_1)$.

3. Simplify the equation to get the standard form of the line's equation.

Let's review an example: According to the following graph, what is the equation of the line in point-slope form?

First, you should find the slope of the line (m). The coordinate of the red point is $(4,6)$. Consider another random point on the line such as $(7,8)$. Put this value in the slope formula: $m = \frac{change\ in\ y}{change\ in\ x} = \frac{8-6}{7-4} = \frac{2}{3} \rightarrow m = \frac{2}{3}$.

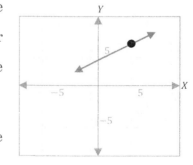

Now, write the equation in point-slope form using the coordinate of the red point is $(4,6)$ and $m = \frac{2}{3}$:

$$y - y_1 = m(x - x_1) \rightarrow y - 6 = \frac{2}{3}(x - 4).$$

Therefore, the equation of the line in point-slope form is

$$y - 6 = \frac{2}{3}(x - 4).$$

Another example: Find the equation of the graph below in point-slope form.

Consider two arbitrary points like $(-5,2)$ and $(2,6)$ on the line graph. (marked points on the line graph).

Then, we calculate the slope of the line passing through these two points such as (x_1, y_1) and (x_2, y_2) using the slope formula: $m = \frac{y_2 - y_1}{x_2 - x_1}$. For the specified

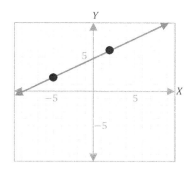

points, we have: $m = \frac{6-2}{2-(-5)} = \frac{4}{7}$. In the next step,

substitute an arbitrary point on the line like $(2,6)$ and the slope obtained $\frac{4}{7}$ in the

point-Slope formula $y - y_1 = m(x - x_1)$. Therefore, the equation of the line in

point-slope form is $y - 6 = \frac{4}{7}(x - 2)$.

 Find the equation of each line.

20) _____

21) _____

22) _____

23) _____

bit.ly/3yaeJ1Q

Find more at

Find $x-$ and $y-$intercepts in the Standard Form of Equation

The standard form of a linear equation, also known as the general form, is written as $Ax + By = C$. In this equation, A, B, and C are integers, and x and y are the variables.

To convert a linear equation to standard form, you can rearrange the equation so that it is in the form $Ax + By = C$. It's important to note that the coefficients A, B, and C should be integers and the variables should be in the proper order as mentioned in the standard form equation.

The $x-$intercept of a line is the point where the line intersects the $x-$axis. At this point, the value of y is equal to zero. The $y-$intercept of a line is the point where the line intersects the $y-$axis. At this point, the value of x is equal to zero.

Let's review an example: Find the $x-$ and $y-$intercepts of the line $6x + 4y = 12$.

To find the $x-$intercept, set y equal to 0 and solve for x:

$6x + 4(0) = 12 \rightarrow 6x = 12 \rightarrow x = 2$

The $x-$intercept is (2,0).

To find the $y-$intercept, set x equal to 0 and solve for y:

$6(0) + 4y = 12 \rightarrow 4y = 12 \rightarrow y = 3$

The $y-$intercept is (0,3).

The $x-$intercept is (2,0) and the $y-$intercept is (0,3).

Another example:

Find the $x-$ and $y-$intercepts of the line $3x - 6y = 0$.

To find the $x-$intercept, set y equal to 0 and solve for x:

$3x - 6(0) = 0 \rightarrow 3x = 0 \rightarrow x = 0$

The x −intercept is $(0,0)$.

To find the y −intercept, set x equal to 0 and solve for y:

$3(0) - 6y = 0 \rightarrow -6y = 0 \rightarrow y = 0$

The y −intercept is $(0,0)$.

Finally, the x − and y −intercept is the origin of the coordinate.

One more example: Find the x − and y −intercepts of the line $2x + 4y = 8$.

To find the x −intercept, set y equal to 0 and solve for x:

$2x + 4(0) = 8 \rightarrow 2x = 8 \rightarrow x = 4$

The x −intercept is $(4,0)$.

To find the y −intercept, set x equal to 0 and solve for y:

$2(0) + 4y = 8 \rightarrow 4y = 8 \rightarrow y = 2$

The y −intercept is $(0,2)$.

The x − and y −intercepts are $(4,0)$ and $(0,2)$, respectively.

For a better understanding, let's solve another example together:

Find the x − and y −intercepts of line $-8x + 16y = 64$.

To find the x −intercept, you can consider y equal to 0 and solve for x:

$-8x + 16y = 64 \rightarrow -8x + 16(0) = 64 \rightarrow -8x = 64 \rightarrow x = -8$

The x −intercept is -8.

To find the y −intercept, you can consider x equal to 0 and solve for y:

$-8x + 16y = 64 \rightarrow -8(0) + 16y = 64 \rightarrow 16y = 64 \rightarrow y = 4$.

The y −intercept is 4.

✒ Find the x −intercept of each line.

24) $21x - 3y = -18$

25) $20x + 20y = -10$

26) $8x + 6y = 16$

27) $2x - 4y = -12$

Graph an Equation in the Standard Form

To graph an equation in standard form, you can follow these steps:

1. Plot the x−intercept and y−intercept. You can find the x−intercept by setting y equal to 0 and solving for x, and you can find the y−intercept by setting x equal to 0 and solving for y. Using the slope-intercept form, find the slope of the line by solving for m from the standard form equation.

2. Using the slope found in step 1, pick a point on the line other than the x−intercept or y−intercept, and use the slope to find another point on the line.

3. Connect the dots you've plotted to form a straight line.

For example, to graph the equation $2x - 4y = 8$:

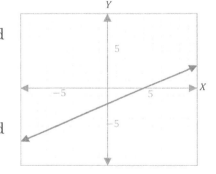

1. To find the x−intercept, set y equal to 0 and solve for x: $2x - 4(0) = 8 \rightarrow x = 4$;

    The x−intercept is $(4,0)$.

2. To find the y−intercept, set x equal to 0 and solve for y: $2(0) - 4y = 8 \rightarrow y = -2$;

    The y−intercept is $(0,-2)$.

3. We can find the slope by dividing both sides by -4, then we have $y = \frac{1}{2}x - 2$, the slope is $\frac{1}{2}$.

4. Using the slope found in step 3, we can pick a point on the line other than the x−intercept or y−intercept, for example $(6,1)$, we can use the slope to find another point on the line $(-4, -4)$, and connect them by a straight line to form a graph.

Another example:

Graph the equation $4x + 2y = 12$:

1. To find the x −intercept, set y equal to 0 and solve for x: $4x + 2(0) = 12 \rightarrow x = 3$;

   The x −intercept is $(3,0)$.

2. To find the y −intercept, set x equal to 0 and solve for y: $4(0) + 2y = 12 \rightarrow y = 6$;

   The y −intercept is $(0,6)$.

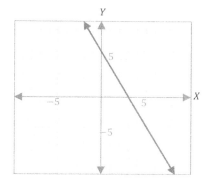

3. We can find the slope by dividing both sides by 4, then we have $y = -2x + 6$, and the slope is -2.

4. Using the slope found in step -2, we can pick a point on the line other than the x −intercept or y −intercept, for example $(2,2)$, we can use the slope to find another point on the line $(4, -2)$, and connect them by a straight line to form a graph.

In this example, we can see that the x −intercept is $(3,0)$, the y −intercept is $(0,6)$, and the slope of the line is -2. By plotting the x −intercept, y −intercept, and any point on the line, we can graph the equation on a coordinate plane.

✎ Graph each equation.

28) $4x - 5y = 40$

29) $9x - 8y = -72$

Equations of Horizontal and Vertical Lines

The equation of a horizontal line is of the form $y = b$, where b is a constant. This is because a horizontal line runs parallel to the x−axis, so its slope (change in y over change in x) is zero. Therefore, the y−value does not change as the x−value changes, and it is equal to a constant value (b).

For example, the equation of a horizontal line that passes through the point (3,4) would be $y = 4$.

On the other hand, the equation of a vertical line is of the form $x = a$, where a is a constant. This is because a vertical line runs parallel to the y−axis, so its slope is undefined. Therefore, the x−value does not change as the y−value changes, and it is equal to a constant value (a).

For example, the equation of a vertical line that passes through the point (3,4) would be $x = 3$.

- The equation of a horizontal line that passes through the point (2,5) would be $y = 5$. This is because the line is parallel to the x−axis, and its slope (change in y over change in x) is zero. Therefore, the y−value does not change as the x−value changes, and it is equal to 5 for all points on the line.

- The equation of a vertical line that passes through the point (−4,3) would be $x = -4$. This is because the line is parallel to the y−axis, and its slope is undefined. Therefore, the x−value does not change as the y−value changes, and it is equal to −4 for all points on the line.

It's worth noting that a horizontal line has a slope of zero, and the x−intercept is undefined, while a vertical line has an undefined slope, and the y−intercept is undefined.

In both cases, the line's equation is in the form of a single variable equals a

constant.

Let's review an example:

Write an equation for the horizontal line that passes through (1,3).

Since the line is horizontal, the equation of the line

is in the form of:

$$y = b,$$

where **y** always takes the same value of 3.

Thus, the equation of the line is:

$$y = 3.$$

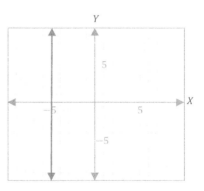

Once more example:

Write an equation for the vertical line that passes through (−5,5).

Since the line is vertical, the equation of the line is

in the form of:

$$x = a,$$

where **x** always takes the same value of −5.

Thus, the equation of the line is: $x = -5$.

 Find the equation of each line.

30) Horizontal line: _____

     Passes through: (1,0)

31) Horizontal line: _____

     Passes through: (0,1)

32) Vertical line: _____

     Passes through: (7,3)

33) Horizontal line: _____

     Passes through: (0,0)

Graph a Horizontal or Vertical Line

A horizontal line is a line that runs along the x −axis, and its slope is equal to zero. To graph a horizontal line, we need to know the y −coordinate of the line, which is also known as the y −intercept.

For example, if we are given the equation of a horizontal line as $y = 3$, we know that the y −intercept is 3, which means that the line passes through the point (0,3) on the coordinate plane. To graph the line, we can simply plot that point and then extend the line horizontally to the right and to the left.

On the other hand, a vertical line is a line that runs along the y −axis. It has an undefined slope, and its x −coordinate is always a constant. To graph a vertical line, we need to know the x −coordinate, which is also known as the x −intercept.

For example, if we are given the equation of a vertical line as $x = 4$, we know that the x −intercept is 4, which means that the line passes through the point (4,0) on the coordinate plane. To graph the line, we can simply plot that point and then extend the line vertically upward and downward.

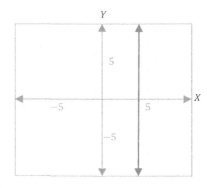

To graph the equation $\boldsymbol{y = -5}$, we can first identify that this is a horizontal line, as the $\boldsymbol{y}$ −value is constant and equal to $\boldsymbol{-5}$. We can then find the $\boldsymbol{y}$ −intercept, which is the point where the line crosses the $\boldsymbol{y}$ −axis. In this case, the $\boldsymbol{y}$ −intercept is $(\boldsymbol{0, -5})$. Then we can plot this point on the coordinate plane and extend the line horizontally, connecting all the points that have the $\boldsymbol{y}$ −value of $\boldsymbol{-5}$. This line will be parallel to the $\boldsymbol{x}$ −axis and at a distance of $\boldsymbol{5}$ units below the $\boldsymbol{x}$ −axis.

Another example:

Graph this equation: $x = 3$.

$x = 3$ is a vertical line and this equation tells you that every x −value is 3. You can consider some points that have an x −value of 3, then draw a line that connects the points.

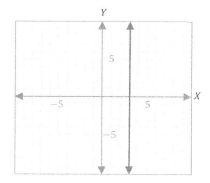

Graph this equation: $x = -2$.

$x = -2$ is a vertical line and this equation tells you that every x −value is −2. You can consider some points that have an x −value of −2, then draw a line that connects the points.

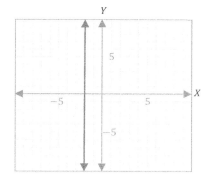

✍ Sketch the graph of each line.

34) Vertical line that

   passes through (2,6)

35) Horizontal line that

   passes through (5,3)

bit.ly/3D61ORj

Find more at

Graph an Equation in Point-Slope Form

To graph an equation in point-slope form, we first need to convert it to slope-intercept form $y = mx + b$. To do this, we can start by isolating y on one side of the equation. The point-slope form is $y - y_1 = m(x - x_1)$, we can add y_1 to both sides and we get $y = m(x - x_1) + y_1$.

For example, if we have an equation in point-slope form $y - 3 = -2(x - 4)$, we can convert it to slope-intercept form by adding 3 to both sides:

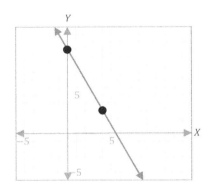

$$y = -2x + 11$$

Now that we have the equation in slope-intercept form, we can graph it by finding the y −intercept, which is the point where the line crosses the y −axis. In this case, the y −intercept is $(0,11)$. We can then plot this point on the coordinate plane and use the slope of the line (-2) to find another point on the line. We can use the point $(x_1, y_1) = (4,3)$ that we had in the point-slope form as another point on the line.

Finally, we can connect the two points with a straight line, and the graph of the equation will be the line that passes through those points.

Another example:

To graph the line $y - 3 = -\frac{1}{3}(x + 5)$, first convert it to point-slope form by writing it as:

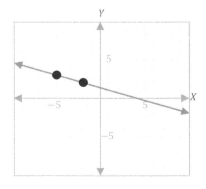

$$y - 3 = -\frac{1}{3}(x + 5)$$

Then, use a point on the line, such as $(-5,3)$, and the slope of $-\frac{1}{3}$ to graph it.

Plot the point $(-5,3)$ on the coordinate plane, then move down 1 unit and right 3 units to find the second point on the line $(-2,2)$. Connect these two points to graph the line.

One more example:

To graph the line $y - 2 = \frac{1}{2}(x + 4)$, first convert it to point-slope form by writing it as:

$$y - 2 = \frac{1}{2}(x + 4)$$

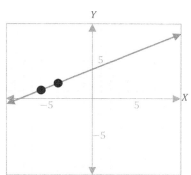

Then, use a point on the line, such as $(-6,1)$, and the slope of $\frac{1}{2}$ to graph it. Plot the point $(-6,1)$ on the coordinate plane, then move up 1 unit and right 2 units to find the second point on the line $(-4,2)$. Connect these two points to graph the line.

✍ Graph each equation.

36) $y + 3 = -\frac{1}{2}(x - 8)$

37) $y - 1 = 3(x + 6)$

38) $y = (x + 11)$

39) $y - 8 = -2(x - 1)$

Equation of Parallel and Perpendicular Lines

The equation of a line in slope-intercept form is $y = mx + b$, where m is the slope of the line and b is the $y-$intercept. To find the equation of a line that is parallel to a given line, you can use the same slope and a different $y-$intercept. For example, if the equation of a given line is $y = 2x + 3$, a line that is parallel to it would have the equation $y = 2x + c$, where c is any real number.

To find the equation of a line that is perpendicular to a given line, you can use the negative reciprocal of the slope and the same $y-$intercept. For example, if the equation of a given line is $y = 2x + 3$, a line that is perpendicular to it would have the equation $y = -\frac{1}{2}x + 3$.

Alternatively, if a line has the equation $y = mx + b$, another line that is parallel to it will have the equation $y = mx + c$ where c is any real number. A line that is perpendicular to it will have the equation $y = -\frac{1}{m}x + d$ where d is any real number.

Let's review an example:

Find equation of a line parallel to $y = 6x + 4$ and passes though the point (0,7).

To find the equation of a line that is parallel to $y = 6x + 4$ and passes through the point (0,7), we can use the point-slope form of a linear equation. The point-slope form is $y - y_1 = m(x - x_1)$, where (x_1, y_1) is a point on the line, and m is the slope of the line. First, we know that the line is parallel to $y = 6x + 4$, which means that the slope of the line is 6.

Next, we can use the point (0,7) to find the $y-$intercept of the line. Substituting the point and the slope into the point-slope form gives: $y - 7 = 6(x - 0)$.

Simplifying this equation gives: $y = 6x + 7$. So, the equation of the line that is parallel to $y = 6x + 4$ and passes through the point (0,7) is $y = 6x + 7$.

One more example:

Perpendicular to $y = -4x + 10$ and passes through the point (7,2).

The slope of $y = -4x + 10$ is -4. The negative reciprocal of that slope is: $m = \frac{(-1)}{(-4)} = \frac{1}{4}$. So, the perpendicular line has a slope of $\frac{1}{4}$.

Then: $y - y_1 = \frac{1}{4}(x - x_1)$ and now put in the point (7,2): $y - 2 = \frac{1}{4}(x - 7)$. Slope intercept $y = mx + b$ form: $y - 2 = \frac{1}{4}x - \frac{7}{4} \rightarrow y = \frac{1}{4}x + \frac{1}{4}$.

Another example:

Find the equation of a line perpendicular to $y = -2x + 7$ and passes through the point (1,3).

To find the equation of a line that is perpendicular to $y = -2x + 7$ and passes through the point (1,3), we can use the point-slope form of a linear equation and the negative reciprocal of the slope of the given line.

First, we know that the line is perpendicular to $y = -2x + 7$, which means that the slope of the line is the negative reciprocal of -2, which is $\frac{1}{2}$.

Next, we can use the point (1,3) to find the $y-$intercept of the line. Substituting the point and the slope into the point-slope form gives: $y - 3 = \frac{1}{2}(x - 1)$.

Simplifying this equation gives: $y = \frac{1}{2}x + 2.5$.

So, the equation of the line that is perpendicular to $y = -2x + 7$ and passes through the point (1,3) is $y = \frac{1}{2}x + 2.5$.

✎ Find the equation of each following.

40) Parallel to $y = -6x + 5$

Passes through (4,4)

41) perpendicular to $y = -\frac{1}{2}x - 4$

Passes through (7,1)

bit.ly/3ke2ieg

Find more at

Compare Linear Function's Graph and Equations

Linear functions are functions that have a constant rate of change, represented by their slope. The slope of a linear function can be positive, negative, zero, or undefined. This slope is represented by the coefficient of the x −term in the equation of the line. The y −intercept of a linear function can be positive, negative, or zero. The y −intercept is represented by the constant term of the equation of the line.

The graph of a linear function is a straight line, and the slope of the line represents the rate of change of the function. A positive slope means that the function increases as x increases, while a negative slope means that the function decreases as x increases. A slope of zero means that the function does not change as x increases.

Two linear functions can have the same slope but different y −intercepts, which means that the two lines are parallel. They will have the same direction but different starting points. Two linear functions can have different slopes and different y −intercepts, which means that the two lines are not parallel. They will have different directions and different starting points.

To summarize, the slope of a linear function represents the rate of change of the function, and the y −intercept represents the starting point of the function. Two linear functions with the same slope but different y −intercepts are parallel, while two linear functions with different slopes are not parallel.

Let's review an example: Here's an example of comparing the equations of two linear functions.

Function 1: $y = 2x + 1$ and Function 2: $y = 2x - 3$

Both function 1 and function 2 have the same slope, which is 2. This means that the rate of change of both functions is the same, and the graph of both functions will have the same direction. However, function 1 has a y −intercept of 1, while function 2 has a y −intercept of −3. This means that the starting point of the two functions is different. The graph of function 1 will start at the point (0,1) and the graph of function 2 will start at the point (0, −3).

The graphs of both lines will be parallel to each other but will be shifted vertically. The graph of function 1 will be above the graph of function 2.

It's important to note that even though the two lines have different y −intercepts, both lines pass through an infinite number of points, so they are not different lines but just different representations of the same line.

Another example: Compare the following linear functions with each other.

Function 1: $x + 3y = 3$ and Function 2: $y = 3x - 2$

To compare, we evaluate the rate of change and y −intercept of two functions. First, we rearrange the given equation and write it in terms of y. So, we have: $y = -\frac{1}{3}x + 3$. We set the value of x to zero to get the y −intercept. Then: $x = 0 \rightarrow 0 + 3y = 9 \rightarrow y = 3$. The y −intercept is (0,3).

Similarly for function 2, the y −intercept is (0, −2), and the slope of the function is 3.

Now, you can see that the slopes are the negative reciprocal of together. This means that two lines are perpendicular.

✍ Compare the slope of the function A and function B.

42)

Function A: $y = 6x - 3$

bit.ly/3XuYCHi

Find more at

Two-variable Linear Equations Word Problems

A two-variable linear equation is a type of equation that involves two variables, usually represented as x and y, with an exponent of 1. The solutions of a two-variable linear equation can be represented as ordered pairs, such as (x, y). These equations can take on several forms, including standard form, point-slope form, and intercept form.

The standard form of a two-variable linear equation is written as $ax + by = c$, where a, b, and c are real numbers and x and y are the variables.

The slope-intercept form of a two-variable linear equation is written as $y = mx + b$, where m represents the slope of the line and b represents the $y-$intercept.

The point-slope form of a two-variable linear equation is written as $y - y_1 = m(x - x_1)$, where (x, y) is a point on the line and m represents the slope of the line.

Solving two-variable linear equations word problems typically involves the following steps:

1. Read and understand the problem: Carefully read the problem and identify what information is given and what is being asked for.

2. Translate the problem into mathematical terms: Use mathematical symbols and equations to represent the information given in the problem.

3. Solve the equation: Use algebraic techniques to solve for the unknown variable.

4. Check your solution: Substitute your solution back into the original equation to make sure it is a valid solution.

5. Interpret the solution: Translate the solution back into the context of the problem and make sure it makes sense.

Here's an example of how to use these steps to solve a word problem:

Problem: A store sells two types of shirts, regular and sale shirts. The store sold a total of 50 shirts and earned $150 in revenue. Regular shirts sell for $10 each and sale shirts sell for $5 each. How many of each type of shirt did the store sell?

1. Read and understand the problem: The problem is asking how many regular and sale shirts the store sold.

2. Translate the problem into mathematical terms: Let x be the number of regular shirts and y be the number of sale shirts. We know that $x + y = 50$ and $10x + 5y = 350$.

3. Solve the equation: We can use either substitution or elimination method to solve for x and y. Using the first equation, we can find that $y = 50 - x$. Substituting this into the second equation we get: $10x + 5(50 - x) = 350$.

4. Check your solution: Once we solve the equation, we get $x = 20$ and $y = 30$, check this solution by plugging it back into the first equation and the second equation.

5. Interpret the solution: The store sold 20 regular shirts and 30 sale shirts.

It's also important to note that word problems could have more than one solution, no solution, or infinitely many solutions based on the given information, so it's important to check whether the solution obtained makes sense in the context of the problem.

✍ Answer the following questions.

43) John has an automated hummingbird feeder. He fills it to capacity, 8 fluid ounces. It releases 1 fluid ounce of nectar every day. Write an equation that shows how the number of fluid ounces of nectar left, y, depends on the number of days John has filled it, x.

44) The entrance fee to Park City is $9. Additionally, skate rentals cost $4 per hour. Write an equation that shows how the total cost, y, depends on the length of the rental in hours, x.

bit.ly/3KD9SwS

Find more at

Chapter 4: Answers

1) 1

2) 2

3) -5

4) -2

5) $-\frac{1}{4}$

6) -6

7) $y = 4x + 16$

8) $y = 3x + 2$

9) $y = -5x - 3$

10) $y = -4x - 22$

11) $y = -3x - 15$

12)

13)

14) y −intercept: -1

   x −intercept: -3

   Slope: $-\frac{1}{3}$

15) y −intercept: 10

   x −intercept: -2

   Slope: 5

16) $y = -\frac{3}{2}x + 4$

17) $y = \frac{5}{3}x$

18) Point-slope form: $y + 6 = -2(x - 6)$

   Slope-intercept form: $y = -2x + 6$

19) Point-slope form: $y - 7 = 4(x + 7)$

   Slope-intercept form: $y = 4x + 35$

20) $y = -(x - 1)$

21) $y + 4 = 3x$

22) $y = \frac{2}{3}(x + 3)$

23) $y - 3 = -2(x + 4)$

24) $-\frac{6}{7}$

25) $-\frac{1}{2}$

26) 2

27) -6

28)

29)

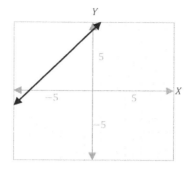

30) $y = 0$

31) $y = 1$

32) $x = 7$

33) $y = 0$

34)

35)

36)

37)

38)

39)

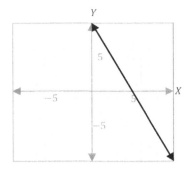

40) $y = -6x + 28$

41) $y = 2x - 13$

42) The absolute value of the slope of function A is 6 and it is steeper than the absolute value of the slope of function B (-1) and the slope of the two functions have different signs.

43) $y = -x + 8$

44) $y = 4x + 9$

CHAPTER

5 Inequalities and System of Equations

Math topics that you'll learn in this chapter:

- ☑ One–Step Inequalities
- ☑ Multi–Step Inequalities
- ☑ Compound Inequalities
- ☑ Write a Linear Inequality from a Graph
- ☑ Graph Solutions to One-step and Two-step Linear Inequalities
- ☑ Solve Advanced Linear Inequalities in Two-Variables
- ☑ Graph Solutions to Advance Linear Inequalities
- ☑ Absolute Value Inequalities
- ☑ Systems of Equations
- ☑ Find the Number of Solutions to a Linear Equation
- ☑ Write a System of Equations Given a Graph
- ☑ Systems of Equations Word Problems Top of Form
- ☑ Solve One-step and Two-step Linear Equations Word Problems
- ☑ Systems of Linear Inequalities
- ☑ Write Two-variable Inequalities in the Form of Word Problems

One–Step Inequalities

One-step inequalities are inequalities that involve a single operation, such as addition, subtraction, multiplication, or division. These inequalities can be solved by isolating the variable on one side of the inequality.

Inequality signs are: "less than" $<$, "greater than" $>$, "less than or equal to" $\leq$, and "greater than or equal to" $\geq$.

When solving one-step inequalities, remember to keep the inequality symbol consistent throughout the solution process. This means that when you multiply or divide both sides of an inequality by a positive number, the inequality symbol stays the same. However, when you multiply or divide both sides of an inequality by a negative number, the inequality symbol must be flipped. For example, if you have the inequality $-\frac{x}{2} > 4$, you would solve it as follows: $-\frac{x}{2} > 4 \rightarrow x < -8$.

Let's review an example:

Solve the inequality: $x + 7 \geq 11$.

To solve the inequality $x + 7 \geq 11$ for x, we need to isolate x on one side of the inequality. To do this, we can subtract 7 from both sides: $x + 7 \geq 11 \rightarrow x \geq 4$.

So, the solution is $x \geq 4$, which means that x can take on any value greater than or equal to 4. This solution can also be represented in interval notation as $x \in [4, \infty)$, which means all real numbers greater than or equal to 4.

One more example:

Solve the inequality: $x - 4 > -7$.

To solve the inequality $x - 4 > -7$ for x, we need to isolate x on one side of the inequality. To do this, we can add 4 to both sides: $x - 4 > -7 \rightarrow x > -3$.

So, the solution is $x > -3$, which means that x can take on any value greater than -3.

Another example:

Solve the inequality: $x + 3 \leq 2$.

The inverse (opposite) operation of addition is subtraction. In this inequality, 3 is added to x. To isolate x, we need to subtract 3 from both sides of the inequality.

Then: $x + 3 \leq 2 \to x + 3 - 3 \leq 2 - 3 \to x \leq -1$.

The solution is: $x \leq -1$.

To better explain the problem, you can draw your attention to these examples:

Solve the inequality: $x - 1 > -7$.

1 is subtracted from x. Add 1 to both sides:

$x - 1 > -7 \to x - 1 + 1 > -7 + 1 \to x > -6$

Solve: $3x > -15$.

3 is multiplied to x. Divide both sides by 3. Then:

$3x > -15 \to \frac{3x}{3} > \frac{-15}{3} \to x > -5$

Solve: $-4x \leq 10$.

-4 is multiplied by x. Divide both sides by -4. Remember when dividing or multiplying both sides of an inequality by negative numbers, flip the direction of the inequality sign. Then:

$-4x \leq 10 \to \frac{-4x}{-4} \geq \frac{10}{-4} \to x \geq -2.5$

✍ Solve the following inequalities.

1) $y - 11 \leq 2$

2) $4x < -8$

3) $2a > 3$

4) $x - \frac{2}{3} \geq -2$

5) $3 + x \geq 7$

6) $-\frac{1}{2}x < -\frac{3}{2}$

7) $b < -2b + 3$

8) $-x \leq 5$

Multi−Step Inequalities

Solving multi-step inequalities is a process that involves several steps, similar to solving multi-step equations. The steps to solving multi-step inequalities are as follows:

1. Isolate the variable on one side of the inequality. This is done by using inverse operations such as addition, subtraction, multiplication, and division.

2. Simplify the inequality by combining like terms, if necessary.

3. Divide or multiply both sides by the same number, if the coefficient of the variable is not 1.

4. Change the direction of the inequality sign, if necessary, when dividing or multiplying both sides by a negative number.

5. Check your solutions by plugging them back into the original inequality and making sure they make the inequality true.

6. Graph the solution on a number line.

For example, consider the inequality: $2x + 4 > 10$.

1. Subtract 4 from both sides: $2x > 6$.

2. Divide both sides by 2: $x > 3$.

3. The solution to the inequality is $x > 3$. To check, we can substitute $x = 4$ into the original inequality and see that it does make the inequality true, $2 \times 4 + 4 > 10$.

When solving an inequality, it is important to remember that multiplying or dividing both sides of an inequality by a negative number changes the direction of the inequality.

Let's review another example:

Solve: $-5x + 12 \leq -2$.

To solve the inequality $-5x + 12 \leq -2$, we will follow these steps:

1. Isolate the variable on one side of the inequality by subtracting 12 from both sides: $-5x \leq -14$.

2. Divide both sides by -5: $x \geq 2.8$.

3. Reverse the inequality sign, as we're dividing by a negative number.

4. Check the solution by plugging it back into the original inequality and making sure it makes the inequality true: $-5(7) + 12 \leq -2 \rightarrow -35 + 12 \leq -2$, which is true.

The solution to this inequality is $x \geq 2.8$.

More examples to better explain:

Solve this inequality. $7x - 3 \geq 11$

In this inequality, 3 is subtracted from $7x$. The inverse of subtraction is addition.

Add 3 to both sides of the inequality: $7x - 3 + 3 \geq 11 + 3 \rightarrow 7x \geq 14$.

Now, divide both sides by 7. Then: $7x \geq 14 \rightarrow x \geq 2$.

The solution of this inequality is $x \geq 2$.

Solve this inequality. $5x - 2 \leq 13$

First, add 2 to both sides: $5x - 2 + 2 \leq 13 + 2$. Then simplify:

$$5x - 2 + 2 \leq 13 + 2 \rightarrow 5x \leq 15.$$

Now divide both sides by 5: $\frac{5x}{5} \leq \frac{15}{5} \rightarrow x \leq 3$.

Solve this inequality. $-2x + 5 < 3$

First, subtract 5 from both sides: $-2x + 5 - 5 < 3 - 5 \rightarrow -2x < -2$.

Divide both sides by -2. Remember that you need to flip the direction of the inequality sign. $-5x < 5 \rightarrow x > 1$.

✎ Solve the following inequalities.

9) $3x + 8 \leq -1$

10) $3 - x \geq 7$

11) $\frac{7 - 2x}{-3} > -1$

12) $-3 + 5x > 2$

13) $7 < -2x - 1$

14) $\frac{x + 2}{5} \leq 1$

Compound Inequalities

Solving compound inequalities is a process that involves breaking down a compound inequality into a combination of two or more simple inequalities, and then solving each one separately.

Here are the steps to solve compound inequalities:

1. Recognize the type of compound inequality you are dealing with. Compound inequalities can be written in two forms: "and" or "or".

2. Break down the compound inequality into two simple inequalities. For example, if the compound inequality is of the form "and", then it will be in the form of "$x < a$ and $x > b$", which can be broken down into two simple inequalities: "$x < a$" and "$x > b$".

3. Solve each of the simple inequalities separately and find the solution set for each one.

4. Combine the solution sets of each of the simple inequalities to get the final solution set for the compound inequality.

5. Graph the solution set on the number line.

For example, consider the compound inequality $3x + 2 < 7$ or $2x - 5 \geq 0$.

1. Break down the compound inequality into two simple inequalities:

    $3x + 2 < 7$ and $2x - 5 \geq 0$.

2. Solve the first inequality: $3x + 2 < 7 \rightarrow 3x < 5 \rightarrow x < \frac{5}{3}$.

3. Solve the second inequality: $2x - 5 \geq 0 \rightarrow 2x \geq 5 \rightarrow x \geq \frac{5}{2}$.

4. The solution set for the compound inequality is $x < \frac{5}{3}$ or $x \geq \frac{5}{2}$.

5. We can graph the solution set on the number line.

Another example: Solve. $12 < -3x \leq 24$

Find more at

To solve the compound inequality $12 < -3x \leq 24$, we will follow these steps:

1. Break down the compound inequality into two simple inequalities, $-3x > 12$ and $-3x \leq 24$.

2. Solve the first inequality: $-3x > 12 \rightarrow x < -4$.

3. Solve the second inequality: $-3x \leq 24 \rightarrow x \geq -8$.

Combine the solution sets of each of the simple inequalities to get the final solution set for the compound inequality: $\boldsymbol{-8 \leq x < -4}$.

Another examples:

Solve. $6 < 3x \leq 24$

To solve this inequality, divide all sides of the inequality by 3. This simplifies the inequality as follows: $2 < x \leq 8$ or $(2,8]$.

Solve. $x - 5 < -9$ or $\frac{x}{5} > 3$.

Solve each inequality by isolating the variable:

$$x - 5 < -9 \rightarrow x - 5 + 5 < -9 + 5 \rightarrow x < -4.$$

Therefore: $\frac{x}{5} > 3 \rightarrow \frac{x}{5} \times 5 > 3 \times 5 \rightarrow x > 15$.

The solution to these two inequalities is:

$$x < -4 \text{ or } x > 15 \text{ or } (-\infty, -4) \cup (15, \infty).$$

✎ Solve the following inequalities.

15) $-4 < 2x < 5$

16) $0 < x - 3 \leq 1$

17) $3 \leq 1 - 2x \leq 5$

18) $\frac{3}{4}x < 2$ or $-x \geq -\frac{1}{3}$

19) $1 < \frac{2x-1}{3} < 2$

20) $-10 < -\frac{2}{5}a < 0$

21) $5x \leq 45$ and $x - 11 > -21$

22) $5x + 1 < 4$ or $-\frac{1}{2}x + 2 > -\frac{3}{2}$

Write a Linear Inequality from a Graph

When comparing two linear expressions using inequality symbols such as $<$, $>$, $\leq$, or $\geq$, they create linear inequalities. The graph of a linear inequality is represented by either a dashed or solid line, and one side is shaded. By analyzing the graph of a linear inequality and considering linear relationships, the equation of the linear inequality can be determined.

To write an equation from a graph of a linear inequality, these steps should be followed:

1. Determine if the inequality line is represented by a dashed or solid line. If it's a dashed line, the inequality symbol is $<$ or $>$. If it's a solid line, the inequality symbol is $\leq$ or $\geq$.

2. Identify two points on the inequality line. These points can be used to determine the equation of the inequality.

3. Find the slope of the inequality line by using the two points identified in step 2. The slope formula is $m = \frac{y_2 - y_1}{x_2 - x_1}$.

4. Use the slope, a point on the line, and the y-intercept formula $y = mx + b$, where m is the slope of the line, (x, y) is a point on the line, and b is the y −intercept.

5. Observe the shaded part of the graph and determine if y is less than or greater than the obtained equation. You can use a point from the shaded part to find the sign of inequality.

Let's review an example: Write the slope-intercept form equation of the following graph.

To write the inequality equation in slope-intercept form, you should find the y −intercept (b), and the slope (m), of the solid line. The value of b is -1 because the solid line passes through the $y-$axis at $(0,-1)$. Now, consider 2 points on the solid line to find the slope. You can use $(0,-1)$ and $(1,2)$: $m = \frac{y_2-y_1}{x_2-x_1} = \frac{2-(-1)}{1-0} = 3 \rightarrow m = 3$.

Now, use the value of b and m and put them into the slope-intercept form formula: $y = mx + b \rightarrow y = 3x - 1$.

Determine the symbol of inequality: you have a solid line and the shaded part is above the line. So, the equation of the inequality is as follows: $y \geq 3x - 1$.

To better explain the problem, you can draw your attention to this example:

Write an equation from the following graph of the linear inequality.

First, find the equation of the dashed line. For this purpose, by using two arbitrary points such as $(-5,8)$ and $(0,7)$ and the formula $m = \frac{y_2-y_1}{x_2-x_1}$, to evaluate the slope of the graph. We have: $m = \frac{7-8}{0-(-5)} = \frac{-1}{5}$. Then, by

substituting in formula $y - y_0 = m(x - x_0)$, where (x_0, y_0) is a point like $(0,7)$ on the line, the equation of the line is obtained: $y - 7 = \frac{-1}{5}(x - 0) \rightarrow y = \frac{-1}{5}x + 7$.

We put a point of the shaded area in the equation to determine the direction of the inequality. Considering point $(0,0)$, we have: $y = 0$ and $x = 0 \rightarrow \frac{-1}{5}(0) + 7 = 7$, which means that $y < \frac{-1}{5}x + 7$.

✍ Solve the following inequalities.

23) _____

24) _____

Graph Solutions to One-step and Two-step Linear Inequalities

Inequalities that you can solve using only one step are called one-step inequalities. Inequalities that you should take two steps to solve are called two-step inequalities.

To graph linear inequalities, use the following steps:

1. First, write the inequality in standard form. This means that the inequality should have the variable on one side and a constant on the other side.

   Example: $2x + 3 < 7$.

2. Next, solve for x by isolating x on one side of the inequality.

   Example: $2x < 4$.

3. Divide or multiply both sides of the inequality by the coefficient of x to get x by itself on one side. Example: $x < 2$.

4. Test a value that is less than the solution to see if it makes the inequality true and test a value that is greater than the solution to see if it makes the inequality false. Example: for $x < 2$, if we test $x = 1$, the inequality is true, and if we test $x = 3$, the inequality is false.

5. Graph the solution on a number line. If the inequality is $<$ or $>$, use a dotted line to show that the solution is not included. If the inequality is $\leq$ or $\geq$, use a solid line to show that the solution is included. Example: $x < 2$ would be graphed as a dotted line with an open circle at 2.

6. Shade the appropriate side of the graph according to the inequality sign. $<$ or $>$ inequalities will be shaded on one side of the line, $\leq$ or $\geq$ will be shaded on both sides of the line. Example: $x < 2$ would be shaded to the left of the line.

For twostep inequalities:

1. Start by solving for x or y by isolating it on one side of the inequality.

2. Then solve for the next variable by substituting the first solution into the other inequality.

3. Test the solution by substituting it back into the original inequalities to see if it makes them true.

4. Graph the solution on a coordinate plane.

5. Shade the appropriate region on the coordinate plane according to the inequality sign.

6. Repeat the steps for any other solution.

Let's review an example: Solve the following inequality and graph the solution.

$$m - 2 \geq 3$$

Solve for m: $m - 2 \geq 3 \rightarrow m \geq 3 + 2 \rightarrow m \geq 5$. Now, graph $m \geq 5$. The inequality $m \geq 5$ means that m can be any number more than or equal to 5. m can be equal to 5, so you should use a filled-in circle located on 5. Also, m can be more than 5, so you should also draw an arrow pointing to the right:

Solve the following inequality and graph the solution: $-3q - 1 < 2$.

$-3q - 1 < 2$ is a two-step inequality. First, solve for q:

$$-3q - 1 < 2 \rightarrow -3q < 2 + 1 \rightarrow -3q < 3 \rightarrow q > -1.$$

Now, graph $q > -1$. The inequality $q > -1$ means that q can be any number more than -1. q can't be equal to -1, so you should use an open circle located on -1. Also, q can be more than -1, so you should also draw an arrow pointing to the right:

🖎 Solve the following inequalities and graph the solution.

25) $x + 3 < 7$ 27) $5 - x > 4$

26) $2x \geq -4$ 28) $-1 < 2a - 7 \leq 3$

Solve Advanced Linear Inequalities in Two-Variables

The general form of a linear inequality in two-variable is $Ax + By < C$. To solve advanced linear inequalities in two variables, you can use the following steps:

1. Get the inequality in standard form, which means having the variables on one side and constants on the other, and the inequality symbol should be either $<$, $>$, $\leq$, or $\geq$.

2. Isolate one of the variables in the inequality by performing the same operation on both sides of the inequality.

3. Plot the inequality on a coordinate plane, using the slope and y −intercept (if possible) of the equation to determine the correct half-plane.

4. Test a point that is not on the line to determine which side of the line to shade.

5. Graph the solution on the coordinate plane, shading the correct half-plane.

6. Write the solution using the inequality sign.

7. For example, consider the inequality: $2x + 3y > 6$.

8. To solve this inequality, we first want to isolate one of the variables on one side of the inequality sign. We can do this by subtracting $3y$ from both sides, resulting in: $2x > 6 − 3y$.

9. Next, we can divide both sides by 2, resulting in: $x > \frac{(6-3y)}{2}$.

10. Now we have the inequality in slope-intercept form, where x is the independent variable and $\frac{(6-3y)}{2}$ is the dependent variable. To graph this inequality, we can use a solid line if the inequality is "less than or equal to" or "greater than or equal to", and a dashed line if the inequality is "less than" or "greater than".

11. To find the solution set, we can pick a test point not on the line and

check whether it satisfies the inequality. For example, if we pick the point $(0,0)$, we can substitute these values into the inequality and get: $0 > \frac{(6-3(0))}{2}$, which is not true. Therefore, the solution set is all the points that are above the line.

Let's review an example:

Solve the inequality $3x + 1 \geq 2y - x$.

First, convert to the general form. Subtract 1 from both sides of the inequality.

So, $3x + 1 - 1 \geq 2y - x - 1 \rightarrow 3x \geq 2y - x - 1$.

Subtract $2y$ to both sides as $3x - 2y \geq 2y - x - 1 - 2y \rightarrow 3x - 2y \geq -x - 1$.

Also, add x to the sides: $3x - 2y + x \geq -x - 1 + x \rightarrow 4x - 2y \geq -1$.

The answer to this inequality is all ordered pairs in the form of (x, y), where $y \leq \frac{4x+1}{2}$. That is, $\left\{(x, y) | x \in \mathbb{R}, y \leq \frac{4x+1}{2}\right\}$.

Another example:

Solve the inequality $y - 5 < x - 3$.

Convert to the general form. Add 3 to both sides. So,

$$y - 5 + 3 < x - 3 + 3 \rightarrow y - 2 < x.$$

Now, subtract y from the sides $y - 2 < x \rightarrow x - y > -2$. The answer to this inequality is all ordered pairs in the form of (x, y), where $x > y - 2$. That is, $\{(x, y) | y \in R, x > y - 2\}$.

✐ Solve the following inequalities.

29) $1 + 2y < 3x + 4$

30) $y - 5x \geq 2y + 7$

31) $\frac{2x-3y}{2} > x - 1$

32) $y + 2 \leq 2x - 3$

33) $\frac{3}{2} > 3y - 2 + x$

34) $6x - 3y + 4 \leq 0$

bit.ly/3Cw38wF

Find more at

Graph Solutions to Advance Linear Inequalities

To graph the solution to an advanced linear inequality in two variables, we can use the following steps:

1. Solve the inequality for one of the variables in terms of the other variable. This will put the inequality in slope-intercept form, where the independent variable is on one side of the inequality sign and the dependent variable is on the other side.

2. Determine the type of inequality. If the inequality is "less than or equal to" or "greater than or equal to", use a solid line to graph the equation. If the inequality is "less than" or "greater than", use a dashed line to graph the equation.

3. Plot the line on a coordinate plane, using the $x-$ and $y-$intercepts as additional points if necessary.

4. Pick a test point not on the line and substitute the coordinates into the inequality. If the inequality is true, the point is in the solution set. If the inequality is false, the point is not in the solution set.

5. Determine the solution set based on the inequality and the type of line used. If the inequality is "greater than" or "solid", the solution set is all the points above the line. If the inequality is "less than" or "dashed", the solution set is all the points below the line. If the inequality is "greater than or equal to" or "less than or equal to" include the line in the solution set.

6. Shade the solution set on the coordinate plane.

Keep in mind that the solution set to an inequality is a region in the coordinate plane and not a single point, this region is represented by shading the area of the coordinate plane that satisfies the inequality.

Here's an example:

Consider the inequality: $2x - 3y \leq 6$.

To solve this inequality, we can start by isolating one of the variables on one side of the inequality sign by adding $3y$ to both sides: $2x \leq 6 + 3y$.

Next, we can divide both sides by 2 to get: $x \leq \frac{(6+3y)}{2}$.

Now, we have the inequality in slope-intercept form, where x is the independent variable and $\frac{(6+3y)}{2}$ is the dependent variable. To graph this inequality, we can use a solid line, since the inequality is "less than or equal to".

To find the solution set, we can pick a test point not on the line and check whether it satisfies the inequality. For example, if we pick the point $(1,1)$, we can substitute these values into the inequality and get: $1 \leq \frac{(6+3(1))}{2} = 4.5$, which is true. Therefore, the point $(1,1)$ is in the solution set.

To graph this, we can plot the y −intercept which is $(0, -2)$ and the x −intercept which is $(3,0)$ and connect them using a dashed line. All the point below the line and on the line are the solution set.

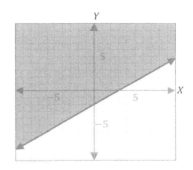

Keep in mind that this is just one example, and the steps for solving and graphing advanced linear inequalities in two variables can vary depending on the specific inequality being solved.

✍ Solve the following inequalities.

35) $3x - 2y > 6$

36) $2y + x < 2x$

Absolute Value Inequalities

An absolute value inequality involves an absolute value expression, denoted by "| |", and a sign of inequality such as $<$, $>$, $\leq$, or $\geq$. To solve an absolute value inequality, the first step is to transform it into a simple inequality by isolating the absolute value expression on one side of the inequality sign. The method used to transform the absolute value inequality into a simple inequality depends on the direction of the inequality. Depending on the direction of the inequality, one of the following methods can be used:

- For an inequality of the form $|a| < b$, we can write two separate inequalities: $a < b$ and $-a < b$.

- For an inequality of the form $|a| > b$, we can write two separate inequalities: $a > b$ and $a < -b$.

- For an inequality of the form $|a| \leq b$, we can write two separate inequalities: $a \leq b$ and $-a \leq b$.

- For an inequality of the form $|a| \geq b$, we can write two separate inequalities: $a \geq b$ and $a \leq -b$. After the inequalities are separated, they can be solved individually and the solution can be represented on a number line.

To solve absolute value inequalities, we can use the following steps:

1. Isolate the absolute value expression on one side of the inequality sign.

2. Split the inequality into two separate inequalities by using the rule that the absolute value of a number is always non-negative.

3. Solve each inequality separately, considering that the absolute value is non-negative.

4. Graph the solution on a number line, remembering that the solution is all the numbers that make the inequality true.

    For example: consider the inequality $|x - 3| \geq 2$.

    - In this example, the expression absolute value is isolated.

- Now we have two inequalities: $x - 3 \geq 2$ or $x - 3 \leq -2$.
- Solving each inequality separately: $x \geq 5$ or $x \leq 1$.
- Graph the solution on a number line: $(-\infty, 1] \cup [5, +\infty)$.

Keep in mind that when solving absolute value inequalities, it is important to remember that the absolute value of a number is always non-negative, and to split the inequality into two separate inequalities. Also, the solution to an absolute value inequality is a set of numbers represented by an interval on the number line.

In other words, to solve the absolute value inequality depending on the direction of the inequality can be used one of the following methods:

- To solve x in the inequality $|ax + b| < c$, you must solve $-c < ax + b < c$.
- To solve x in the inequality $|ax + b| > c$ you must solve $ax + b > c$ and $ax + b < -c$.

For better explain, consider the following example:

Solve: $|2x + 1| < 7$.

Since the inequality sign is $<$, rewrite the inequality to: $-7 < 2x + 1 < 7$. Then, solve the inequality: $-7 - 1 < 2x + 1 - 1 < 7 - 1 \rightarrow -8 < 2x < 6$. Now, divide each section by 2: $-8 < 2x < 6 \rightarrow -4 < x < 3$.

You can also write this solution using the interval symbol: $(-4, 3)$.

✎ Solve the following inequalities and graph the solution.

37) $|2 + x| < 1$

38) $\left| -\frac{2}{3}x \right| \geq 2$

39) $|3x - 1| \leq 3$

40) $|-2x + 3| > 1$

System of Equations

A system of equations is a set of two or more equations that contain multiple variables. To solve a system of equations, one common method is the elimination method. The elimination method uses the property of equality that allows you to add or subtract the same value from both sides of an equation.

For example, consider the system of equations: $x - y = 1$ and $x + y = 5$.

To use the elimination method, we can start by adding the same value to both sides of each equation. In this case, we can subtract x from both sides of the first equation and y from both sides of the first equation. Now, we have: $x - x - y = -x + 1 \rightarrow -y = -x + 1$, and $-y - y = -x - y + 1 \rightarrow -2y = -x - y + 1$. Next, you can see that there is the expression $x + y$ from the first side of the second equation on the left side of the obtained equation as follows:

$-2y = -x - y + 1 \rightarrow -2y = -(x + y) + 1$.

Now, substitute 5 instead of $x + y$: $-2y = -(5) + 1 \rightarrow -2y = -4 \rightarrow y = 2$.

Now we can substitute the value of y into the second equation:

$y = 2 \rightarrow x + 2 = 5 \rightarrow x = 3$.

So, the solution to this system of equations is $(x, y) = (3, 2)$.

Here's another example of a system of equations and how to solve it using the elimination method:

Consider the system of equations: $2x + y = 12$ and $4x + 6y = 24$.

1. To use the elimination method, we can start by multiplying one of the equations by a constant. In this case, we can multiply the first equation by 2. Now, we have: $4x + 2y = 24$ and $4x + 6y = 24$.

2. Next, we can subtract the first equation from the second equation. This will eliminate one of the variables and leave us with a simpler equation: $4x + 6y - (4x + 2y) = 24 - (24) \rightarrow 2y = 0 \rightarrow y = 0$.

3. Now, we can solve for y: $y = 0$.

4. Now that we know the value of y, we can substitute it back into one of the original equations to find the value of x. In this case, we can substitute $y = 0$ into the first equation: $2x + (0) = 12 \rightarrow 2x = 12 \rightarrow x = 6$.

5. So, the solution to this system of equations is $(x, y) = (6,0)$.

Keep in mind that there are many methods for solving systems of equations, and the elimination method is just one of them. Depending on the specific system of equations, some methods may be more efficient or easier to use than others.

As another example:

What is the value of xy in this system of equations? $\begin{cases} -x + 3y = -2 \\ 3x + y = -2 \end{cases}$

Solving a System of Equations by Elimination: multiply the first equation by (3) then add it to the second equation.

$\begin{array}{l} 3(-x + 3y = -2) \\ 3x + y = -2 \end{array} \rightarrow \begin{array}{l} -3x + 9y = -6 \\ 3x + y = -2 \end{array} \rightarrow 3x + y + (-3x + 9y) = -2 + (-6)$

$$\rightarrow 10y = -8 \rightarrow y = -\frac{4}{5}$$

Plug in the value of y into one of the equations and solve for x.

$-x + 3\left(-\frac{4}{5}\right) = -2 \rightarrow -x + \left(-\frac{12}{5}\right) = -2 \rightarrow -x = -2 + \frac{12}{5} \rightarrow x = -\frac{2}{5}.$

Thus, $xy = -\frac{2}{5} \times \left(-\frac{4}{5}\right) = +\frac{8}{25} = 0.32.$

✍ Solve the following system of equations.

41) $2x - y = 3$ and $x + 2y = -1$

42) $\begin{cases} x + 2y = 4 \\ 3x - y = 6 \end{cases}$

43) $\begin{cases} 3x + y = 6 \\ x - y = -2 \end{cases}$

44) $4x + 3y = 12$ and $2x - y = 18$

45) $\begin{cases} 2a + b = 7 \\ 4a - b = 5 \end{cases}$

46) $\begin{cases} x - y = 4 \\ 2x - 2y = 10 \end{cases}$

bit.ly/3mPGO6k

Find the Number of Solutions to a Linear Equation

The linear equation is a kind of equation with the highest degree of 1. In other words, in a linear equation, there is no variable with an exponent more than 1. A linear equation's graph always is in the form of a straight line, it's called a "linear equation".

The linear equation has no solution if by solving a linear equation you get a false statement as an answer.

The linear equation has one solution if by solving a linear equation you get a true statement for a single value for the variable.

The equation has infinitely many solutions if by solving a linear equation you get a statement that is always true.

Let's review an example:

How many solutions does the following equation have?

$$7 - 4p = -4p$$

Solve for p: $7 - 4p = -4p \rightarrow 7 = -4p + 4p \rightarrow 7 = 0$.

$7 = 0$ is a false statement. The linear equation has no solution because by solving the linear equation you get a false statement as an answer.

For another example:

How many solutions does the following equation have?

$$12h = 3h + 27$$

Solve for h: $12h = 3h + 27 \rightarrow 12h - 3h = 27 \rightarrow 9h = 27 \rightarrow h = 3$.

$h = 3$ is a true statement for a single value for the variable. So, the linear equation has one solution because by solving a linear equation you get a true statement for a single value for the variable.

One more example:

How many solutions does the following equation have?

$$8n - 2n = 6n$$

Simplify the left side of the equation: $8n - 2n = 6n \rightarrow 6n = 6n$.

$6n = 6n$ is a statement that is always true. So, the equation has infinitely many solutions because by solving a linear equation you get a statement that is always true.

For more explanation about the problem, pay attention to the following example:

How many solutions does the following equation have?

$$42 - 4x = 2(x - 6)$$

Solve for x:

$$42 - 4x = 2(x - 6) \rightarrow 42 - 4x = 2x - 12$$

$$\rightarrow 42 - 4x - 42 = 2x - 12 - 42$$

$$\rightarrow -4x = 2x - 54$$

$$\rightarrow -4x - 2x = 2x - 54 - 2x$$

$$\rightarrow -6x = -54$$

$$\rightarrow x = 9$$

$x = 9$ is a true statement for a single value for the variable. So, the linear equation has one solution.

✎ How many solutions do the following equations have?

47) $2x + 3 = 14$

48) $5a = 9a - 6a$

49) $1 - c + 4 = -c - 3$

50) $2y + 5y = -3y$

51) $-x + 8 + 5x = 4x - 2$

52) $3x + 2 = x - 4$

bit.ly/3iWpa57

Find more at

Write a System of Equations Given a Graph

A system of equations is a group of two or more equations that share the same variables. In particular, a system of linear equations is a set of equations that can be satisfied by the same set of values for the variables.

To write a system of equations given a graph, it is important to understand that each line in the graph represents a linear equation. By determining the equation of each line, you can create a system of equations.

To write the equation of a line, you can use the slope-intercept form, $y = mx + b$. To find the slope (m) of a line, you can use two points on the line and plug them into the slope equation: $m = \frac{change\ in\ y}{change\ in\ x}$. To determine the $y-$intercept (b), you can see at which point the line crosses the $y-$axis. Then you can use the value of the slope and $y-$intercept to construct the line's equation in slope-intercept form. Repeat this process for the second line to get the second equation of the system of equations.

Let's review an example:

Write a system of equations for the following graph.

First, look at the red line. write its equation by identifying the slope (m) and $y-$intercept (b): to find the slope, you can use any two points on the line and plug in the slope equation: $m = \frac{change\ in\ y}{change\ in\ x}$. Here choose

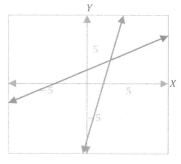

the points $(0,2)$ and $(-4,0)$: $m = \frac{0-2}{-4-0} = \frac{1}{2}$. The red line crosses the $y-$axis at $(0,2)$, so the $y-$intercept is $b = 2$. Now, write the equation of the red line: $y = \frac{1}{2}x + 2$.

You can find the blue line's equation in the same way. Use the points $(0, -8)$ and $(2,0)$: $m = \frac{0-(-8)}{2-0} = 4$. The blue line crosses the $y-$axis at $(0, -8)$, so the $y-$intercept is $b = -8$. Now, write the equation of the blue line:

$y = 4x - 8$. Therefore, the graph shows the following system of equations:

$$\begin{cases} y = \frac{1}{2}x + 2 \\ y = 4x - 8 \end{cases}.$$

For another example:

Write the system of equations of the following graph.

Consider two arbitrary points on each of the lines.

Then calculate the slope of the lines using the formula:

$m = \frac{y_2 - y_1}{x_2 - x_1}$, where (x_1, y_1) and (x_2, y_2) are two points on

the line. Therefore,

Red line: $(-1,0)$ and $(0,-1) \rightarrow m = -1$

Blue line: $(-3,0)$ and $(0,5) \rightarrow m = \frac{5}{3}$

Now, find the equation of each line by using the point-slope form of a line $(y - y_0) = m(x - x_0)$ and having the slope of the line and a point. We have:

Red line: $m = -1$ and $(0,-1) \rightarrow y - (-1) = -1(x - 0) \rightarrow y + 1 = -x$

Blue line: $m = \frac{5}{3}$ and $(-3,0) \rightarrow y - 0 = \frac{5}{3}(x - (-3)) \rightarrow y = \frac{5}{3}x + 5$

Finally, the system of linear equations shown in the above graph is as follows:

$$\begin{cases} y + 1 = -x \\ y = \frac{5}{3}x + 5 \end{cases}$$

✍ Solve the following system of equations.

53) _____

54) _____

Systems of Equations Word Problems Top of Form

To solve systems of equations word problems, follow these steps:

1. Read the problem carefully and identify the variables and the information given.

2. Translate the information from the problem into equations. This will typically involve writing an equation for each piece of information given.

3. Write the system of equations using the equations you just created.

4. Solve the system of equations using one of the methods (substitution, elimination, or graphing)

5. Check your solution by substituting it back into the original equations and making sure it makes sense in the context of the problem.

Here is an example:

A company produces two products, x and y. Each unit of x costs \$20 and each unit of y costs \$30. The company's daily revenue is \$700. How many units of x and y the company should produce to maximize the revenue?

1. Identify the variables: x (number of units of product x) and y (number of units of product y)

2. Translate the information into equations: $20x + 30y = 700$ (the revenue of the company)

3. Write the system of equations: $20x + 30y = 700$.

4. Solve the system of equations: You can use any method you prefer, in this case, I will use substitution: $x = \frac{700-30y}{20}$.

5. Check your solution: Now, you know that $x = \frac{700-30y}{20}$ and you can substitute this into the equation $20x + 30y = 700$, and check if the equation holds true.

6. Now you can use this information to find the values of x and y that maximize the revenue.

Note that in this example you can use the graph method and find the solution that way too, it's your choice. Also, sometimes the word problems will be a bit more complex, and you may need to use multiple equations or algebraic manipulations to solve them.

One more example:

Tickets to a movie cost $7 for adults and $4 for students. A group of friends purchased 24 tickets for $123. How many adult tickets did they buy?

Let x be the number of adult tickets and y be the number of student tickets. There are 24 tickets.

Then: $x + y = 24$. The cost of adults' tickets is $7 and for students, it is $4, and the total cost is $123. So, $7x + 4y = 123$.

Now, we have a system of equations: $\begin{cases} x + y = 24 \\ 7x + 4y = 123 \end{cases}$.

To solve this system of equations, multiply the first equation by -4 and add it to the second equation: $-4(x + y = 24) \rightarrow -4x - 4y = -96$. So, we have:

$7x + 4y = 123 + (-4x - 4y) = 123 - 96 \rightarrow 3x = 27 \rightarrow x = 9$.

Now, substitute the obtained value of x in one of the equations to get the value of y. Use the first equation. Therefore, $x = 9 \rightarrow 9 + y = 24 \rightarrow y = 15$.

There are 9 adult tickets and 15 student tickets. Now, check your answers by substituting solutions into the original equations.

$x + y = 24 \rightarrow 9 + 15 = 24,\ 7x + 4y = 123 \rightarrow 7(9) + 4(15) = 123 \rightarrow 63 + 60 = 123$.

The solutions are correct in both equations.

✍ Solve the following word problem.

55) Sara and Jack are saving money. Sara starts with $40 and saves $25 per week. Jack starts with $110 and saves $15 per week. After how many weeks do they have the same amount of money?

bit.ly/3koWCP3

Find more at

Solve One-step and Two-step Linear Equations Word Problems

To solve one-step and two-step linear equations word problems, you should follow these steps:

1. Read the problem carefully and identify the variables and the information given.
2. Translate the information from the problem into an equation. This will typically involve writing an equation for each piece of information given.
3. Solve the equation using one of the methods (addition, subtraction, multiplication, or division)
4. Check your solution by substituting it back into the original equation and making sure it makes sense in the context of the problem.

Here is an example of a one-step linear equation word problem:

A store is selling a shirt for $20. If you apply a discount of 20%, how much will the shirt cost?

1. Identify the variables: x (cost of the shirt).
2. Translate the information into an equation: $x = 20$.
3. Solve the equation: $x = 20 \times \left(\frac{80}{100}\right) = 16$.
4. Check your solution: The shirt costs $16 after the discount.

Here is an example of a two-step linear equation word problem:

John has two times more money than Jane. If John has $120, how much money does Jane have?

1. Identify the variables: x (amount of money Jane has) and y (amount of money John has).
2. Translate the information into an equation: $y = 2x$.
3. Solve the equation:

$$y = 2x, \text{ and } y = 120 \rightarrow 120 = 2x \rightarrow x = \frac{120}{2} \rightarrow x = 60.$$

bit.ly/47lQ9vr

Find more at

4. Check your solution: If John has $120, then Jane has $60.

It's worth mentioning that it's important to pay attention to the units of measurement when solving word problems. Make sure to convert units of measurement if necessary, and always include the units in your final answer.

Also, when solving two-step linear equation word problems, you will often need to use inverse operations (addition, subtraction, multiplication, or division) to isolate the variable. Remember that to undo an operation, you should do the opposite operation.

In addition, be mindful of the signs of inequalities if the problem is asking for a range of solutions or solutions that are greater or lesser than a certain value.

One more example:

Larry is in a chocolate shop and is going to buy some chocolates for his friends. He chooses 7 chocolates with a flower design and in addition, he also chooses some packs of five chocolates. If the total number of chocolates he has bought is 32, write an equation that you can use to find c, the number of packs of three chocolates. How many packs of three chocolates has Larry bought?

Larry chooses some packs of three chocolates and n is the number of packs of three chocolates. We can write it as follows: $5c$. He also chooses 7 chocolates with a flower design. The total number of chocolates he has bought is 32. Therefore, we can complete the equation as follows: $5c + 7 = 32$. The equation $5c + 7 = 32$ can be used to find how many packs of three chocolates Larry bought. Solve the equation for c: $5c + 7 = 32 \rightarrow 5c = 32 - 7 \rightarrow 5c = 25 \rightarrow c = 25 \div 5 = 5 \rightarrow c = 5$. So, he bought 5 packs of five chocolates.

✍ Solve each word problem.

56) A rectangle is $3\,m$ tall and $5\,m$ wide. if its width is enlarged to $2\,m$ without changing its perimeter, then find the new length of the rectangle?

Systems of Linear Inequalities

A system of linear inequalities is a group of two or more linear inequalities that share one or more variables. The goal of solving a system of linear inequalities is to find the values of the variables that satisfy all of the inequalities in the system. To solve a system of linear inequalities, one can use a variety of methods, such as graphing or substitution.

Graphing is a common method used to solve systems of linear inequalities. This method involves plotting each inequality on a coordinate plane and finding the region where the solutions to all of the inequalities overlap. The solutions to the system of inequalities are the points that lie within the region where the solutions of the inequalities overlap.

Another method is Substitution, this is where we substitute the expression of one equation of the system in the other one, then solve for the variable and substitute back in the first equation and solve for the other variable.

In general, solving a system of linear inequalities can be a bit more complex than solving a single linear inequality, but with the right methods and strategies, it can be done. And it's important to understand that the solutions to a system of linear inequalities are not a single value, but a set of values (a range) that make the system true.

Let's review an example:

Solve the following system of inequalities:

$$\begin{cases} 8x - 4y \leq 12 \\ 3x + 6y \leq 12 \\ \quad\ y \geq 0 \end{cases}$$

To solve this system of inequalities, we can use the method of graphing.

First, we'll graph the first inequality: $8x - 4y \leq 12$. We can start by putting it in slope-intercept form: $y = 2x - 3$. We can see that the inequality is pointing towards the direction of "less than or equal to", thus we'll shade the side of the line that does not include the line.

Second, we'll graph the second inequality: $3x + 6y \leq 12$. We can start by putting it in slope-intercept form: $y = -\frac{x}{2} + 2$. As the inequality is also pointing towards the direction of "less than or equal to", we'll shade the side of the line that does not include the line.

Finally, the third inequality is a non-strict inequality, $y \geq 0$, which means that **y** is greater than or equal to 0.

Now, we'll look at the graph, where the intersection of the shaded areas gives us the solution of the system of inequalities. And the answer is the solution is the area of intersection between the two shaded areas, which is the area above the line $y = 2x - 3$ and below the line $y = -\frac{x}{2} + 2$, and $y \geq 0$.

We can also represent the solution of the system by writing the ordered pair (x, y) that makes all the inequalities true.

The solution to the system is the set of all ordered pairs (x, y) that

____ $8x - 4y \leq 12$, ____ $3x + 6y \leq 12$, ____ $y \geq 0$

satisfies the system of inequalities. It's a set of points that form the shaded area on the graph.

✍ Solve each following system of inequalities.

57) $\begin{cases} 3x - 2y \geq -1 \\ x + y < -2 \\ y > \frac{5}{3}x - 4 \end{cases}$

58) $\begin{cases} 3x + y \geq -3 \\ x - 2y < 2 \end{cases}$

59) $\begin{cases} y \leq 2 \\ 2x + y < -2 \\ x - y \leq -1 \end{cases}$

60) $\begin{cases} x + y > -3 \\ x - y \leq -2 \end{cases}$

Write Two-variable Inequalities in Form of Word Problems

The two-variable linear inequalities describe a not equal relationship between 2 algebraic statements which contain two different variables. A Two-variables linear inequality is created when two variables are involved in the equation and inequality symbols ($<$, $>$, $\leq$, or $\geq$) are used to connect 2 algebraic expressions.

The two-variables linear inequalities solution can be expressed as an ordered pair (x, y). When the x and y values of the ordered pair are replaced in the inequality they make a correct expression.

The method of solving a linear inequality is like the method of solving a linear equation. The difference between these two methods is in the symbol of inequality. You solve linear inequalities word problems in the same way as linear equations word problems:

Step 1: First, read the problem and try to write an inequality in words in a way that expresses the situation well.

Step 2: Represent each of the given information with numbers, symbols, and variables.

Step 3: Compare the inequality you've written in words with the given information that you've represented with numbers, symbols, and variables. Then rewrite what you've found out in form of an inequality expression.

Step 4: Simplify both sides of the inequality. Once you find the values, you have one of these inequalities:

   o Strict inequalities: In this case, both sides of the inequalities can't be equal to each other.

   o Non-strict inequalities: In this case, both sides of the inequalities can be equal.

bit.ly/41YQNMP

Find more at

Let's review an example:

Sara plans to hold a party. She plans to order pizza and pasta from a restaurant for dinner. The cost of each pizza is $45 and the cost of each pasta is $30. She hopes to spend no more than $400 on dinner. Write a linear inequality so that x represents the number of pizzas and y represents the number of pasta.

First, try to write an inequality in words in a way that expresses the situation well: The cost of the pizzas plus the cost of the pasta is no more than $400. Now, represent each of the given information with numbers, symbols, and variables: The cost of the pizzas is $45 times the number of pizzas, which is x. The product is $45x$. The cost of the pasta is $30 times the number of pasta, which is y. The product is $30y$. No more than means less than or equal ($\leq$). Rewrite what you've found out in form of an inequality expression: $45x + 30y \leq 400$.

✍ Solve.

61) A baker is buying barley flour and wheat flour and can spend no more than $840. Each kilogram of wheat flour costs $2.5, and each kilogram of barley flour costs $5.8.

Write an inequality that represents all possible combinations of x, the amount of wheat flour, and y, the amount of barley flours the customer can buy.

62) An influencer has two different jobs. His combined work schedules consist of less than 48 hours in week.

Write an inequality that shows the best solution set for all possible combinations of x, the number of hours she worked at her first job, and y, the number of hours she worked at her second job, in one week?

bit.ly/41YQNMP

Find more at

Chapter 5: Answers

1) $y \leq 13$

2) $x < -2$

3) $a > \frac{3}{2}$

4) $x \geq -\frac{4}{3}$

5) $x \geq 4$

6) $x > 3$

7) $b < 1$

8) $x \geq -5$

9) $x \leq -3$

10) $x \leq -4$

11) $x > 2$

12) $x > 1$

13) $x < -4$

14) $x \leq 3$

15) $\left(-2, \frac{5}{2}\right)$

16) $(3, 4]$

17) $[-2, -1]$

18) $\left(-\infty, \frac{8}{3}\right]$

19) $\left(2, \frac{7}{2}\right)$

20) $(0, 25)$

21) $(-10, 9]$

22) $(-\infty, 7)$

23) $y \leq -x - 5$

24) $y \leq 2x - 2$

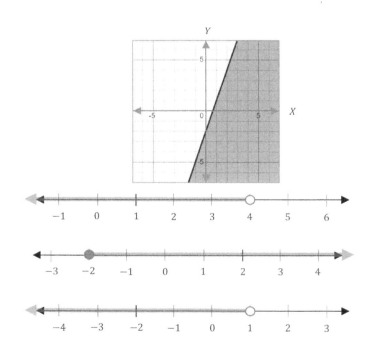

25) $x + 3 < 7$

26) $2x \geq -4$

27) $5 - x > 4$

28) $-1 < 2a - 7 \leq 3$

29) $\left\{(x,y)|x \in \mathbb{R}, y < \frac{3}{2}(x+1)\right\}$

30) $\{(x,y)|x \in \mathbb{R}, y \leq -(5x+7)\}$

31) $\left\{(x,y)|x \in \mathbb{R}, y < \frac{2}{3}\right\}$

32) $\{(x,y)|x \in \mathbb{R}, y \leq 2x - 5\}$

33) $\left\{(x,y)|y \in \mathbb{R}, x < \frac{7}{2} - 3y\right\}$

34) $\left\{(x,y)|y \in \mathbb{R}, x \leq \frac{3y-4}{6}\right\}$

35) $3x - 2y > 6$

36) $2y + x < 2x$

37) $-3 < x < -1$

38) $x \leq -3$ or $x \geq 3$

39) $-\frac{2}{3} \leq x \leq \frac{4}{3}$

40) $x > 2$ or $x < 1$

41) $x = 1$ and $y = -1$

42) $x = \frac{16}{7}$ and $y = \frac{6}{7}$

43) $x = 1$ and $y = 3$

44) $x = 6.6$ and $y = -4.8$

45) $a = 2$ and $b = 3$

46) No solution

47) One solution

48) One solution

49) No solution

50) One solution

51) No solution

52) One solution

Effortless
Math
Education

53) $\begin{cases} x - 2y = -8 \\ 9x + 2y = -12 \end{cases}$

54) $\begin{cases} y = -3 \\ -x + y = 2 \end{cases}$

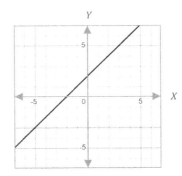

55) 7 weeks

56) $1\ m$

57)

58)

59)

60)

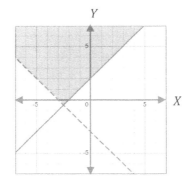

61) $2.5x + 5.8y \le 840$

62) $x + y \le 48$

CHAPTER

6 Quadratic

Math topics that you'll learn in this chapter:

- ☑ Solving Quadratic Equations
- ☑ Graphing Quadratic Functions
- ☑ Solve a Quadratic Equation by Factoring
- ☑ Transformations of Quadratic Functions
- ☑ Quadratic Formula and the Discriminant
- ☑ Characteristics of Quadratic Functions: Equations
- ☑ Characteristics of Quadratic Functions: Graphs
- ☑ Complete a Function Table: Quadratic Functions
- ☑ Domain and Range of Quadratic Functions: Equations
- ☑ Factor Quadratics: Special Cases
- ☑ Factor Quadratics Using Algebra Tiles
- ☑ Write a Quadratic Function from Its Vertex and Another Point

Solving Quadratic Equations

To solve a quadratic equation, first write the equation in the form of:

$$ax^2 + bx + c = 0,$$

where a, b, and c are coefficients and x is the variable. This is called the standard form of a quadratic equation.

Once you have the equation in this form, you can use the quadratic formula:

$$x = \frac{-b \pm \sqrt{b^2 - 4ac}}{2a}$$

To find the solutions (also known as roots or zeros) of the equation. If you can factor the equation, you can also set each factor equal to zero and solve for x.

For example, if the equation is $x^2 + 3x = 4$, you can write it in the standard form of a quadratic equation: $x^2 + 3x - 4 = 0$.

Then use the quadratic formula to find the solutions.

$$x = \frac{-b \pm \sqrt{b^2 - 4ac}}{2a}$$

Where $a = 1$, $b = 3$, and $c = -4$.

$$x = \frac{-3 \pm \sqrt{3^2 - 4(1)(-4)}}{2(1)} = \frac{-3 \pm \sqrt{9 + 16}}{2} = \frac{-3 \pm 5}{2}$$

So, the solutions are: $x = \frac{-3+5}{2} = 1$ and $x = \frac{-3-5}{2} = -4$.

The solutions to this equation are $x = 1$ and $x = -4$.

We can also use factoring to solve this equation. To solve the equation by factoring, we need to find two numbers that multiply by -4 and add to 3. These numbers are -1 and -4, so we can factor the equation as:

$$x^2 + 3x - 4 = (x - 1)(x + 4) = 0$$

So, we have $x - 1 = 0$ and $x + 4 = 0$.

So, the solutions to this equation are $x = 1$ and $x = -4$.

A few more examples:

Find the solutions of the following quadratic equation.

$$x^2 - x - 12 = 0.$$

Factor the quadratic by grouping. We need to find two numbers whose sum is -1 (from $-x$) and whose product is -12. Those numbers are 3 and -4. Then:

$$x^2 - x - 12 = 0 \rightarrow x^2 + 3x - 4x - 12 = 0 \rightarrow (x^2 + 3x) + (-4x - 12) = 0.$$

Now, find common factors: $(x^2 + 3x) = x(x + 3)$ and $(-4x - 12) = -4(x + 3)$. We have two expressions $(x^2 + 3x)$ and $(-4x - 12)$ and their common factor is $(x + 3)$. Then:

$$(x^2 + 3x) + (-4x - 12) = 0 \rightarrow x(x + 3) - 4(x + 3) = 0$$

$$\rightarrow (x + 3)(x - 4) = 0.$$

The product of two expressions is 0. Then:

$$(x + 3) = 0 \rightarrow x = -3 \text{ or } (x - 4) = 0 \rightarrow x = 4.$$

Solve the equation below:

$$x^2 + 4x + 3 = 0$$

Use quadratic formula: $x_{1,2} = \frac{-b \pm \sqrt{b^2 - 4ac}}{2a}$, $a = 1$, $b = 4$ and $c = 3$.

Then: $x_{1,2} = \frac{-4 \pm \sqrt{4^2 - 4 \times 1(3)}}{2(1)} = \frac{-4 \pm \sqrt{16 - 12}}{2} = \frac{-4 \pm 2}{2}$,

$$x_1 = \frac{-4 + 2}{2} = -1, \quad x_2 = \frac{-4 - 2}{2} = -3.$$

Find the zeros of the quadratic:

$$x^2 + 9x + 8 = 0$$

Factor: $x^2 + 9x + 8 = 0 \rightarrow (x + 8)(x + 1) = 0 \rightarrow x = -8$, or $x = -1$.

✎ Solve each equation .

1) $x^2 - x - 2 = 0$

2) $x^2 - 6x + 8 = 0$

3) $x^2 - 4x + 3 = 0$

4) $x^2 + x - 12 = 0$

5) $x^2 + 7x - 18 = 0$

6) $x^2 - 2x - 15 = 0$

7) $x^2 + 6x - 40 = 0$

8) $x^2 - 9x - 36 = 0$

Graphing Quadratic Functions

Graphing a quadratic function involves plotting the points that satisfy the equation and then connecting them to form a parabola. The general form of a quadratic function is $y = ax^2 + bx + c$, where a, b, and c are constants.

The graph of a quadratic function is a parabola that opens either upward or downward, depending on the value of a. If a is positive, the parabola opens upward and if a is negative, the parabola opens downward. The vertex of the parabola is the point where it changes direction and it is given by the coordinates

$$\left(-\frac{b}{2a}, f\left(-\frac{b}{2a}\right)\right),$$

where $f(x)$ is the quadratic function.

The x −intercepts of the parabola are the solutions of the equation $y = 0$. We can find them by setting $y = 0$ and solving for x. They are given by

$$x = \frac{-b \pm \sqrt{b^2 - 4ac}}{2a}$$

To graph a quadratic function, we can use the vertex and the x −intercepts as key points and then plot several other points to complete the graph. Graphing calculators and software also can help to graph a quadratic function. (Remember that the graph of a quadratic function is a U −shaped curve and it is called a "parabola".)

Consider that quadratic functions in vertex form: $y = a(x - h)^2 + k$ where (h, k) is the vertex of the function. The axis of symmetry is $x = h$. The sign of a determines the direction of the corresponding graph. So that:

- If $a > 0$, then it opens upwards.
- If $a < 0$, then it opens downwards.

Let's review an example to better explanation:

        Sketch the graph of $y = (x + 2)^2 - 3$.

The graph of $y = (x + 2)^2 - 3$ is a parabola that opens upward because a is positive. To sketch the graph, we can use the following steps:

Find the vertex: The vertex of the parabola is given by $(-2, -3)$.

Find the $x-$intercepts: We can set $y = 0$ and solve for x.

We will have $(x + 2)^2 = 3$, then $x^2 + 4x + 4 = 3$, so $x^2 + 4x + 1 = 0$, this equation has two negative solutions as

$x = \frac{-4 \pm \sqrt{4^2 - 4(1)(1)}}{2(1)} = \frac{-4 \pm \sqrt{12}}{2} = -2 \pm \sqrt{3}$.

Plot several points to complete the graph: we can pick several $x-$values, substitute them into the equation, and find the corresponding $y-$values.

For example, we can take $x = -5, -4, -3, -2, -1, 0,$ and 1, and substitute them into the equation. We will have $y = 6, 1, -2, -3, -2, 1,$ and 6 respectively.

Sketch the graph: Using the vertex and the points we found above, we can sketch the graph of the parabola. The vertex is the lowest point on the parabola and the parabola opens upward. The parabola doesn't cross the $x-$axis.

Note: The graph will be a parabola shape symmetric around $x = -2$.

✎ Draw the graph of the following functions.

9) $y = (x - 4)^2 - 2$

10) $y = 2(x + 2)^2 - 3$

Solve a Quadratic Equation by Factoring

To solve a quadratic equation by factoring, we need to factor the left-hand side of the equation into the form of $(x - a)(x - b) = 0$, where a and b are the solutions of the equation. We can then set each factor equal to zero and solve for x.

For example, let's solve the equation $x^2 - 5x + 6 = 0$. We can factor it as:

$$x^2 - 5x + 6 = (x - 2)(x - 3) = 0$$

Now, we set each factor equal to zero and solve for x:

$$x - 2 = 0 \rightarrow x = 2 \text{ and } x - 3 = 0 \rightarrow x = 3.$$

So, the solutions of the equation $x^2 - 5x + 6 = 0 \rightarrow x = 2$ and $x = 3$.

Another example, let's solve the equation $x^2 + 2x - 8 = 0$. We can factor it as:

$$x^2 + 2x - 8 = (x + 4)(x - 2) = 0.$$

Now, we set each factor equal to zero and solve for x:

$$x + 4 = 0 \rightarrow x = -4 \text{ and } x - 2 = 0 \rightarrow x = 2.$$

So, the solutions of the equation $x^2 + 2x - 8 = 0$ are $x = -4$ and $x = 2$.

It's important to remember that factoring a quadratic equation requires finding two numbers that multiply to give the constant term and add to give the coefficient of x.

Here are some examples of solving a quadratic equation by factoring:

Solve the equation $x^2 - 8x + 12 = 0$.

Step 1: Factor the left-hand side of the equation:

$$x^2 - 8x + 12 = (x - 6)(x - 2) = 0.$$

Step 2: Set each factor equal to zero and solve for x:

$$x - 6 = 0 \rightarrow x = 6 \text{ and } x - 2 = 0 \rightarrow x = 2.$$

Step 3: Check the solution by substituting it back into the original equation:

$$x = 6: (6)^2 - 8(6) + 12 = 36 - 48 + 12 = 0$$

$$x = 2: (2)^2 - 8(2) + 12 = 4 - 16 + 12 = 0$$

So, the solutions of the equation $x^2 - 8x + 12 = 0$ are $x = 6$ and $x = 2$.

Find the solutions of $x^2 + 5x = 0$.

The greatest common factor of the two terms is x.

Take the common factor out: $x(x + 5) = 0$.

Using MPZ, which states that either $x = 0$ or $x + 5 = 0$.

In the second equation, the value of x equals -5. So, $x + 5 = 0 \rightarrow x = -5$.

To solve a quadratic equation as $ax^2 + bx + c = 0$ by factoring, if $a \neq 1$. In this case, it is enough to find two numbers whose product is ac and whose sum is b.

To better explain, pay attention to the following example:

Find the solutions of $2x^2 + 3x - 9 = 0$.

Since $a \neq 1$, determine two factors of the product of $ac = 2 \times (-9) = -18$ and add up to 3.

$$2x^2 + 3x - 9 = 0 \rightarrow 2x^2 - 3x + 6x - 9 = 0 \rightarrow x(2x - 3) + 3(2x - 3) = 0$$

$$\rightarrow (2x - 3)(x + 3) = 0$$

Lastly, by setting each factor to 0, we have:

$2x - 3 = 0 \rightarrow x = \frac{3}{2}$, or $x + 3 = 0 \rightarrow x = -3$.

So, the solutions of the equation $2x^2 + 3x - 9 = 0$ are $x = \frac{3}{2}$ and $x = -3$.

✎ Find the solution of the following equations.

11) $x^2 - 2x - 3 = 0$

12) $x^2 + 9x + 20 = 0$

13) $6x^2 + x - 5 = 0$

14) $x^2 - 2x - 4 = 12$

15) $x^2 + 1 = 2x$

16) $x^2 - 16 = 0$

17) $5x^2 + 7x + 2 = 0$

18) $x^2 + x + 2 = 0$

bit.ly/3K4phDi

Find more at

Transformations of Quadratic Functions

Quadratic functions are functions of the form $f(x) = ax^2 + bx + c$, where a, b, and c are constants. The graph of a quadratic function is a parabola. The shape of the parabola can be changed by changing the values of a, b, and c. These changes are known as transformations of quadratic functions.

1. Vertical shifts: We can change the y −coordinate of the vertex of the parabola by adding or subtracting a constant to the function.

$y = f(x) + k$:

Moves up	if	k is positive
Moves down	if	k is negative

2. Horizontal shifts: We can change the x −coordinate of the vertex of the parabola by adding or subtracting a constant to the x −term.

$y = f(x + k)$:

Moves left	if	k is positive
Moves right	if	k is negative

3. Stretch or compression: We can change the width of the parabola by multiplying or dividing the x −term by a constant.

$y = f(x) + k$:

Compressed in direction y	if	$0 < k < 1$
Stretched in direction y	if	$k > 1$

As the same:

$y = f(kx)$:

Compressed in direction x	if	$0 < k < 1$
Stretched in direction x	if	$k > 1$

4. Reflection: We can reflect the parabola over the x −axis or y −axis by changing the sign of the leading coefficient (a) or by multiplying the x −term by −1.

$y = -f(x)$:   Reflection over x − axis
$y = f(-x)$:   Reflection over y − axis

It's important to note that when we make these transformations, the vertex of the parabola will change. The vertex is the point at the bottom or top of the parabola. The standard form of the vertex form of a quadratic function is $y = a(x - h)^2 + k$, where (h, k) is the vertex of the parabola. By analyzing the vertex form we can understand the shift of the parabola.

Here are some examples of how to apply transformations to a quadratic function:
$$y = x^2 + 2x - 3$$

- To shift the parabola upward by 2 units, we add 2 to the $y-$coordinate:
$$y = x^2 + 2x - 3 + 2 \rightarrow y = x^2 + 2x - 1$$

- To shift the parabola to the left by 1 unit, we subtract 1 from the $x-$coordinate: $y = (x + 1)^2 + 2(x + 1) - 3 \rightarrow y = x^2 + 4x$.

- To stretch the parabola horizontally by a factor of 2, we multiply the $x-$term by 2: $y = (2x)^2 + 2(2x) - 3 \rightarrow y = 4x^2 + 4x - 3$.

- To reflect the parabola over the $x-$axis, we change the sign of the leading coefficient: $y = -(x^2 + 2x - 3) \rightarrow y = -x^2 - 2x + 3$.

✍ State the transformations and sketch the graph of the following function.

19) $y = 2(x - 3)^2 + 1$

✍ Write the equation for the function $y = x^2$ with the following transformations.

20) reflect across the $x-$axis and vertically compress by a factor of $\frac{3}{2}$

21) shift down 2

22) reflect across the $y-$axis, shift up 1

23) vertically stretch by a factor of 3, shift left 4 and up 1

bit.ly/3s7MG0o
Find more at

Quadratic Formula and the Discriminant

The quadratic formula is a method for solving a quadratic equation of the form $ax^2 + bx + c = 0$. The formula is:

$$x = \frac{-b \pm \sqrt{b^2 - 4ac}}{2a}$$

The discriminant of the quadratic equation is the expression under the square root sign in the quadratic formula and is indicated by the notation Δ:

$$\Delta = b^2 - 4ac$$

The discriminant determines the nature of the solutions of the quadratic equation.

- If the discriminant is positive, the equation has two distinct real solutions.
- If the discriminant is zero, the equation has one repeated real solution.
- If the discriminant is negative, the equation has no real solutions.

In other words, the discriminant helps us understand the behavior of the graph of the equation, whether it has two distinct roots, one repeated root, or no real roots.

For more explanation, pay attention to the following examples:

Solve equation $4x^2 + 3x - 1 = 0$.

To solve a quadratic equation, first find the values of a, b, c.

By comparing the mentioned equation with the equation $ax^2 + bx + c = 0$, the values a, b, c are equal to: $a = 4, b = 3, c = -1$.

Now, calculate the discriminant of the equation (Δ). Given the values of a, b, and c, the value of Δ is equal to:

$\Delta = b^2 - 4ac = 3^2 - 4 \times 4 \times (-1) = 25$.

25 is a positive number. Therefore, this equation will have two

different solutions: $x = \frac{-3 \pm \sqrt{25}}{2(4)} \rightarrow x = \frac{-3 \pm 5}{8} \rightarrow x = -1$, or $x = \frac{1}{4}$.

Find the solutions of the equation $x^2 + x + 1 = 0$.

In the equation, the values of a, b, c are: $a = 1$, $b = 1$, $c = 1$.

$$\Delta = b^2 - 4ac = 1^2 - 4 \times 1 \times 1 = 1 - 4 = -3.$$

The value of the discriminant (Δ) is negative; Therefore, this equation has no solution in real numbers.

Solve the following quadratic equation:

$$x^2 + 4x + 4 = 0$$

In order to solve the problem, we evaluate the value of the discriminant (Δ). For this purpose, we determine the values of a, b, and c corresponding to the standard form of the quadratic equation $ax^2 + bx + c = 0$ and put them in the formula $\Delta = b^2 - 4ac$.

According to the given equation $x^2 + 4x + 4 = 0$, we get: $a = 1$, $b = 4$, and $c = 4$. Then, $\Delta = 4^2 - 4(1)(4) = 0$. So, the equation has one repeated real solution as:

$$x = \frac{-b}{2a} \rightarrow x = \frac{-4}{2(1)} \rightarrow x = -2$$

✎ How many solutions do the following equations have?

24) $x^2 + 2x + 4 = 0$

25) $x^2 - 4x - 5 = 0$

26) $3x^2 + x - 1 = 0$

27) $x^2 + 1 = 0$

✎ Find the answers to the questions below.

28) $2x^2 - 7x + 3 = 0$

29) $x^2 + 8x - 9 = 0$

30) $2x^2 + 5x - 3 = 0$

31) $x^2 + 6x + 9 = 0$

bit.ly/3LdZauS

Find more at

Characteristics of Quadratic Functions: Equations

By analyzing the equation of a quadratic function, we can determine various characteristics of the corresponding parabolic graph, including:

- Direction of the parabola: The direction of the parabola refers to whether the parabola opens upwards or downwards. This can be determined by the sign of the leading coefficient 'a' in the equation of the quadratic function. If 'a' is positive, the parabola opens upwards, and if 'a' is negative, the parabola opens downwards.

- Vertex: The vertex of a parabola is the highest or lowest point of the graph, and it can be determined by using the vertex form of the equation:

$$y = a(x - h)^2 + k,$$

where (h, k) is the vertex of the parabola or using formula $\left(-\frac{b}{2a}, f\left(-\frac{b}{2a}\right)\right)$ for the standard form of a quadratic equation $y = ax^2 + bx + c$.

- Axis of symmetry: The axis of symmetry of a parabola is a vertical line that separates the parabola into two mirror-image halves. It can be determined by using the vertex form of the equation, the axis of symmetry is the line $x = h$, where h is the $x-$coordinate of the vertex.

- $x-$intercept(s): The $x-$intercepts of a quadratic function are the points at which the parabola crosses the $x-$axis. These can be found by setting $y = 0$ and solving for x.

- $y-$intercept: The $y-$intercept of a quadratic function is the point at which the parabola crosses the $y-$axis, this point is represented by $(0, c)$ in the equation $y = ax^2 + bx + c$.

- Range: The range of a quadratic function is the set of all possible $y-$values of the function. It can be determined by analyzing the vertex and the direction of the parabola.

- Minimum/maximum value: The minimum or maximum value of a

quadratic function can be found by using the vertex form of the equation, it is the $y-$coordinate of the vertex (h, k), and it indicates the lowest or highest value of the function, depending on the direction of the parabola. If the parabola opens upwards, the vertex represents the minimum value, and if it opens downwards, the vertex represents the maximum value. This can also be determined by looking at the leading coefficient, if a is positive, the vertex is a minimum point, if a is negative, the vertex is a maximum point.

Let's review an example:

Specify characteristics of the vertex, direction, and $y-$intercept for the quadratic function $f(x) = x^2 + 3x + 2$.

In the standard form of a quadratic function $f(x) = ax^2 + bx + c$, the vertex is not immediately obvious. The $x-$coordinate for the vertex can be obtained by using the formula $x = -\frac{b}{2a}$. So, $x = -\frac{3}{2}$.

Now, substitute it into the equation of function to obtain the $y-$coordinate:

$$y = f\left(-\frac{3}{2}\right) = \left(-\frac{3}{2}\right)^2 + 3\left(-\frac{3}{2}\right) + 2 = \left(\frac{9}{4}\right) - \frac{9}{2} + 2 = -\frac{1}{4}.$$

So, the vertex of the function $f(x) = x^2 + 3x + 2$ is the ordered pair $\left(-\frac{3}{2}, -\frac{1}{4}\right)$.

Remember that the sign of the coefficient x^2 indicates the direction of the quadratic equation. Since the coefficient of x^2 is $+1$, then it is upward.

To find the $y-$intercept of a function, evaluate the output at $f(0)$.

$$f(0) = (0)^2 + 3(0) + 2 = 2.$$

✍ Solve.

32) Find the equation of the axis of symmetry for the parabola $y = x^2 + 7x + 3$.

33) Find the $y-$intercept of the parabola $y = x^2 + 25x + 7$.

34) Find the vertex of the parabola $y = x^2 - 4x + 3$.

bit.ly/3iRGJU7

Find more at

Characteristics of Quadratic Functions: Graphs

When graphed, quadratic functions take the shape of a parabola, which is a symmetric, U−shaped curve. The graph of a quadratic function has several key characteristics that can be determined from the equation of the function:

- Vertex: The vertex is the highest or lowest point of the parabola.

- Axis of Symmetry: The axis of symmetry of a parabola is a vertical line that separates the parabola into two mirror-image halves. The axis of symmetry is the line $x = h$, where h is the x−coordinate of the vertex.

- x−intercepts: The x−intercepts are the points at which the parabola crosses the x−axis.

- y−intercept: The y−intercept is the point at which the parabola crosses the y−axis, it is represented by $(0, c)$ in the equation $y = ax^2 + bx + c$.

- Minimum/maximum: The minimum or maximum value of a quadratic function is equivalent to the vertex of the function, which can be clearly identified from the graph.

- Increase/decrease: According to the parabolic form of a quadratic function, the increasing or decreasing of the graph at the vertex changes according to the sign of the leading coefficient of the equation. This property can be seen in the graph.

- Concavity: The parabola of a quadratic function is either concave up or concave down, depending on the sign of the leading coefficient of the equation. If the leading coefficient is positive, the parabola is concave up, and if it is negative, the parabola is concave down. The direction of concavity of a parabola can be determined by evaluating the graph.

All of these characteristics can be used to analyze and interpret the behavior of a quadratic function and its corresponding graph. The shape and position of the graph can give insight into the properties of the function and how it behaves in different situations. Look at the following graphs to understand more:

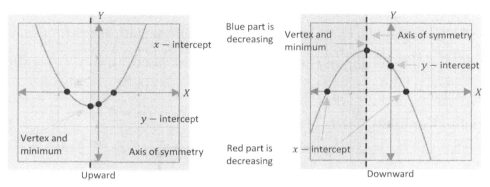

For example:

Considering the following graph, determine the following characteristics:

vertex, axis of symmetry, x −intercepts, y −intercept,

Max/minimum point, concavity

According to the graph, see that a point at the coordinate $(2,4)$ is the vertex. So, the line $x = 2$ is the axis of symmetry.

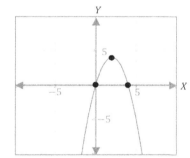

Since the graph intersects the x −axis at points 0 and 4, the mentioned points are x −intercepts. In the same way, the point $(0,0)$ is the y −intercept.

In addition, this is clear that the vertex is the maximum point. Clearly, the graph is downward.

✍ Considering the following graph, determine the following:

35) vertex

36) axis of symmetry

37) y −intercepts

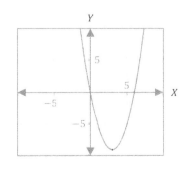

Complete a Function Table: Quadratic Functions

A function table is a tool that can be used to organize and display the inputs and outputs of a function. To complete a function table for a quadratic function, you need to know the equation of the function and the set of inputs (x −values) that you want to use.

For example: Complete the table.

$g(x) = -2x^2 + 4x + 1$	
x	$f(x)$
-2	
0	
1	
4	

According to the function table, the first value of the input in the table is -1. Evaluate $g(x) = -2x^2 + 4x + 1$ for $t = -2$.

$g(-2) = -2(-2)^2 + 4(-2) + 1$

$\qquad = -2(4) - 8 + 1 = -15$

When $t = -2$, then $g(-2) = -15$.

$g(x) = -2x^2 + 4x + 1$	
x	$f(x)$
-2	-15
0	
1	
4	

Complete the first row of the table.

In the same way, evaluate $g(x) = -2x^2 + 4x + 1$ for $t = 0$, $t = 1$, and $t = 4$, respectively. So,

$g(0) = -2(0)^2 + 4(0) + 1 = 1$

$g(1) = -2(1)^2 + 4(1) + 1 = 3$

$g(4) = -2(4)^2 + 4(4) + 1 = -15$

Enter the obtained values in the table.

$g(x) = -2x^2 + 4x + 1$	
x	$f(x)$
-2	-15
0	1
1	3
4	-15

Here's another example:

Let's say we have the quadratic function: $y = x^2 + 2x - 3$.

And we want to create a function table with $x-$values of $-2, -1, 0$, and 3. The completed function table would look like this:

$f(x) = x^2 + 2x - 3$	
x	$f(x)$
-2	-3
-1	-4
0	-3
3	12

To complete the table, we substitute each $x-$value into the equation and solve for y. You can use a similar approach for any quadratic function, just substitute the equation you have into the table, and for each $x-$value in the table, substitute it in the equation and solve for y.

✎ Complete the following tables.

38)

$g(t) = t^2 + 7$	
t	$g(t)$
-1	
0	
1	

39)

$f(p) = 4p^2$	
p	$f(p)$
-2	
0	
2	

Domain and Range of Quadratic Functions: Equations

The domain of a function is the set of all possible input values (x −values) for which the function produces a valid output (y −value). The range of a function is the set of all possible output values (y −values) that the function can produce.

For a quadratic function in the form of $y = ax^2 + bx + c$, the domain is all real numbers, because any value of x can be plugged into the equation and produce a valid output.

The range of a quadratic function can be found by examining the leading coefficient of the equation.

- If the leading coefficient (a) is positive, the parabola opens upwards and the vertex is a minimum point, the range is all real numbers greater than the y −coordinate of the vertex.

- If the leading coefficient (a) is negative, the parabola opens downwards and the vertex is a maximum point, the range is all real numbers less than the y −coordinate of the vertex.

For example: What is the domain and range of the function to the equation?

$$y = x^2 + 2x + 1$$

The function is quadratic, then the domain is all real numbers. Because every value of x is a valid input of the quadratic function. Now, to find the range of the function, rewrite the equation as a perfect square. That is, $y = (x + 1)^2$.

Since the value of the expression $(x - 1)^2$ is always greater than and equal to 0. Then the range of the function includes all non-negative real numbers.

Here's another example:

If we have the quadratic function $y = 2x^2 - 4x - 6$, the leading coefficient is positive, so the parabola opens upward and the vertex is a minimum point. By completing the square, we can find that the vertex is located at $(1, -8)$, which is the minimum point of the graph. Therefore, the range is all real numbers greater than -8.

More examples:

Let's say we have the quadratic function: $y = -2x^2 - 4x + 5$.

In this equation, the leading coefficient (a) is negative, so the parabola opens downward and the vertex is a maximum point. By completing the square, we can find that the vertex is located at $(-1, 7)$, which is the maximum point of the graph. Therefore, the range is all real numbers less than 7.

So, the domain of this function is all real numbers, and the range is all real numbers less than 7.

It's good to note that in some cases, the range may not be restricted to a certain set of numbers. In those cases, the range would be all real numbers.

Find the range of the function $y = x^2 - 5x + 3$.

Rewrite the equation of the function as a perfect square. So,

$$x^2 - 5x + 3 = \left(x^2 - 5x + \frac{25}{4} - \frac{25}{4}\right) + 3 = \left(x - \frac{5}{2}\right)^2 - \frac{25}{4} + 3 = \left(x - \frac{5}{2}\right)^2 - \frac{13}{4}.$$

According to the obtained equation, since the domain of the function is all real numbers, so, we have: $\left(x - \frac{5}{2}\right)^2 \geq 0 \rightarrow \left(x - \frac{5}{2}\right)^2 - \frac{13}{4} \geq -\frac{13}{4}$. Therefore, the range of the function is the set of $\left\{y \in \mathbb{R} \mid y \geq -\frac{13}{4}\right\}$.

Evaluate the range of the following function: $y = -3x^2 + x - 1$.

Rewrite the equation of function as

$$-3x^2 + x - 1 = -3\left(x^2 - \frac{1}{3}x\right) - 1 = -3\left(x^2 - \frac{1}{3}x + \frac{1}{36} - \frac{1}{36}\right) - 1 = -3\left(x - \frac{1}{3}\right)^2 - 3\left(-\frac{1}{36}\right) - 1 = -3\left(x - \frac{1}{3}\right)^2 - \frac{11}{12}.$$

Since $\left(x - \frac{1}{3}\right)^2 \geq 0 \rightarrow -3\left(x - \frac{1}{3}\right)^2 \leq 0 \rightarrow -3\left(x - \frac{1}{3}\right)^2 - \frac{11}{12} \leq -\frac{11}{12} \rightarrow y \leq -\frac{11}{12}$.

Therefore, the range of the function is the set of $\left\{y \in \mathbb{R} \mid y \leq -\frac{11}{12}\right\}$.

✎ Find the domain and range.

40) $y = x^2 + 5x + 6$

41) $y = -x^2 + 4$

Find more at

Factor Quadratics: Special Cases

The special cases for factoring quadratics are when the equation has a square or difference of squares.

- When factoring a square, the equation is of the form $a^2 \pm 2ab + b^2$. In this case, you can factor it as $(a \pm b)^2$.

- When factoring a difference of squares, the equation is of the form $a^2 - b^2$. In this case, you can factor it as $(a + b)(a - b)$.

It's important to note that these special cases only work when the equation is in a specific form and you cannot always factor a quadratic equation using this method.

Here are a couple of examples:

Factor the equation $9x^2 - 36$.

Notice that $9x^2$ and 36 are perfect squares, because $9x^2 = (3x)^2$, and $36 = 6^2$. By using the formula $a^2 - b^2 = (a + b)(a - b)$.

Let $a = 3x$, and $b = 6$. The represented equation can be rewritten as follow:

$9x^2 - 36 = (3x + 6)(3x - 6) = 9(x + 2)(x - 2)$.

Factor $25n^2 - 10n + 1$.

First, consider that this formula $a^2 - 2ab + b^2 = (a - b)^2$. Since $25n^2 = (5n)^2$, then $25n^2$ and 1 are perfect squares. This means that $a = 5n$, and $b = 1$. Next, check to see if the middle term is equal to $2ab$, which it is: $2ab = 2(5n)(1) = 10n$. Therefore, the square equation can be rewritten as,

$25n^2 - 10n + 1 = (5n - 1)^2$.

Factor $49\alpha^2 + 28\alpha\beta + 4\beta^2$.

First, notice that $49\alpha^2$ and $4\beta^2$ are perfect squares because $49\alpha^2 = (7\alpha)^2$ and $4\beta^2 = (2\beta)^2$. Let $a = 7\alpha$, and $b = 2\beta$. Now, evaluate the middle term

$28\alpha\beta$. Then, you can write as $28\alpha\beta = 2(7\alpha)(2\beta) = 2ab$. Using this formula:

$$a^2 + 2ab + b^2 = (a + b)^2.$$

Therefore, we have: $49\alpha^2 + 28\alpha\beta + 4\beta^2 = (7\alpha + 2\beta)^2$.

Factor the equation $3x^2 - 12x + 12$.

First, rewrite the equation as $3x^2 - 12x + 12 = 3(x^2 - 4x + 4)$. According to the x^2 and 4 are perfect squares. That is, $a = x$, and $b = 2$. Now, check to see if the middle term is equal to $2ab$: $2ab = 2(x)2 = 4x$. Using this formula:

$a^2 - 2ab + b^2 = (a - b)^2$.

Therefore, we have: $3x^2 - 12x + 12 = 3(x^2 - 4x + 4) = 3(x - 2)^2$.

Factor the equation $5x^2 - 80$.

By factoring from 5, rewrite the equation as $5x^2 - 90 = 5(x^2 - 16)$. We see that this expression in the parentheses is a difference of squares because it can be written as $(x + 4)(x - 4)$, so the factored form of this equation is:

$5x^2 - 80 = 5(x + 4)(x - 4)$.

Expand the expression: $(x + 5)^2$.

Using this formula: $(a + b)^2 = a^2 + 2ab + b^2$. So, the expnded form of this equation is $(x + 5)^2 = x^2 + 10x + 25$.

✎ Factor the following expressions.

42) $25x^2 + 20x + 4$

43) $9x^2 - 1$

44) $3 + 6x + 3x^2$

45) $b^4 - 36$

✎ Expand the following expressions.

46) $(2 - x)(x + 2)$

47) $(x - 2y)(x + 2y)$

48) $(7 - 2r)^2$

49) $(x + 2)(x + 2)$

bit.ly/3VTKoxQ

Find more at

Factor Quadratics Using Algebra Tiles

To factor quadratic expressions like $ax^2 + bx + c$ using algebraic tiles, follow the steps below:

- Model the polynomials with tiles.
- Arrange the tiles into a rectangle grid. Start with the x^2 tiles from the upper left corner so that the number of horizontal and vertical divisions is equal to the multiples of a. Add the integer tiles in the lower right corner. Here, the number of horizontal and vertical divisions should be equal to integer multiples. Make sure to choose horizontal and vertical divisions from possible multiples of a and c that will fill the remaining empty grid tiles.
- The product of expressions related to horizontal and vertical divisions is equal to the answer.
- Check the answer.

For example, to better explanation:

Use algebra tiles to factor: $3x^2 - 7x + 2$.

Model the polynomials with tiles:

In this case, arrange the tiles into a rectangle grid.

Determine both binomials relate to the divisions, such that $3x - 1$ for the horizontal division and $x - 2$ for the vertical. As follow:

In the end, multiply two expressions and check the answer:

$(3x - 1)(x - 2) = 3x^2 - 7x + 2$.

Use algebra tiles to factor $2x^2 + x - 3$.

Represent this expression using the number of 2 tiles x^2 ($2x^2$), and 1 tile x, and 3 negative integer tiles (-3).

In this case, arrange the tiles into a rectangle grid. Note that there aren't enough x tiles to correctly fit all of the integer tiles into the larger rectangle.

To fix this problem, we need to add some tiles in the empty spaces of the grid so that the sum of the positive and negative tiles is zero. Adding 2 positive x tiles and 2 negative x tiles does not change the value of the original expression. Since $-2x + 2x = 0$. These pairs cancel the combination. Make sure you place the negative x tiles on one side of the x^2 tile and all the positive x tiles on the other side.

Determine both binomials relate to the divisions, such that $2x + 3$ for the horizontal division and $x - 1$ for the vertical. Finally, check the answer.

$$(2x + 3)(x - 1) = 2x^2 + x - 3.$$

✍ Use algebra tiles to factor the following equations.

50) $x^2 - 3x + 2$ 51) $x^2 + 5x + 6$

Write a Quadratic Function from Its Vertex and Another Point

To write a quadratic function from its vertex and another point, you can use the vertex form of the equation which is $y = a(x - h)^2 + k$.

Here, (h, k) is the vertex of the parabola and a is the leading coefficient of the equation.

You can use the following steps to write the quadratic function:

1. Identify the vertex of the parabola: The vertex is the turning point of the parabola, and it is the point of minimum or maximum value.

2. Identify the other point: This can be any point on the parabola.

3. Substitute the coordinates of the vertex and the other point into the vertex form of the equation: $y = a(x - h)^2 + k$.

4. Solve for a: Once you have the equation set up with the vertex and another point, you can solve for the leading coefficient.

5. Write the final equation: Once you have solved for a, you can write the final equation in the form $y = a(x - h)^2 + k$.

For example, if the vertex of the parabola is $(-1,2)$ and the other point on the parabola is $(1,6)$, the steps would be:

1. Identify the vertex: $(-1,2)$.

2. Identify the other point: $(1,6)$.

3. Substitute the coordinates into the vertex form: $y = a(x + 1)^2 + 2$.

4. Solve for a: $6 = a(1 + 1)^2 + 2 \rightarrow 6 = 4a + 2 \rightarrow a = 1$.

5. Write the final equation: $y = 1(x + 1)^2 + 2$.

So, the final equation is $y = (x + 1)^2 + 2$.

Let's review an example:

bit.ly/3XLDlc7

Find more at

A quadratic function opening up or down has a vertex $(0, -4)$ and passes through $(4,0)$. Write its equation in vertex form.

Use the vertex form of the quadratic function as $y = a(x - h)^2 + k$. Substitute the coordinate of the vertex $(0, -4)$ in the vertex form:

$y = a(x - 0)^2 + (-4) \rightarrow y = ax^2 - 4$.

To find a substitute $(4,0)$ in this equation and calculate. Then,

$(4,0) \rightarrow 0 = a(4 - 0)^2 - 4 \rightarrow 0 = 16a - 4 \rightarrow 16a = 4 \rightarrow a = \frac{1}{4}$.

Therefore, the equation of the quadratic function in the vertex form is as follows:

$y = \frac{1}{4}x^2 - 4$.

A quadratic function has a vertex $\left(-\frac{1}{4}, -\frac{25}{8}\right)$ and passes through $(2,7)$. Write its equation in vertex form.

By using the vertex form formula: $y = a(x - h)^2 + k$. So, we have:

$\left(-\frac{1}{4}, -\frac{25}{8}\right) \rightarrow y = a\left(x - \left(-\frac{1}{4}\right)\right)^2 + \left(-\frac{25}{8}\right) \rightarrow y = a\left(x + \frac{1}{4}\right)^2 - \frac{25}{8}$.

Substitute $(2, 7)$ in the obtained equation, then:

$7 = a\left(2 + \frac{1}{4}\right)^2 - \frac{25}{8} \rightarrow 7 = \frac{81}{16}a - \frac{25}{8} \rightarrow \frac{81}{16}a = \frac{81}{8} \rightarrow a = 2$.

Therefore, $y = 2\left(x + \frac{1}{4}\right)^2 - \frac{25}{8}$.

✍ Find the quadratic equations that passes through the given vertex and another point.

52) A parabola opening or down has vertex $(0,0)$ and passes through $(8, -16)$.

53) A parabola opening up or down has a vertex $(0,2)$ and passes through $(-2,5)$.

Chapter 6: Answers

1) $x = 2, x = -1$

2) $x = 2, x = 4$

3) $x = 3, x = 1$

4) $x = 3, x = -4$

5) $x = 2, x = -9$

6) $x = 5, x = -3$

7) $x = 4, x = -10$

8) $x = 12, x = -3$

9)

10)

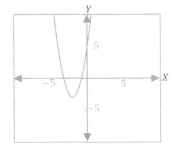

11) $\{-1, 3\}$

12) $\{-5, -4\}$

13) $\left\{-1, \frac{5}{6}\right\}$

14) $\left\{1 - \sqrt{17}, 1 + \sqrt{17}\right\}$

15) $\{1\}$

16) $\{-4, 4\}$

17) $\left\{-1, -\frac{2}{5}\right\}$

18) No real solution

19) The graph stretches vertically by a factor of 2.

Move 3 units to the right and 1 unit up.

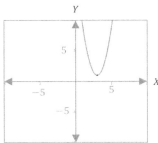

20) $y = -\frac{2}{3}x^2$

21) $y = x^2 - 2$

22) $y = x^2 + 1$

23) $y = 3(x + 4)^2 + 1$

24) No solution

25) Two different solutions

26) Two different solutions

27) No solution

28) $x_1 = 3, x_2 = \frac{1}{2}$

29) $x_1 = -9, x_2 = 1$

30) $x_1 = -3, x_2 = \frac{1}{2}$

31) $x_1 = x_2 = -3$

32) $x = -\frac{7}{2}$

33) 7

34) $(2, -1)$

35) $(3, -9)$

36) $x = 3$

37) 0

38)

$g(t) = t^2 + 7$	
t	$g(t)$
-1	8
0	7
1	8

39)

$f(p) = 4p^2$	
p	$f(p)$
-2	16
0	0
2	16

40) $D = \{x | x \in R\}$,

$R = \{y \in R | y \geq -\frac{1}{4}\}$

41) $D = \{x | x \in R\}$,

$R = \{R | y \leq 4\}$

42) $(5x + 2)^2$
43) $(3x - 1)(3x + 1)$
44) $3(x + 1)^2$
45) $(b^2 + 6)(b^2 - 6)$
50) $x^2 - 3x + 2 = (x - 1)(x - 2)$

46) $-x^2 + 4$
47) $x^2 - 4y^2$
48) $4r^2 - 28r + 49$
49) $x^2 + 4x + 4$
51) $x^2 + 5x + 6 = (x + 2)(x + 3)$

52) $y = -\frac{1}{4}x^2$

53) $y = \frac{3}{4}x^2 + 2$

CHAPTER

7 Polynomials

Math topics that you'll learn in this chapter:

- ☑ Simplifying Polynomials
- ☑ Adding and Subtracting Polynomials
- ☑ Add and Subtract Polynomials Using Algebra Tiles
- ☑ Multiplying Monomials
- ☑ Dividing Monomials
- ☑ Multiplying a Polynomial and a Monomial
- ☑ Multiply Polynomials Using Area Models
- ☑ Multiplying Binomials
- ☑ Multiply two Binomials Using Algebra Tiles
- ☑ Factoring Trinomials
- ☑ Factoring Polynomials
- ☑ Use a Graph to Factor Polynomials
- ☑ Factoring Special Case Polynomials
- ☑ Add Polynomials to Find Perimeter

Simplifying Polynomials

Simplifying polynomials is the process of combining like terms and reducing the degree of the polynomial.

To simplify a polynomial, you can follow these steps:

Step 1: Identify the like terms: These are terms that have the same variables raised to the same powers. For example, $3x^2$ and $5x^2$ are like terms.

Step 2: Combine the like terms: Add or subtract the numerical coefficients of the like terms. For example, you can combine $3x^2$ and $5x^2$ to get $8x^2$.

Step 3: Write the polynomial in descending order of exponents: This is done by arranging the terms in decreasing order of exponents, starting with the term with the highest exponent.

Step 4: Check for any remaining like terms, and combine them.

Step 5: Simplify any constants or coefficients that can be simplified.

For example, to simplify the polynomial $3x^2 + 2x^2 + 5x - 7x - 4x + 6$,

Step 1: Identify the like terms: $3x^2$ and $2x^2$, $5x$, $-7x$, and $-4x$.

Step 2: Combine the like terms: $3x^2 + 2x^2 = 5x^2$, $5x - 7x - 4x = -6x$.

Step 3: Write the polynomial in descending order of exponents: $5x^2 - 6x + 6$.

Step 4: Check for any remaining like terms and combine them: $5x^2 - 6x + 6$ (No more like terms).

Step 5: Simplify any constants or coefficients that can be simplified: $5x^2 - 6x + 6$ (No constants or coefficients can be simplified).

So, the simplified polynomial is $5x^2 - 6x + 6$.

Here's another example:

Simplify the polynomial $2x^3 - x + 5x^2 - 3x^2 - 8 + 6x$.

Step 1: Identify the like terms: $5x^2$ and $-3x^2$, $6x$ and $-x$.

Step 2: Combine the like terms: $5x^2 - 3x^2 = 2x^2$, and $6x - x = 5x$.

Step 3:   Write the polynomial in descending order of exponents:

$$2x^3 + 2x^2 + 5x - 8.$$

Step 4: Check for any remaining like terms and combine them:

$$2x^3 + 2x^2 + 5x - 8 \text{ (No more like terms)}.$$

Step 5: Simplify any constants or coefficients that can be simplified:

$$2x^3 + 2x^2 + 5x - 8$$

(No constants or coefficients can be simplified).

So, the simplified polynomial is $2x^3 + 2x^2 + 5x - 8$.

Some more examples:

Simplify this expression. $3x(2x - 5) + 7x =$

Use Distributive Property: $3x(2x - 5) = 6x^2 - 15x$.

Now, combine like terms:

$$3x(2x - 5) + 7x = 6x^2 - 15x + 7x = 6x^2 - 8x.$$

Simplify this expression. $(x + 3)(x - 5) - 2x^2 + 2x =$.

First, apply the FOIL method:

$$(a + b)(c + d) = ac + ad + bc + bd.$$

Therefore, use the Distributive Property: $(x + 3)(x - 5) = x^2 - 5x + 3x - 15$.

Next, substitute the obtained expression in the original expression:

$$(x + 3)(x - 5) - 2x^2 + 2x = x^2 - 5x + 3x - 15 - 2x^2 + 2x.$$

.Now combine like terms: $x^2 - 2x^2 = -x^2$, and $-5x + 3x + 2x = 0$.

The simplified form of the expression: $(x + 3)(x - 5) - 2x^2 + 2x = -x^2 - 15$.

✐ Simplify the following expressions.

1) $3(6x + 4) =$

2) $5(3x - 8) =$

3) $x(7x + 2) + 9x =$

4) $6x(x + 3) + 5x =$

5) $6x(3x + 1) - 5x =$

6) $x(3x - 4) + 3x^2 - 6 =$

7) $x^2 - 5 - 3x(x + 8) =$

8) $2x^2 + 7 - 6x(2x + 5) =$

Adding and Subtracting Polynomials

Adding and subtracting polynomials involves combining like terms, just as simplifying polynomials does. The process is the same, but instead of simplifying a single polynomial, you are combining two or more polynomials.

For example, to add the polynomials $2x^3 + 3x^2 - x - 8$ and $3x^3 - 4x^2 + 8x + 4$:

1. Identify the like terms: $2x^3$ and $3x^3$, $3x^2$ and $-4x^2$, $-x$ and $8x$, -8 and 4.

2. Add the like terms together:

$$2x^3 + 3x^3 = 5x^3, 3x^2 - 4x^2 = -x^2, -x + 8x = 7x, \text{ and } -8 + 4 = -4.$$

3. Write the polynomial in descending order of exponents: $5x^3 - x^2 + 7x - 4$.

4. Check for any remaining like terms and combine them: $5x^3 - x^2 + 7x - 4$

   (No more like terms).

5. Simplify any constants or coefficients that can be simplified:

   $5x^3 - x^2 + 7x - 4$

   (No constants or coefficients can be simplified).

So, the sum of the polynomials is $5x^3 - x^2 + 7x - 4$.

You can do the same process of subtracting polynomials, by replacing the addition with subtraction of the like terms.

Let's another example:

$$(4x^4 - 3x^3 + 2x^2 - x - 6) - (2x^4 + x^3 - 5x^2 + 4x + 2)$$

To subtract the polynomials $4x^4 - 3x^3 + 2x^2 - x - 6$ and $2x^4 + x^3 - 5x^2 + 4x + 2$:

1. Identify the like terms:

   $4x^4$ and $2x^4$, $-3x^3$ and x^3, $2x^2$ and $-5x^2$, $-x$ and $4x$, -6 and 2.

2. Subtract the like terms: $4x^4 - 2x^4 = 2x^4$, $-3x^3 - x^3 = -4x^3$, $2x^2 -$

   $(-5x^2) = 7x^2$, $-x - 4x = -5x$, $-6 - 2 = -8$.

3. Write the polynomial in descending order of exponents:

   $2x^4 - 4x^3 + 7x^2 - 5x - 8$.

4. Check for any remaining like terms and combine them:

$$2x^4 - 4x^3 + 7x^2 - 5x - 8 \text{ (No more like terms)}.$$

5. Simplify any constants or coefficients that can be simplified:

$$2x^4 - 4x^3 + 7x^2 - 5x - 8$$

(No constants or coefficients can be simplified).

So, the subtraction of the polynomials is $2x^4 - 4x^3 + 7x^2 - 5x - 8$.

Simplify the expressions. $(5 + x^2 - 2x^3) - (x^3 - 3x^2 - 3) =$

First, use the Distributive Property:

$$-(x^3 - 3x^2 - 3) = -x^3 + 3x^2 + 3.$$

Substitute the last expression in the given expression:

$$(5 + x^2 - 2x^3) - (x^3 - 3x^2 - 3) = 5 + x^2 - 2x^3 - x^3 + 3x^2 + 3.$$

Now, combine like terms: $-2x^3 - x^3 = -3x^3$, $x^2 + 3x^2 = 4x^2$ and $5 + 3 = 8$.

Then: $(5 + x^2 - 2x^3) - (x^3 - 3x^2 - 3) = -3x^3 + 4x^2 + 8$.

Simplify the expressions. $(8x^2 - 3x^3) + (2x^2 + 5x^3) =$

Since the operation between the parentheses is summation, remove parentheses:

$$(8x^2 - 3x^3) + (2x^2 + 5x^3) = 8x^2 - 3x^3 + 2x^2 + 5x^3.$$

Now, combine like terms and write in standard form:

$$8x^2 - 3x^3 + 2x^2 + 5x^3 = 10x^2 + 2x^3 = 2x^3 + 10x^2.$$

✍ Simplify the following expressions.

9) $(x^2 + 3) + (2x^2 - 4) =$

10) $(3x^2 - 6x) - (x^2 + 8x) =$

11) $(4x^3 - 3x^2) + (2x^3 - 5x^2) =$

12) $(6x^3 - 7x) - (5x^3 - 3x) =$

13) $(10x^3 + 4x^2) + (14x^2 - 8) =$

14) $(4x^3 - 9) - (3x^3 - 7x^2) =$

15) $(9x^3 + 3x) - (6x^3 - 4x) =$

16) $(7x^3 - 5x) - (3x^3 + 5x) =$

Add and Subtract Polynomials Using Algebra Tiles

To better understand and visualize the addition and subtraction of algebraic expressions, you can use Algebra tiles as follows:

- Model the polynomials using tiles.
- For algebraic subtraction, change the color of the tiles on the second side.
- Cross out the same number of negative or positive tiles on both sides of the equation.
- Write the answer by determining the number of remaining tiles.

Let's review an example:

Use algebra tiles to simplify: $(x^2 - x + 3) + (2x^2 + 3x - 2)$.

Model the given polynomials using algebra tiles.

Here, cross out one x tile on the left side and do the same on the other side. In the same way, cancel two 1 tiles on the left side and do the same on the right side.

That is, count the number of remaining tiles.

So, $3x^2 + 2x + 1$.

Simplify the polynomial $(2x^2 + 3x - 1) - (x^2 - 2x - 2)$ using algebra tiles.

Model the polynomials with tiles.

Change the color of the tiles on the second side, then add them to the first side.

EffortlessMath.com

Now, simplify the obtained algebraic tiles by canceling negative and positive tiles of the same size. As follow:

Finally, by counting the remaining tiles, the following expression obtains:

$$x^2 + 5x + 1$$

One more example:

Use algebra tiles to simplify: $(2x^2 - 5x + 3) - (x^2 - 3x + 6)$.

Model the given expression using algebra tiles.

Change the color of the tiles related to the second side to show the negative sign applied to the second side term, then add them to the first side:

Next, cancel the same tiles with the different colors (negative and positive tiles) from the sides.

Now, count the number of remaining tiles.

$$x^2 - 2x - 3$$

✒ Use algebra tiles to simplify the following expressions.

17) $(2x^2 - 3x + 3) - (x^2 - x - 1)$

18) $(2x^2 + 2x + 5) + (x^2 + 2x + 1)$

bit.ly/3J7x2eP

Find more at

Multiplying Monomials

When multiplying monomials, the process involves first multiplying the coefficients and then using the multiplication property of exponents for the variables.

- A monomial is a polynomial with just one term. For example, $2x$ or $7x^2$.
- When you multiply monomials, first multiply the coefficients (a number placed before and multiplying the variable) and then multiply the variables using the multiplication property of exponents.

$$x^a \times x^b = x^{a+b}$$

To illustrate this, consider the example of multiplying $3x^2$ and $4x^3$, you would first multiply the coefficients $3 \times 4 = 12$, then add the exponents of x, $2 + 3 = 5$, resulting in the product $12x^5$ ($x^2 \times x^3 = x^{2+3} = x^5$).

Here are a few examples with explanations:

$$(2x)(3x) = 6x^2$$

In this case, we have two monomials, $2x$ and $3x$. To multiply them, we simply multiply the numerical coefficients (2 and 3), which is $2 \times 3 = 6$.

Next, combine the variables (x) by using the formula $x^a \times x^b = x^{a+b}$ as

$$x \times x = x^{1+1} = x^2$$

The result is $6x^2$, which is a monomial with a numerical coefficient of 6 and a variable of x raised to the power of 2.

$$(-5y)(2y) = -10y^2$$

In this case, we have two monomials, $-5y$ and $2y$. To multiply them, we again multiply the numerical coefficients (-5 and 2) and combine the variables (y). The result is $-10y^2$, which is a monomial with a numerical coefficient of -10 and a variable of y raised to the power of 2.

$$(4)(-3) = -12$$

In this case, we have two monomials, 4 and -3. To multiply them, we again multiply the numerical coefficients (4 and -3) and combine the variables. The result is -12, which is a monomial with a numerical coefficient of -12 and no variable.

$$(2x^2)(3x^3) = 6x^5$$

In this case, we have two monomials, $2x^2$ and $3x^3$. To multiply them, we again multiply the numerical coefficients (2 and 3) and combine the variables (x) with their exponents (2 and 3) as follows: $x^2 \times x^3 = x^{2+3} = x^5$.

The result is $6x^5$, which is a monomial with a numerical coefficient of 6 and a variable of x raised to the power of 5.

Some more examples:

Multiply expressions. $2xy^3 \times 6x^4y^2$.

Find the same variables (x and x^4), and (y^3 and y^2). Then, use the multiplication property of exponents for multiplying the same variables: $x^a \times x^b = x^{a+b}$.

So, we have: $x \times x^4 = x^{1+4} = x^5$ and $y^3 \times y^2 = y^{3+2} = y^5$.

Then, multiply coefficients and variables: $2xy^3 \times 6x^4y^2 = 12x^5y^5$.

Multiply. $-5x^2z^3 \times 4z^5y^7$.

Use the multiplication property of exponents: $x^a \times x^b = x^{a+b}$. First multiply the same variable(s): $z^3 \times z^5 = z^{3+5} = z^8$. Then: $-5x^2z^3 \times 4z^5y^7 = -20x^2y^7z^8$.

Simplify. $(-6a^7b^4)(4a^8b^5) =$

Use the multiplication property of exponents: $x^a \times x^b = x^{a+b}$. $a^7 \times a^8 = a^{7+8} = a^{15}$ and $b^4 \times b^5 = b^{4+5} = b^9$. Then: $(-6a^7b^4)(4a^8b^5) = -24a^{15}b^9$.

✎ Multiply the following expressions.

19) $3x^2 \times 8x^3 =$

20) $2x^4 \times 9x^3 =$

21) $-4a^4b \times 2ab^3 =$

22) $(-7x^3yz) \times (3xy^2z^4) =$

23) $-2a^5bc \times 6a^2b^4 =$

24) $9u^3t^2 \times (-2ut) =$

25) $12x^2z \times 3xy^3 =$

26) $11x^3z \times 5xy^5 =$

27) $-6a^3bc \times 5a^4b^3 =$

28) $-4x^6y^2 \times (-12xy)$

Dividing Monomials

When dividing monomials, divide the numerical coefficients and divide the exponents with the same variable each other. For example, $6x^2 \div 2x = 3x$. It's important to make sure that the divisor and dividend have the same base before dividing.

It's also important to note that when dividing monomials, we can also use fractions. For example, $6x^2 \div 2x = \frac{6x^2}{2x} = 3x$.

If you divide a monomial with an exponent by another monomial with the same base, you subtract the exponent of the divisor from the exponent of the dividend. For example, $\frac{8x^3}{2x^2} = 4x^{(3-2)} = 4x$.

Summarily, keep in mind the following when working with monomials:

- When you divide two monomials, you need to divide their coefficients and then divide their variables.

- In the case of exponents with the same base, for Division, subtract their powers, for Multiplication, add their powers.

- Exponent's Division rules:

$$\frac{x^a}{x^b} = x^{a-b}$$

Here are a few samples:

Divide $18x^4$ by $6x^2$.

To divide these two monomials, we first make sure that they have the same base, which in this case is x. Then, we divide the numerical coefficients (18 and 6). So, $18 \div 6 = 3$. Next, divide the variables (x) with their exponents (4 and 2):

$$x^4 \div x^2 = x^{(4-2)} = x^2.$$

The result is, $(18x^4) \div (6x^2) = 3x^2$.

Divide $\frac{12y^3}{-3y^4}$.

To divide these two monomials, we first make sure that they have the same base, which in this case is y. Then we divide the numerical coefficients (12 and -3), which is $12 \div (-3) = -4$, and divide the variables (y) with their exponents (3 and 4) as $y^3 \div y^4 = y^{(3-4)}$. The result is $\frac{12y^3}{-3y^4} = -4y^{(3-4)} = -4y^{-1} = -\frac{4}{y}$.

Divide expressions: $\frac{12x^4 y^6}{6xy^2}$.

Use the division property of exponents:

$$\frac{x^a}{x^b} = x^{a-b}.$$

Divide the exponent with the same base:

$\frac{x^4}{x} = x^{4-1} = x^3$, and $\frac{y^6}{y^2} = y^{6-2} = y^4$.

Now, substitute the obtained expression in the original expression. Then:

$\frac{12x^4 y^6}{6xy^2} = 2x^3 y^4$.

Divide the expressions: $(3a^5) \div \left(\frac{1}{9}a^4\right)$.

First, divide the numerical coefficient: $3 \div \frac{1}{9} = 3 \times 9 = 27$.

Next, use the multiplication property of exponents:

$\frac{x^a}{x^b} = x^{a-b} \rightarrow a^5 \div a^4 = a^1 = a$. Then: $(3a^5) \div \left(\frac{1}{9}a^4\right) = 27a$.

Divide expressions: $\frac{49a^6 b^9}{7a^3 b^4}$

Use the division property of exponents:

$\frac{x^a}{x^b} = x^{a-b} \rightarrow \frac{a^6}{a^3} = a^{6-3} = a^3$ and $\frac{b^9}{b^4} = b^{9-4} = b^5$.

Then: $\frac{49a^6 b^9}{7a^3 b^4} = 7a^3 b^5$.

✎ Divide the following expressions.

29) $\frac{42x^4 y^2}{6x^3 y} =$

30) $\frac{49x^5 y^6}{7x^2 y} =$

31) $\frac{63x^{15} y^{10}}{9x^8 y^6} =$

32) $\frac{35x^8 y^{12}}{5x^4 y^8} =$

Multiplying a Polynomial and a Monomial

To multiply a polynomial and a monomial, you simply multiply each term of the polynomial by the monomial. For example, if the polynomial is $2x^2 + 3x - 4$ and the monomial is $5x$, the product would be:

$(2x^2 + 3x - 4)(5x) = 10x^3 + 15x^2 - 20x$.

In general, the distributive property applies to any polynomial and monomial multiplication. The monomial $(5x)$ is distributed to every term in the polynomial, and the exponent of the variable in the monomial is added to the exponent of the variable in each term of the polynomial. So, when you multiply $2x^2$ and $5x$, the result is $(2x^2)(5x) = (2 \times 5)x^{2+1} = 10x^3$, similarly for other terms.

Notice that the order of the terms in the polynomial doesn't change during this operation, the result is still a polynomial.

Here are some examples of polynomial and monomial multiplication problems with detailed solutions:

Multiply $(3x^2 - 2x + 5)$ and $(3x)$.

By using the distributive property, we have:

$(3x^2 - 2x + 5)(3x) = (3x^2 \times 3x) - (2x \times 3x) + (5 \times 3x)$

Calculate the product of each of the monomial multiplications inside the parentheses:

$3x^2 \times 3x = (3 \times 3)x^{2+1} = 9x^3$,

$2x \times 3x = (2 \times 3)x^{1+1} = 6x^2$,

$5 \times 3x = (5 \times 3)x = 15x$

Put these expressions:

$(3x^2 - 2x + 5)(3x) = 9x^3 - 6x^2 + 15x$

Multiply $(2x^3 - 4x^2 + 5x + 3)$ and $(3x^2)$.

Use the distributive property:

$$(2x^3 - 4x^2 + 5x + 3)(3x^2) = (2x^3 \times 3x^2) - (4x^2 \times 3x^2)$$
$$+(5x \times 3x^2) + (3 \times 3x^2)$$

Multiply the monomials in parentheses:

$2x^3 \times 3x^2 = 6x^5$, $4x^2 \times 3x^2 = 12x^4$, $5x \times 3x^2 = 15x^3$, and $3 \times 3x^2 = 9x^2$.

Next, substitute them:

$(2x^3 - 4x^2 + 5x + 3)(3x^2) = 6x^5 - 12x^4 + 15x^3 + 9x^2$.

Multiply $(6x^4 + x^2 - 7)$ and (6).

To multiply these two expressions, we use the distributive property:

$(6x^4 + x^2 - 7)(6) = (6x^4 \times 6) + (x^2 \times 6) - (7 \times 6) = 36x^4 + 6x^2 - 42$

As you can see in each example, the distributive property is used to distribute the monomial to each term of the polynomial, and the exponents of the variable in the monomial are added to the exponents of the variable in each term of the polynomial.

Keep in mind that in the last example, the monomial is a constant, in this case, the constant is multiplied by each term of the polynomial.

Also, pay attention to the following examples:

Multiply expressions: $6x(2x + 5)$.

Use Distributive Property:

$6x(2x + 5) = (6x \times 2x) + (6x \times 5) = 12x^2 + 30x$.

Multiply: $-x(-2x^2 + 4x + 5)$.

Use Distributive Property:

$-x(-2x^2 + 4x + 5) = (-x) \times (-2x^2) + (-x) \times (4x) + (-x) \times (5) = 2x^3 - 4x^2 - 5x$

✍ Multiply the following expressions.

33) $3x(5x - y) =$

34) $2x(4x + y) =$

35) $7x(x - 3y) =$

36) $x(2x^2 + 2x - 4) =$

37) $5x(3x^2 + 8x + 2) =$

38) $7x(2x^2 - 9x - 5) =$

Multiply Polynomials Using Area Models

To multiply polynomials using area models, you can follow these steps:

Step 1: Create a rectangular area with one side corresponding to each of the polynomials.

Step 2: Divide each side of the rectangle corresponding to the polynomials into the monomial factors.

Step 3: Multiply the monomials in each area to complete the rectangle.

Step 4: To find the product of the polynomials, add the resulting expressions.

Let's review some examples:

Use the area model to find the product $2x(x + 1)$.

Model a rectangular area,

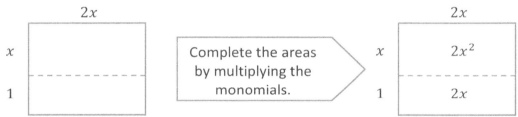

Last, combine terms to find the polynomial product.

$$2x(x + 1) = 2x^2 + 2x.$$

Use an area model to multiply these binomials.

$$(a - 2)(3a + 1)$$

Draw an area model representing the product $(a - 2)(3a + 1)$.

Now, add the partial products to find the product and simplify,

$$3a^2 + a - 6a - 2 = 3a^2 - 5a - 2.$$

Therefore, $(a - 2)(3a + 1) = 3a^2 - 5a - 2$.

Multiply$(3x^2 - 2x - 1)(1 - 3x)$, using the area model.

For this purpose, we model the multiplication as below.

Multiply the monomials in each area to complete the rectangle.

	$3x^2$	$-2x$	-1
1	$3x^2$	$-2x$	-1
$-3x$	$-9x^3$	$6x^2$	$+3x$

Now, add the obtained expressions on the grid, to find the product and simplify.

Therefore:

$$(3x^2 - 2x - 1)(1 - 3x) = 3x^2 - 9x^3 - 2x + 6x^2 - 1 + 3x$$
$$= -9x^3 + (3x^2 + 6x^2) + (-2x + 3x) - 1$$
$$= -9x^3 + 9x^2 + x - 1$$

✍ Multiply the following expressions with the area model.

39) $3x(x + 2)$

40) $(a - 3)(2a + 2)$

✍ Complete the model area below and write the multiplication.

41)

Multiplying Binomials

Multiplying binomials is a specific case of polynomial multiplication, where the polynomials are two terms polynomials, called binomials. The most common method of multiplying binomials is the FOIL method (First, Outer, Inner, Last). FOIL method is used to multiply two binomials of the form $(a + b)$ and $(c + d)$ as follows:

$$(a + b)(c + d) = ac + ad + bc + bd$$

It's based on distributing each term of the first binomial to each term of the second binomial. The acronym FOIL stands for:

- First: Multiply the first term of the first binomial by the first term of the second binomial.
- Outer: Multiply the first term of the first binomial by the second term of the second binomial.
- Inner: Multiply the second term of the first binomial by the first term of the second binomial.
- Last: Multiply the second term of the first binomial by the second term of the second binomial.

For example, to multiply $(x + 2)$ and $(x - 3)$, using the FOIL method:

$$(x + 2)(x - 3) = x(x) + x(-3) + 2(x) + 2(-3)$$
$$= x^2 - 3x + 2x - 6 = x^2 - x - 6$$

Another method to multiply binomials is using distributive property and combining like terms, but FOIL is the most widely used method.

It's important to notice that, when multiplying binomials, the order of terms in the binomials doesn't change, the result is still a polynomial.

bit.ly/3aCs0FL

Find more at

Here's another example of multiplying binomials using FOIL method:

Multiply $(3a - 2)$ and $(4a + 5)$.

Using the FOIL method:

$$(3a - 2)(4a + 5) = 3a(4a) + 3a(5) + (-2)(4a) + (-2)(5)$$

$$= 12a^2 + 15a - 8a - 10$$

$$= 12a^2 + 7a - 10$$

So, the product of $(3a - 2)$ and $(4a + 5)$ is $12a^2 + 7a - 10$.

Likewise, see some other examples:

Multiply Binomials. $(1 - x)(x - 2) =$

Use "FOIL". (First–Out–In–Last):

$$(1 - x)(x - 2) = x - 2 - x^2 + 2x.$$

Then combine like terms: $x - 2 - x^2 + 2x = -x^2 + 3x - 2$.

Therefore, the product of this multiplication is,

$$(1 - x)(x - 2) = -x^2 + 3x - 2.$$

Multiply Binomials. $(2a^3 - a)(a + 1) =$

Use "FOIL". (First–Out–In–Last):

$$(2a^3 - a)(a + 1) = 2a^4 + 2a^3 - a^2 - a.$$

So, the answer is this expression.

Multiply. $(x - 2y)(2x + 1) =$

Use "FOIL". (First–Out–In–Last):

$$(x - 2y)(2x + 1) = 2x^2 + x - 4xy - 2y.$$

Then simplify: $2x^2 + x - 4xy - 2y = 2x^2 - 4xy + x - 2y$.

✎ Multiply the following binomials.

42) $(x - 3)(x + 3) =$

43) $(x - 6)(x + 6) =$

44) $(x + 10)(x + 4) =$

45) $(x - 6)(x + 7) =$

46) $(x + 2)(x - 5) =$

47) $(x - 10)(x + 3) =$

Multiply two Binomials Using Algebra Tiles

To multiply two binomials using algebra tiles, you can follow these steps:

1. Place one binomial on the left side of the board and the other binomial on the right side of the board.

2. Take the first term of the left binomial and match it with the first term of the right binomial. This will create a rectangle tile with the product of the two terms.

3. Take the first term of the left binomial and match it with the second term of the right binomial. This will create a rectangle tile with the product of the two terms.

4. Take the second term of the left binomial and match it with the first term of the right binomial. This will create a rectangle tile with the product of the two terms.

5. Take the second term of the left binomial and match it with the second term of the right binomial. This will create a rectangle tile with the product of the two terms.

6. Arrange the rectangle tiles in a square array and add the products together to get the final result.

Pay attention an example for further explanation:

Use algebra tiles to simplify: $(x - 2)(2x + 1)$.

Set up the grid as follow:

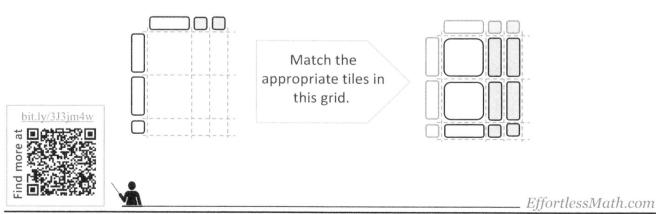

Match the appropriate tiles in this grid.

Here, cross out one x tile on the first column and do the same on the second column.

Count the like terms inside the grid. Since the number of x^2 tiles = 2, the number of $-x$ tiles = 3, and the number of -1 tiles = 2, then, sum the like terms inside the grid. So, $2x^2 - 3x - 2$

One more example:

Use algebra tiles to multiply $(2x - 1)$ to $(x - 3)$.

First, we set the binomial multiplication of a grading.

Match the appropriate tiles in this grid.

We see that there is no similar tile with the opposite sign in the grading.

Therefore, the number of tiles is obtained by multiplication.

Finally, we have:

$$(2x - 1)(x - 3) = 2x^2 - 7x + 3$$

✍ Multiply the following expressions by using the algebra tiles.

48) $(x + 1)(x + 6)$ 49) $(2x + 1)(x - 4)$

bit.ly/3J3jm4w
Find more at

Factoring Trinomials

Factoring trinomials is the process of expressing a trinomial, which is a polynomial with three terms, as the product of two binomials. One method for factoring trinomials is the "AC method", which involves identifying the coefficient of the squared term (a) and the constant term (c) and then finding two numbers whose product is c and whose sum is the coefficient of the x term (b). These two numbers can be used as the factors of the trinomial. Another method is known as "grouping" where you factor out the greatest common factor from the first two terms and the last two terms and then factor those two binomials.

For example, to factor the trinomial $x^2 - 5x + 6$, we could use the AC method by identifying $a = 1$, $b = -5$, and $c = 6$. The two numbers whose product is 6 and whose sum is -5 are -2 and -3, so we can factor the trinomial as $(x - 2)(x - 3)$. Alternatively, we could use the grouping method. First, rewrite the expression as $x^2 - 3x - 2x + 6$. Next, we factor out the greatest common factor of x^2 and $3x$ which is x, this gives us $x(x - 3) - 2x + 6$. Now we can factor the remaining binomial $-2x + 6$ which gives us $x(x - 3) - 2(x - 3)$ and thus the original trinomial can be written as $x(x - 3) - 2(x - 3) = (x - 3)(x - 2)$.

Let's review two examples:

Factor $x^2 + 7x + 10$.

We can use the AC method to factor this trinomial. The coefficient of the squared term is $a = 1$, the coefficient of the x term is $b = 7$, and the constant term is $c = 10$. We can find two numbers whose product is 10 and whose sum is 7: 2 and 5. So, we can factor the trinomial as $(x + 2)(x + 5)$.

To factor trinomials, you can use the following methods:

- "FOIL": $(x + a)(x + b) = x^2 + (b + a)x + ab$.
  - "Difference of Squares":
    $$a^2 + 2ab + b^2 = (a + b)(a + b)$$

$$a^2 - 2ab + b^2 = (a - b)(a - b)$$

- "Reverse FOIL": $x^2 + (b + a)x + ab = (x + a)(x + b)$.

Some another examples:

Factor this trinomial. $x^2 - 2x - 8$

Break the expression into groups. You need to find two numbers that their product is -8 and their sum is -2.

(Remember "Reverse FOIL": $x^2 + (b + a)x + ab = (x + a)(x + b)$).

Those two numbers are 2 and -4. Then: $x^2 - 2x - 8 = (x^2 + 2x) + (-4x - 8)$.

Now factor out x from $x^2 + 2x$: $x(x + 2)$, and factor out -4 from $-4x - 8$: $-4(x + 2)$; Then: $(x^2 + 2x) + (-4x - 8) = x(x + 2) - 4(x + 2)$.

Now factor out like term: $(x + 2)$. Then: $(x + 2)(x - 4)$.

Factor this trinomial. $4x^2 + 4x - 8$

First, factor -4 from the trinomial and rewrite as $4(x^2 + x - 2)$. Next, use the AC method for $x^2 + x - 2$. Find two numbers whose product is -2 and whose sum is 1 are 2 and -1, so we can factor the trinomial. Therefore,

$$4x^2 + 4x - 8 = 4(x - 1)(x + 2).$$

Factor this trinomial. $4x^6 - 10x^3 + 6$

Comparing the given trinomial and the "Reverse FOIL" method

$$x^2 + (b + a)x + ab = (x + a)(x + b),$$

we find that by substituting $2x^3$ for x and rewriting the trinomial as we get: $(2x^3)^2 - 5(2x^3) + 6$. Next, use the "AC method" for resulting trinomial, we have: $4x^6 - 10x^3 + 6 = (2x^3 - 2)(2x^3 - 3)$.

✍ Factor the following expressions.

50) $x^2 + 6x + 8 =$

51) $x^2 + 3x - 10$

52) $x^2 + 2x - 48 =$

53) $x^2 - 10x + 16 =$

54) $2x^2 - 10x + 12 =$

55) $3x^2 - 10x + 3 =$

Factoring Polynomials

Factoring polynomials is the process of expressing a polynomial as the product of simpler polynomials. There are several methods for factoring polynomials, including:

1. Factoring by grouping: This method involves grouping the terms of the polynomial into pairs and factoring out the greatest common factor from each pair.

2. Factoring by using the difference of squares: This method involves identifying two binomials that when multiplied together give the polynomial, and are each the square of the difference of two terms.

3. Factoring by using the sum and difference of cubes: This method involves identifying two binomials that when multiplied together give the polynomial, and are each the cube of the sum or difference of two terms.

4. Factoring by using the Rational Root Theorem: This method involves finding the possible rational roots of the polynomial, and testing them to see if they divide the polynomial.

5. Factoring by synthetic division: This method involves dividing the polynomial by a linear factor using synthetic division.

For example, to factor the polynomial $x^3 + 6x^2 - x - 6$, we could use factoring by grouping. We would group the first two terms, $x^3 + 6x^2$, and the last two terms, $-x - 6$, and find that both pairs share a common factor of $x + 6$. So, we can factor out $x + 6$ and get:

$x^3 + 6x^2 - x - 6 = (x^3 + 6x^2) - x - 6 = x^2(x + 6) - x - 6$

$$= x^2(x + 6) - (x + 6) = (x + 6)(x^2 - 1).$$

Now, we can factor the remaining binomial $x^2 - 1$ as $(x-1)(x+1)$, and the original polynomial can be written as $(x+6)(x+1)(x-1)$.

Another example is to factor the polynomial $x^4 - 16$, we can use the difference of squares method by noticing that $x^4 - 16 = (x^2 + 4)(x^2 - 4)$.

It's worth noting that not all polynomials can be factored and the method of factoring will depend on the polynomial you are trying to factor.

Some more examples:

Factor each polynomial.

$$6x^3 - 6x$$

To factorize the expression $6x^3 - 6x$, first factor out the largest common factor, $6x$, and then you will see that you have the pattern of the difference between two complete squares: $(a-b)(a+b) = a^2 - b^2$,

then: $6x^3 - 6x = 6x(x^2 - 1) = 6x(x-1)(x+1)$.

$$x^2 + 9x + 20$$

To factorize the expression $x^2 + 9x + 20$, you need to find two numbers whose product is 20 and sum is 9. You can get the number 20 by multiplying 1×20, 2×10, 4×5. The last pair will be your choice, because $4 + 5 = 9$.

Then: $x^2 + 9x + 20 = (x+4)(x+5)$.

✎ Factor each expression.

56) $4x^2 - 4x - 8$

57) $6x^2 + 37x + 6$

58) $16x^2 + 60x - 100$

59) $4x^2 - 17x + 4$

Use a Graph to Factor Polynomials

If a polynomial includes the factor of the form $(x - h)^p$, you can determine the behavior near the x −intercept by the power p. It can be said that $x = h$ is a zero of multiplicity p:

- If a polynomial function graph touches the x −axis, it's a zero with even multiplicity.

- If a polynomial function graph crosses the x −axis, it's a zero with odd multiplicity.

- A polynomial function graph gets flattered at zero if the multiplicity of the zero is higher.

- The sum of the multiplicities of the zero is the polynomial function's degree.

To check factorization using a graphing calculator, follow these steps:

Step 1: Press the $Y =$ button and enter the given equation for $Y1$.

Step 2: Press the GRAPH button to see the equation's graph.

Step 3: Press the TRACE button and by the left and right buttons move the cursor along the graph. You can see at which points the graph crosses the x −axis.

Step 4: To find the y −values at the x −values when the graph crosses the x −axis, enter the value of x at this point and press the ENTER button while in Trace mode. The calculator finds the y −value for you. The calculator tells you that in these values of x, the y −values are equal to zero.

Step 5: Remember that for functions with binomial factors of the form $(x - a)$, a is an x −intercept.

Let's review an example:

Use a graph to factor following polynomial: $y = x^2 - x - 2$

First, graph the polynomial. Then find the points where the polynomial function graph crosses the x −axis. These points are the zeros of the polynomial function. For $y = x^2 - x - 2$, $x = -1$ and $x = 2$ are the zeros of the polynomial function.

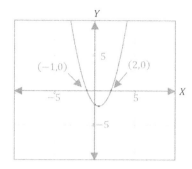

Therefore, two binomials $(x + 1)$ and $(x - 2)$ are the factors of the given trinomial. So, we can write as follows:

$$x^2 - x - 2 = (x + 1)(x - 2).$$

Use the following graph to find the polynomial factors below:

$$y = 2x^4 - 7x^3 + 6x^2 + x - 2$$

To solve, we first find the zeros of the polynomial from the graph. We can see that the graph intersects the x −axis at points $-\frac{1}{2}$ and 2 (with odd multiplicity) and

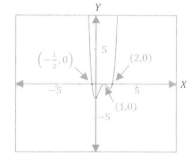

touches at point 1 (with even multiplicity).

So, you can write the given polynomial in the form:

$$y = Q(x)\left(x + \frac{1}{2}\right)^r (x - 1)^s (x - 2)^t,$$

where r and t are odd positive integers and s is an even positive integer, and $r + s + t \leq 4$. $Q(x)$ is a non-zero polynomial whose power of the leading term is $4 - (r + s + t)$. Clearly, we have: $r = 1$, $s = 2$, and $t = 1$. Then, Q is a constant number such as k. Because every polynomial with zero degree is a constant number. So, we get: $y = k\left(x + \frac{1}{2}\right)(x - 1)^2(x - 2)$.

To find k, the factors can be multiplied together and compared with the initial polynomial. $y = 2\left(x + \frac{1}{2}\right)(x - 1)^2(x - 2)$.

✐ Use a graph to find zeros of following polynomials.

60) $y = x^2 - 4$

61) $y = -(x + 2)^2$

bit.ly/3D5vQom

Find more at

Factoring Special Case Polynomials

There are several special cases of polynomials that can be factored using specific methods. These include:

1. Factoring perfect square trinomials: A trinomial of the form $a^2 + 2ab + b^2$ or $a^2 - 2ab + b^2$ is a perfect square trinomial, which can be factored as $(a + b)^2$ or $(a - b)^2$ respectively.

2. Factoring a difference of squares: A polynomial of the form $a^2 - b^2$ can be factored as $(a + b)(a - b)$ using the difference of squares identity.

3. Factoring a sum of cubes: A polynomial of the form $a^3 + b^3$ can be factored as $(a + b)(a^2 - ab + b^2)$ using the sum of cubes identity.

4. Factoring a difference of cubes: A polynomial of the form $a^3 - b^3$ can be factored as $(a - b)(a^2 + ab + b^2)$ using the difference of cubes identity.

5. Factoring by grouping: A polynomial of the form $ax^3 + bx^2 + cx + d$ can be factored by grouping the first two terms and the last two terms and factoring out the greatest common factor from each pair.

6. Factoring by synthetic division: You can use synthetic division to divide the polynomial by a linear factor.

For example, to factor the trinomial $x^2 - 4x + 4$, we can see that it's a perfect square trinomial and we can factor it as $(x - 2)^2$.

Another example: to factor the polynomial $x^3 + 8$, we can factor it as $(x + 2)(x^2 - 2x + 4)$ by using the difference of cubes identity.

It's important to note that not all polynomials will have special cases that can be used to factor them, and it's not always the most efficient method. It's also important to check the solutions of the polynomial equation before applying the factoring methods because that can make the process easier.

Here are some more examples for further explanation:

Factor completely: $x^3 - x^2 - 9x + 9$.

Looking at the given equation, we can see that the factor x^2 can be factored from two monomials with the largest degree $(x^3 - x^2)$. Thus:

$x^3 - x^2 - 9x + 9 = x^2(x - 1) - 9x + 9$.

Also, we can see factor from the coefficient -9 of this part of the polynomial $-9x + 9$ to get binomial $(x - 1)$. So, we have:

$x^2(x - 1) - 9x + 9 = x^2(x - 1) - 9(x - 1)$.

In this step, we separate factor $(x - 1)$ as a coefficient from the whole polynomial.

$x^2(x - 1) - 9(x - 1) = (x - 1)(x^2 - 9)$

Looking more closely at the result, we can see that the monomial $(x^2 - 9)$ can be factored using the formula $a^2 - b^2 = (a + b)(a - b)$. Therefore, we get:

$x^2 - 9 = (x + 3)(x - 3)$.

Finally, substitute the obtained polynomial in the original expression to get the answer: $x^3 - x^2 - 9x + 9 = (x - 1)(x + 3)(x - 3)$.

Factor: $36y^2 - 25x^4$.

Phrase $36y^2$ can be written in form $(6y)^2$ and phrase $25x^4$ in form $(5x^2)^2$. Now, according to the formula $a^2 - b^2 = (a + b)(a - b)$. Put the values of $a = 6y$ and $b = 5x^2$.

Therefore, the relation of the question form is as follows:

$$(6y)^2 - (5x^2)^2 = (6y - 5x^2)(6y + 5x^2).$$

✎ Factor each completely.

62) $36x^2 - 121 =$

63) $-36x^4 + 4x^2 =$

64) $-36x^2 + 400 =$

65) $49x^2 - 56x + 16 =$

66) $1 - x^2 =$

67) $81x^4 - 900x^2 =$

bit.ly/3KCrd6g

Find more at

Add Polynomials to Find Perimeter

When working with polynomials, adding them is a process of combining like terms. This can be done by adding the coefficients of the same degree together.

To add polynomials to find the perimeter of a shape, you will need to first identify the polynomials that represent the lengths of the sides of the shape.

For example, let's say we have a rectangle with sides of length $x + 2$ and $x - 3$. To find the perimeter of this rectangle, we would add the polynomials representing the lengths of the sides:

$2\big((x + 2) + (x - 3)\big) = 2(2x - 1) = 4x - 2.$

So, the perimeter of the rectangle is represented by the polynomial $4x - 2$.

For another example, let's say we have a square with side length $2x + 3$. To find the perimeter of this square, we would add the polynomials representing the lengths of the sides: $4(2x + 3) = 8x + 12$.

So, the perimeter of the square is represented by the polynomial $8x + 12$.

It's worth noting that the perimeter is a scalar value, so the polynomial representing it will be a constant, and it's not dependent on the variable.

Also, the same process can be used for different shapes and different dimensions, you just need to identify the polynomials that represent the lengths of the sides and then add them together to find the perimeter.

Here's another example:

Find the perimeter. Simplify your answer.

The perimeter of the shape is the sum of the sides. So,

Perimeter $= (x - 2) + (2x) + (3x - 1) + (2x)$

$\qquad = x - 2 + 2x + 3x - 1 + 2x.$

Group and add like terms,

Perimeter $= (x + 2x + 3x + 2x) + (-2 - 1) = 8x - 3.$

What is the perimeter of the rectangle if the length is $2x^2 - 1$ and the width is

$4(x + 1)$?

The perimeter of the rectangle is,

$$\text{Perimeter} = 2\big((2x^2 - 1) + 4(x + 1)\big)$$

Expand the expression and simplify,

$$\text{Perimeter} = 2\big((2x^2 - 1) + (4x + 4)\big)$$

$$= 2(2x^2 - 1 + 4x + 4)$$

$$= 2(2x^2 + 4x + 3)$$

$$= 4x^2 + 8x + 6.$$

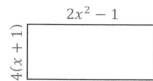

✎ What is the perimeter of the following shapes.

68) Perimeter =

69) Perimeter =

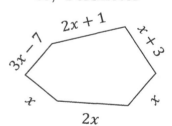

✎ Based on the information in each case, find the value of x.

70) $a =$ _____

Perimeter $= 36$

71) $x =$ _____

Perimeter $= 42$

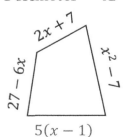

Chapter 7: Answers

1) $18x + 12$

2) $15x - 40$

3) $7x^2 + 11x$

4) $6x^2 + 23x$

5) $18x^2 + x$

6) $6x^2 - 4x - 6$

7) $-2x^2 - 24x - 5$

8) $-10x^2 - 30x + 7$

17) $x^2 - 2x + 4$

19) $24x^5$

20) $18x^7$

21) $-8a^5b^4$

22) $-21x^4y^3z^5$

23) $-12a^7b^5c$

24) $-18u^4t^3$

25) $36x^3y^3z$

26) $55x^4y^5z$

27) $-30a^7b^4c$

28) $48x^7y^3$

9) $3x^2 - 1$

10) $2x^2 - 14x$

11) $6x^3 - 8x^2$

12) $x^3 - 4x$

13) $10x^3 + 18x^2 - 8$

14) $x^3 + 7x^2 - 9$

15) $3x^3 + 7x$

16) $4x^3 - 10x$

18) $3x^2 + 4x + 6$

29) $7xy$

30) $7x^3y^5$

31) $7x^7y^4$

32) $7x^4y^4$

33) $15x^2 - 3xy$

34) $8x^2 + 2xy$

35) $7x^2 - 21xy$

36) $2x^3 + 2x^2 - 4x$

37) $15x^3 + 40x^2 + 10x$

38) $14x^3 - 63x^2 - 35x$

39) $3x^2 + 6x$

40) $2a^2 - 4a - 6$

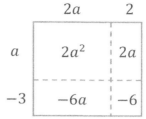

41) $(x - 1)(y + 2x) = xy + 2x^2 - y - 2x$

42) $x^2 - 9$

43) $x^2 - 36$

44) $x^2 + 14x + 40$

45) $x^2 + x - 42$

46) $x^2 - 3x - 10$

47) $x^2 - 7x - 30$

48) $x^2 + 7x + 6$

49) $2x^2 - 7x - 4$

50) $(x + 4)(x + 2)$

51) $(x + 5)(x - 2)$

52) $(x - 6)(x + 8)$

53) $(x - 8)(x - 2)$

54) $2(x - 2)(x - 3)$

55) $(3x - 1)(x - 3)$

56) $4(x + 1)(x - 2)$

57) $(x + 6)(6x + 1)$

58) $4(x + 5)(4x - 5)$

59) $(x - 4)(4x - 1)$

60) $x = \pm 2$

61) $x = -2$

62) $(6x - 11)(6x + 11)$

63) $-4x^2(3x + 1)(3x - 1)$

64) $-4(3x + 10)(3x - 10)$

65) $(7x - 4)^2$

66) $(1 + x)(1 - x)$

67) $9x^2(3x + 10)(3x - 10)$

68) 10

69) $10x - 3$

70) $a = 9\sqrt{2}$

71) $x = 4$

CHAPTER

8 Relations and Functions

Math topics that you'll learn in this chapter:

- ☑ Function Notation and Evaluation
- ☑ Adding and Subtracting Functions
- ☑ Multiplying and Dividing Functions
- ☑ Composition of Functions
- ☑ Evaluate an Exponential Function
- ☑ Function Inverses
- ☑ Domain and Range of Relations
- ☑ Interval Notation
- ☑ Rate of Change and Slope
- ☑ Complete a Function Table from an Equation

191

Function Notation and Evaluation

Function notation is a way to express a mathematical function using a specific symbol, usually denoted by "$f(x)$" or "$g(x)$" where "x" is the input (also called the independent variable) and "$f(x)$" or "$g(x)$" is the output (also called the dependent variable). The notation is read as "f of x" or "g of x", and it's used to indicate that the value of "$f(x)$" or "$g(x)$" is determined by the value of "x".

For example, if we have a function $f(x) = 2x + 3$, this means that for any value of x, the corresponding value of $f(x)$ is found by plugging that value of x into the equation and solving for the output. So, if we plug in $x = 2$, we would get:

$f(2) = 2(2) + 3 = 4 + 3 = 7$.

Evaluation of a function is the process of determining the value of the function at a specific input.

For example, if we have a function $g(x) = x^2$, and we want to find the value of $g(-1)$, we would substitute -1 for x in the equation and solve for the output:

$g(-1) = (-1)^2 = 1$. So, the value of $g(-1)$ is 1.

It's worth noting that in the function notation, the letter "f" or "g" is arbitrary and can be replaced by any other letter.

Also, you can have a function with more than one variable. Like $f(x, y) = x^2 + y^2$, where x and y are the independent variable and $f(x, y)$ is the dependent variable.

Furthermore, you can have a function defined by a table of values, where you have the function inputs and their corresponding outputs, and the function can be defined by the relation between the inputs and the outputs.

Let's review an example:

Find the value of the function $f(x) = 2x^2 + 4$ for -1 and 1.

For this purpose, plug the value of $x = -1$ into the function $f(x) = 2x^2 + 4$, as $f(-1) = 2(-1)^2 + 4$. Then, calculate the value of expression:

$2(-1)^2 + 4 = 2(1) + 4 = 2 + 4 = 6.$

Here, I see that the value of the function $f(x)$ for -1 is 6.

Similarly, we find the value of the function for 1.

$x = 1 \rightarrow f(1) = 2(1)^2 + 4 = 2(1) + 4 = 2 + 4 = 6.$

We see that the function values for -1 and 1 are equal to each other.

Look at some other examples:

Evaluate: $f(x) = x + 6$, find $f(2)$.

Substitute x with 2. Then:

$f(x) = x + 6 \rightarrow f(2) = 2 + 6 \rightarrow f(2) = 8.$

Therefore, the corresponding value of $f(x) = x + 6$ for $x = 2$ is 8.

Evaluate: $w(x) = 3x - 1$, find $w(4)$.

Substitute x with 4. Then: $w(x) = 3x - 1 \rightarrow w(4) = 3(4) - 1 = 12 - 1 = 11.$

So, the value of $w(4)$ is 11.

Evaluate: $h(x) = 4x^2 - 9$, find $h(2a)$.

Substitute x with $2a$. Then:

$h(x) = 4x^2 - 9 \rightarrow h(2a) = 4(2a)^2 - 9 \rightarrow h(2a) = 4(4a^2) - 9 = 16a^2 - 9.$

Here, the value of the function $h(x)$ is a combination of the value $2a$ evaluated the values of h by putting different values for a.

✎ Evaluate each function.

1) $f(x) = x - 2$, find $f(-1)$

2) $g(x) = 2x + 4$, find $g(3)$

3) $g(n) = 2n - 8$, find $g(-1)$

4) $h(n) = n^2 - 1$, find $h(-2)$

5) $f(x) = x^2 + 12$, find $f(5)$

6) $g(x) = 2x^2 - 9$, find $g(-2)$

7) $w(x) = 2x^2 - 4x$, find $w(2n)$

8) $p(x) = 4x^3 - 10$, find $p(-3a)$

Adding and Subtracting Functions

When adding or subtracting functions, we combine the expressions for each function and simplify the result.

To add two functions, we simply add their expressions together. For example, if we have two functions $f(x) = 2x + 3$ and $g(x) = x - 4$, we can add them together to get:

$$f(x) + g(x) = (2x + 3) + (x - 4) = 2x + 3 + x - 4 = (2x + x) + (3 - 4) = 3x - 1$$

The addition of two functions f and g is represented by the notation $f + g$.

$$(f + g)(x) = f(x) + g(x)$$

To subtract two functions, we subtract the expressions for one function from the other. For example, if we have two functions $f(x) = 2x + 3$ and $g(x) = x - 4$, we can subtract them to get:

$$f(x) - g(x) = (2x + 3) - (x - 4) = 2x + 3 - x + 4 = (2x - x) + (3 + 4) = x + 7$$

The subtraction of two functions f and g is represented by the notation $f - g$.

$$(f - g)(x) = f(x) - g(x)$$

It's worth noting that the same process can be applied to functions with more than one variable, you just need to combine the expressions of the functions and simplify the result.

Also, when you are working with different functions, you need to make sure that the domain of the function and the range of the function are the same, otherwise, the operation is not defined.

Additionally, if you want to add or subtract functions with different variables, you can use the principle of the change of variables.

For example, if you want to add $f(x) = 2x + 3$ and $g(y) = y - 4$, you can change the variable of $g(y)$ to $g(x) = x - 4$, and then add the two functions.

Some examples:

Let $g(x) = 2x - 2$, and $f(x) = x + 1$. Find: $(g + f)(x)$.

In order to, use the relation: $(f + g)(x) = f(x) + g(x)$. Then:

$(g + f)(x) = g(\boldsymbol{x}) + f(x) = (2x - 2) + (x + 1) = 2x - 2 + x + 1$

$\qquad = (2x + x) + (-2 + 1) = 3x - 1.$

Therefore, the equation of the function $g + f$ is $(g + f)(x) = 3x - 1$.

Find $(f - g)(x)$, for the functions $f(x) = 4x - 3$, and $g(x) = 2x - 4$.

Given that $(f - g)(x) = f(x) - g(x)$. Then:

$(f - g)(x) = (4x - 3) - (2x - 4) = 4x - 3 - 2x + 4 = 2x + 1.$

If $h(x) = x^2 + 2$, and $k(x) = x + 5$. Find: $(h + k)(x)$.

According to the $(g + f)(x) = g(x) + f(x)$, we have:

$(h + k)(x) = h(x) + k(x) = (x^2 + 2) + (x + 5) = x^2 + x + 7.$

Evaluate: $f(x) = 5x^2 - 3$, $g(x) = 3x + 6$. Find: $(f - g)(3)$.

Then: $(f - g)(x) = (5x^2 - 3) - (3x + 6) = 5x^2 - 3 - 3x - 6 = 5x^2 - 3x - 9.$

Substitute x with 3: $(f - g)(3) = 5(3)^2 - 3(3) - 9 = 45 - 9 - 9 = 27.$

$g(x) = x^2 - 4$, $f(x) = 2x + 3$, Find: $(g + f)(x)$. Since $(g + f)(x) = g(x) + f(x)$.

Then: $(g + f)(x) = (x^2 - 4) + (2x + 3) = x^2 - 4 + 2x + 3 = x^2 + 2x - 1.$

✎ **Perform the indicated operation.**

9) $g(x) = x - 2$,

$\quad h(x) = 2x + 6$

$\quad$ Find: $(h + g)(3)$

10) $f(x) = 3x + 2$,

$\quad g(x) = -x - 6$

$\quad$ Find: $(f + g)(2)$

11) $f(x) = 5x + 8$,

$\quad g(x) = 3x - 12$

$\quad$ Find: $(f - g)(-2)$

12) $h(x) = 2x^2 - 10.$

$\quad g(x) = 3x + 12$

$\quad$ Find: $(h + g)(3)$

13) $g(x) = 12x - 8$,

$\quad h(x) = 3x^2 + 14$

$\quad$ Find: $(h - g)(x)$

14) $h(x) = -2x^2 - 18$,

$\quad g(x) = 4x^2 + 15$

$\quad$ Find: $(h - g)(a)$

bit.ly/3hdeFVO

Find more at

Multiplying and Dividing Functions

When multiplying or dividing functions, we use the standard rules of algebra to simplify the result.

To multiply two functions, we simply multiply their expressions together. For example, if we have two functions $f(x) = 2x + 3$ and $g(x) = x - 4$, we can multiply them together to get:

$f(x) \cdot g(x) = (2x + 3) \cdot (x - 4) = 2x^2 - 8x + 3x - 12 = 2x^2 - 5x - 2.$

The multiplication of two functions f and g is represented by the notation $f \cdot g$.

$$(f \cdot g)(x) = f(x) \cdot g(x)$$

To divide two functions, we divide the expression of one function by the other. For example, if we have two functions $f(x) = 2x + 3$ and $g(x) = x - 4$, we can divide them to get: $\left(\frac{f}{g}\right)(x) = \frac{f(x)}{g(x)} = \frac{2x+3}{x-4}.$

The division of two functions as g by f is represented by the notation $\frac{f}{g}$.

$$\left(\frac{f}{g}\right)(x) = \frac{f(x)}{g(x)}$$

It's worth noting that when you divide two functions, you should check that the denominator is not equal to zero since it would mean that the division is not defined.

It's also worth noting that the same process can be applied to functions with more than one variable, you just need to combine the expressions of the functions and simplify the result.

Also, when you are working with different functions, you need to make sure that the domain of the function and the range of the function are the same, otherwise, the operation is not defined.

Additionally, if you want to multiply or divide functions with different variables, you can use the principle of the change of variables. For example, if you want to multiply $f(x) = 2x + 3$ and $g(y) = y - 4$, you can change the variable of $g(y)$ to $g(x) = x - 4$, and then multiply the two functions.

Let's review some examples:

Let's $g(x) = x + 3$, and $f(x) = x + 4$. Find: $(g.f)(x)$.

Use the formula: $(f \cdot g)(x) = f(x) \cdot g(x)$. Instead of $f(x)$ and $g(x)$, put $g(x) = x + 3$ and $f(x) = x + 4$, respectively. So, we get:

$(g.f)(x) = g(x).f(x) = (x + 3)(x + 4) = x^2 + 4x + 3x + 12 = x^2 + 7x + 12$.

Evaluate: $f(x) = x + 6$, and $h(x) = x - 9$. Find: $\left(\frac{f}{h}\right)(x)$.

Since $\left(\frac{f}{g}\right)(x) = \frac{f(x)}{g(x)}$. Therefore, $\left(\frac{f}{h}\right)(x) = \frac{x+6}{x-9}$.

If $g(x) = x + 7$, and $f(x) = x - 3$. Find: $(g.f)(2)$.

To solve it, we can get the equation of function $(g.f)(x)$. Therefore, $(g.f)(x) = g(x).f(x) = (x + 7)(x - 3) = x^2 - 3x + 7x - 21$.

Then: $g(x).f(x) = x^2 + 4x - 21$.

Next, substitute x with 2: $(g.f)(2) = (2)^2 + 4(2) - 21 = 4 + 8 - 21 = -9$.

$f(x) = x + 3$, $h(x) = 2x - 4$. Find: $\left(\frac{f}{h}\right)(3)$.

Since $\left(\frac{f}{h}\right)(x) = \frac{f(x)}{h(x)} = \frac{x+3}{2x-4}$. Substitute x with 3: $\left(\frac{f}{h}\right)(3) = \frac{3+3}{2(3)-4} = \frac{6}{2} = 3$.

✎ Perform the indicated operation.

15) $g(x) = x - 5$, $h(x) = x + 6$

   Find: $(g.h)(-1) =$

16) $f(x) = 2x + 2$, $g(x) = -x - 6$

   Find: $\left(\frac{f}{g}\right)(-2) =$

17) $f(x) = 5x + 3$, $g(x) = 2x - 4$

   Find: $\left(\frac{f}{g}\right)(5) =$

18) $h(x) = x^2 - 2$, $g(x) = x + 4$

   Find: $(g.h)(3) =$

19) $g(x) = 4x - 12$, $h(x) = x^2 + 4$

   Find: $(g.h)(-2) =$

20) $h(x) = 3x^2 - 8$, $g(x) = 4x + 6$

   Find: $\left(\frac{h}{g}\right)(-4) =$

bit.ly/3ph7kHA

Find more at

Composition of Functions

The composition of functions is a way to combine two or more functions to create a new function. It is denoted by the symbol $fog(x)$, and it is read as "f composed with g".

The composition of two functions $f(x)$ and $g(x)$ is defined as the function $h(x) = f(g(x))$, where $h(x)$ is the new function formed by the composition. This means that the output of function $g(x)$ is used as the input to function $f(x)$, and the final output of the composition is $h(x)$. Thus, it can be said:

$$fog(x) = f(g(x))$$

For example, if we have two functions $f(x) = 2x + 3$ and $g(x) = x^2$, we can compose them together to get: $h(x) = f(g(x)) = f(x^2) = 2(x^2) + 3 = 2x^2 + 3$.

It's worth noting that when you compose two functions, the domain of the composed function is the intersection of the domain of the two functions being composed. The range of the composed function is the range of the first function. Also, you can compose multiple functions together.

For example, if you have three functions: $f(x) = 2x + 3$, $g(x) = x^2$, and $h(x) = x^3$, you can compose them together in the order of $hogof(x) = h\left(g(f(x))\right)$. So, the output of $f(x)$ would be the input of $g(x)$, the output of $g(x)$ would be the input of $h(x)$, and the final output is the composition of all the functions.

Finally, it is worth noting that the composition of functions is not commutative, meaning that $f(g(x))$ is not the same as $g(f(x))$, and it is not associative meaning that $(fog)oh(x)$ is not the same as $fo(goh)(x)$.

Additionally, it is important to note that when composing functions, the order of the functions matters. The composition of two functions $f(x)$ and $g(x)$ is not the same as the composition of the same two functions in reverse order, i.e., $g(f(x))$. This is because the output of one function is used as the input of the other function, so the order in which they are composed affects the final output. For example, if we have two functions $f(x) = 2x + 3$, and $g(x) = x^2$, then the composition of $f(g(x)) = f(x^2) = 2x^2 + 3$, while the composition of $g(f(x)) = g(2x + 3) = (2x + 3)^2 = 4x^2 + 12x + 9$.

Let's review an example:

Using $f(x) = x + 3$ and $g(x) = 5x$, find: $(fog)(x)$.

According to $(fog)(x) = f(g(x))$. Then: $(fog)(x) = f(g(x)) = f(5x)$.

Now, find $f(5x)$ by substituting x with $5x$ in the $f(x)$ function.

Therefore, $f(x) = x + 3$; $(x \to 5x) \to f(5x) = (5x) + 3 = 5x + 3$.

Another example:

Using $f(x) = 3x - 1$ and $g(x) = 2x - 2$, find: $(gof)(5)$.

Using $(fog)(x) = f(g(x))$. Then: $(gof)(x) = g(f(x)) = g(3x - 1)$,

Now, substitute x in $g(x)$ by $(3x - 1)$.

Then: $g(3x - 1) = 2(3x - 1) - 2 = 6x - 2 - 2 = 6x - 4$.

Substitute x with 5: $(gof)(5) = g(f(5)) = 6(5) - 4 = 30 - 4 = 26$.

✎ Solve.

21) $f(x) = 2x$, $g(x) = x + 3$

    Find: $(fog)(2) =$

22) $f(x) = x + 2$, $g(x) = x - 6$

    Find: $(fog)(-1) =$

23) $f(x) = 3x$, $g(x) = x + 4$

    Find: $(gof)(4) =$

24) $h(x) = 2x - 2$, $g(x) = x + 4$

    Find: $(goh)(2) =$

25) $f(x) = 2x - 8$, $g(x) = x + 10$

    Find: $(fog)(-2) =$

26) $f(x) = x^2 - 8$, $g(x) = 2x + 3$

    Find: $(gof)(4) =$

Evaluate an Exponential Function

For any real number x, an exponential function is an equation with the form $f(x) = ab^x$, where a is a non-zero real number and b is a positive real number.

For example, $f(x) = 2^x$, $g(x) = -3\left(\frac{1}{2}\right)^x$, and $h(x) = 5\left(\frac{7}{2}\right)^x$.

To evaluate the value of an exponential function, it's enough to substitute the given input for the independent variable. For example, the value of the function $f(x) = \frac{1}{2}(3)^x$ for the value of $x = 0$ is $f(0) = \frac{1}{2}$.

It is worth noting that exponential functions can be added and subtracted or combined with other functions.

Pay attention to the following explanations:

Find the value of the exponential function of $f(x) = 3^x$ for $x = 2$.

To solve, it is enough to substitute $x = 2$, in the equation $f(x) = 3^x$.

So, $f(2) = 3^2 = 9$.

Let $f(x) = 7(2)^x$. Evaluate $f(3)$.

To evaluate $f(3)$, plug 3 in equation $f(x) = 7(2)^x$ instead of the independent variable x. Therefore, $f(3) = 7(2)^3 = 7(8) = 56$.

Use the following function to find $f(6)$.

$$f(x) = -2(3)^{\frac{x}{2}-1}$$

First, substitute $x = 6$ in the equation,

$f(6) = -2(3)^{\frac{6}{2}-1} = -2(3)^{3-1} = -2(3)^2 = -2(9) = -18$.

Use the following function to find $f(2)$.

$$f(x) = 9\left(\frac{1}{3}\right)^{2x-1} + 1$$

To solve, plug 2 into $f(x) = 9\left(\frac{1}{3}\right)^{2x-1} + 1$ instead of x. So,

$f(2) = 9\left(\frac{1}{3}\right)^{2(2)-1} + 1 = 9\left(\frac{1}{3}\right)^{2(2)-1} + 1 = 9\left(\frac{1}{3}\right)^{4-1} + 1 = 9\left(\frac{1}{3}\right)^{3} + 1$

$$= 9\left(\frac{1}{27}\right) + 1 = \frac{1}{3} + 1 = \frac{4}{3}.$$

Therefore, the value of $f(2)$ is $\frac{4}{3}$.

Another example:

Let $f(x) = 2x\left(\frac{3}{2}\right)^{x-2}$. What is $f(2)$?

The function f is multiplication of two function $g(x) = 2x$, and $h(x) = \left(\frac{3}{2}\right)^{x-2}$.

Now, to evaluate $f(2)$, you can put the value of $x = 2$ in the function f:

$$x = 2 \rightarrow f(2) = 2(2)\left(\frac{3}{2}\right)^{(2)-2} = 4\left(\frac{3}{2}\right)^{0} = 4(1) = 4.$$

In another way, you can find the value of $g(x) = 2x$ and $h(x) = \left(\frac{3}{2}\right)^{x-2}$ for $x = 2$

and multiply the result. Therefore,

$$g(2) = 2 \times 2 = 4$$

$$h(2) = \left(\frac{3}{2}\right)^{2-2} = \left(\frac{3}{2}\right)^{0} = 1$$

Finally, $f(2) = g(2) \times h(2) \rightarrow f(2) = 4 \times 1 = 4$.

✎ Evaluate.

27) $f(x) = 3^x$

   Find: $f(-1)$

28) $g(x) = \frac{1}{2}(2)^x$

   Find: $g(2)$

29) $f(x) = -3\left(\frac{1}{2}\right)^{x-1}$

   Find: $f(0)$

30) $r(x) = 5x(2)^x$

   Find: $r(-1)$

31) $h(x) = x - \left(\frac{3}{2}\right)^x + 1$

   Find: $h(1)$

32) $f(x) = 2^{2x-3}$

   Find: $f(a)$

33) $f(x) = 3x\left(\frac{1}{2}\right)^{2x+2}$

   Find: $f(2)$

34) $f(x) = 3x\left(\frac{1}{2}\right)^{2x+2}$

   Find: $f(4)$

Find more at

Function Inverses

A function inverse, also known as the reciprocal function, is a function that "undoes" the effect of another function. If two functions $f(x)$ and $g(x)$ are inverses of each other, then $f(g(x)) = x$ and $g(f(x)) = x$. This means that applying function f followed by function g will give you the original input, and applying function g followed by function f will also give you the original input.

For example, the inverse of the function $f(x) = 2x + 3$ is $g(x) = \frac{x-3}{2}$. Because,

$$f(g(x)) = f\left(\frac{x-3}{2}\right) = 2\left(\frac{x-3}{2}\right) + 3 = x$$

$$g(f(x)) = g(2x + 3) = \frac{(2x+3)-3}{2} = \frac{2x}{2} = x$$

It is important to note that not all functions have inverse functions. For a function to have an inverse, it must be a one-to-one function, which means that for every y in the range of the function, there can be only one x in the domain that corresponds to it.

To find the inverse of a function, you can follow these steps:

Step 1: Replace the function notation with $y = f(x)$.

Step 2: Interchange x and y to get $x = f(y)$.

Step 3: Solve for y to get $y = f^{-1}(x)$.

Step 4: Replace y with the original function notation to get the inverse function $f^{-1}(x)$.

It's also worth noting that not all functions have inverse functions. for instance, functions that are not one-to-one, such as $y = x^2$, do not have an inverse function.

Here is an example of how to find the inverse of a function:

Find the inverse of the function $f(x) = 2x + 3$.

Step 1: Replace the function notation with $y = f(x)$ so $y = 2x + 3$.

Step 2: Interchange x and y to get $x = f(y)$ so $x = 2y + 3$.

Step 3: Solve for y to get $y = f^{-1}(x)$: $x = 2y + 3 \rightarrow x - 3 = 2y \rightarrow y = \frac{x-3}{2}$

Step 4: Replace y with the original function notation to get the inverse function $f^{-1}(x)$ so $f^{-1}(x) = \frac{x-3}{2}$.

So, the inverse of the function $f(x) = 2x + 3$ is $f^{-1}(x) = \frac{x-3}{2}$.

It's worth noting that the function $f(x) = 2x + 3$ is a one-to-one function, so it has an inverse function.

You can also check if the inverse function is correct by plugging in a value for x and seeing if it gives the original input when plugged back into the original function. For example, $f(f^{-1}(3)) = f\left(\frac{x-3}{2}\right) = \left(2\left(\frac{x-3}{2}\right) + 3\right) = 3$, which is the original input.

Other examples:

Find the inverse of the function: $f(x) = \frac{1}{2}x - 1$.

First, replace $f(x)$ with y: $y = \frac{1}{2}x - 1$.

Then, replace all x's with y and all y's with x: $x = \frac{1}{2}y - 1$.

Now, solve for y: $x = \frac{1}{2}y - 1 \rightarrow x + 1 = \frac{1}{2}y \rightarrow 2(x + 1) = y \rightarrow y = 2x + 2$.

Finally, replace y with $f^{-1}(x)$: $f^{-1}(x) = 2x + 2$.

Find the inverse of the function: $h(x) = \sqrt{x} + 6$.

Replace the function notation with $y = h(x)$: $h(x) = \sqrt{x} + 6 \rightarrow y = \sqrt{x} + 6$.

Next, replace all x's with y and all y's with x;

$x = \sqrt{y} + 6 \rightarrow x - 6 = \sqrt{y} \rightarrow (x - 6)^2 = (\sqrt{y})^2 \rightarrow x^2 - 12x + 36 = y$.

Then: $h^{-1} = x^2 - 12x + 36$.

✑ Find the inverse of the following functions.

35) $f(x) = -\frac{1}{x} - 9$

36) $g(x) = \sqrt{x} - 2$

37) $h(x) = -\frac{5}{x+3}$

38) $f(x) = 6x + 6$

bit.ly/3fmumtj

Find more at

Domain and Range of Relations

A relation is a set of ordered pairs that shows the connection or correspondence between elements of two sets. The ordered pair, typically represented as (x, y), contains an input or "x" value and an output or "y" value. Essentially, a relation is a rule that links a value or element from one set to a value or element from another set.

In other words, a relation is defined as a set or the desired set(s) connection. An ordered pair, commonly named as a point and a relation is a set of these ordered pairs. In fact, inputs and outputs values in a relationship is are shown in ordered pairs. Actually, a relation is a kind of rule that connects a component or value from one set to a component or value from the other set.

The domain of a relation is the set of all input (x) values for which the relation is defined. The range of a relation is the set of all output (y) values that can be achieved by the relation.

To find the domain and range of a relation, you can follow these steps:

Step 1: Identify the set of all x −values in the relation. These values make up the domain of the relation.

Step 2: Identify the set of all y −values in the relation. These values make up the range of the relation.

Step 3: Look for any x −values that are not allowed in the relation. These values are excluded from the domain.

Step 4: Look for any y −values that are not possible in the relation. These values are excluded from the range.

Let's review an example:

Find the domain and range of the relation $y = 2x + 3$.

Step 1: Identify the set of all x −values in the relation. The domain is all real numbers.

Step 2: Identify the set of all y −values in the relation. The range is all real numbers.

Step 3: Look for any x −values that are not allowed in the relation. There are no x −values that are not allowed in the relation.

Step 4: Look for any y −values that are not possible in the relation. There are no y −values that are not possible in the relation.

So, the domain of the relation $y = 2x + 3$ is all real numbers and the range is all real numbers.

Another example:

What is the domain and range of the following relation?

$$\{(7,2), (-3,4), (4,-1), (5,3), (8,5)\}$$

The domain contains x −values of a relation and the range includes y −values of a relationship. So, Domain $= \{7, -3, 4, 5, 8\}$ and Range $= \{2, 4, -1, 3, 5\}$.

Find the domain and range of the following relation:

$$R = \{(4n + 1, n - 2): n \in \{-1, -2, 0, 2\}\}$$

In the question we have given $n = \{-1, -2, 0, 2\}$. So, put these values in two equations $4n + 1$ and $n - 2$ of the relation R to find the domain and range of the relation:

$$n = -1 \rightarrow \begin{matrix} 4(-1) + 1 = -3 \\ (-1) - 2 = -3 \end{matrix}, \quad \text{and} \quad n = -2 \rightarrow \begin{matrix} 4(-2) + 1 = -7 \\ (-2) - 2 = -4 \end{matrix}$$

$$n = 0 \rightarrow \begin{matrix} 4(0) + 1 = 1 \\ (0) - 2 = -2 \end{matrix}, \quad \text{and} \quad n = 2 \rightarrow \begin{matrix} 4(2) + 1 = 9 \\ (2) - 2 = 0 \end{matrix}$$

Therefore, the domain of the relation R is the set $\{-3, -7, 1, 9\}$ and the range of R is $\{-3, -4, -2, 0\}$.

✎ Write the domain and the range of the following.

39) $\{(1, -1), (2, -4), (0,5), (-1,6)\}$

40) $\{(10, -5), (-16, -8), (-4,19), (16,7), (6, -14)\}$

41) $\{(4,7), (-15,6), (-20,9), (13,8), (7,5)$

Interval Notation

Interval notation is a way of expressing a set of numbers in a concise and precise manner. It is commonly used to express the domain and range of a function.

For example, if the domain of a function is all real numbers greater than or equal to 3 and less than or equal to 5, the interval notation for the domain would be [3,5].

The notation for the domain is [a,b], where a and b are the lower and upper bounds of the domain, respectively.

Similarly, if the range of a function is all real numbers greater than −3 and less than 4, the interval notation for the range would be (−3,4).

The notation for the range is (a,b), where a and b are the lower and upper bounds of the range, respectively.

It's important to note that when the interval notation is used to express a set of numbers, the square brackets "[ ]" indicate that the set includes the endpoint values, while the round parentheses "( )" indicate that the set does not include the endpoint values.

For example, the interval notation [2,5] means that the set of numbers includes 2 and 5, while the interval notation (2,5) means that the set of numbers does not include 2 and 5.

Here are some more examples of interval notation for the domain and range of a function:

- If the domain of a function is all real numbers greater than −2 and less than or equal to 3, the interval notation for the domain would be (−2,3].

- If the range of a function is all real numbers greater than or equal to 0 and less than 4, the interval notation for the range would be [0,4).

- If the domain of a function is all real numbers less than or equal to −1, the interval notation for the domain would be (−∞, −1].

    o If the range of a function is all real numbers greater than 2, the interval notation for the range would be $(2, +\infty)$.

It's also possible to use interval notation to express multiple intervals.

To express multiple intervals using interval notation, we can use the union symbol "∪" to combine the different intervals.

For example, consider the following function:

$$f(x) = x^2 - 4x + 2$$

The domain of this function is all real numbers, but the range is restricted to values greater than or equal to -2. The interval notation for the domain would be $(-\infty, +\infty)$ and the interval notation for the range would be $[-2, +\infty)$.

Another example:

Write the set $\{x \mid -3 < x \leq 1\}$ in the form of an interval notation.

To write this interval in interval notation, use the half-open and half-closed as $(-3, 1]$.

One more example:

Write as an interval notation.

We use the union operator to represented this set in the form of an interval notation: $(-\infty, -3) \cup (-1, 0]$.

✎ Write the following in the form of interval notation.

42) The set of all real numbers less than or equal to 1 and greater than -1.

43) The set of all real numbers greater than or equal to 3.

44) The set $\{x \in \mathbb{R} \mid 1 < x < 4, -2 \leq x \leq -1\}$.

✎ Write the domain and the following as an interval.

45) $f(x) = (x + 1)^2$ 46) $g(x) = 3x - 1$

bit.ly/43Z9EqE

Find more at

Rate of Change and Slope

The rate of change, also known as the slope, is a ratio used to compare the change in y −values to the change in x −values. The y −values, also known as dependent variables, are dependent on the x −values, or independent variables. When the rate of change is constant and linear, the slope of a line can be represented as a number. The slope can be positive, negative, zero, or undefined.

The direction of a line's slope can also be described by its slope. A line with a positive slope rises from left to right, while a line with a negative slope falls from left to right. A line with a slope of zero is a horizontal line, indicating no change in the y −value. A vertical line, on the other hand, represents a relationship that is not a function, and the slope is undefined as there are many y −values for one x −value. It's because there are many y −values for one x −value.

The variable m is used to represent the slope of a line. It is calculated as the ratio of the change in y −values to the change in x −values. If the coordinates of two points on a line are (x_1, y_1) and (x_2, y_2), then the slope m is calculated as

$$m = \frac{y_2 - y_1}{x_2 - x_1}$$

For example, consider the line represented by the equation $y = 2x + 3$.

In this equation, the slope m is 2, which means for every unit increase in x, the y −value increases by 2 units. This slope is positive, indicating that the line rises from left to right.

You can also find the slope of a line by finding the slope between two points on the line. For example, if we have two points on this line, $(2,7)$ and $(5,13)$. The coordinates of these two points are $(x_1, y_1) = (2,7)$ and $(x_2, y_2) = (5,13)$. The slope between these two points is $m = \frac{y_2 - y_1}{x_2 - x_1} = \frac{13-7}{5-2} = \frac{6}{3} = 2$, which is the same as the slope of the line represented by the equation $y = 2x + 3$.

Let's review an example:

The following table shows the number of cars sold by a company in different years. Find the rate of change in car sales for each time interval. Determine which time interval has the greatest rate.

Year	2005	2010	2015	2020	2022
Number of Sold Cars	35	45	47	67	85

First, find the dependent and independent variables: years are independent variables and the number of sold cars are dependent variables. Now, find the rate of changes:

2005 to 2010: $\frac{change\ in\ the\ number\ of\ sold\ cars}{change\ in\ years} = \frac{45-35}{2010-2005} = 2.$

2010 to 2015: $\frac{change\ in\ the\ number\ of\ sold\ cars}{change\ in\ years} = \frac{47-45}{2015-2010} = 0.4.$

2015 to 2020: $\frac{change\ in\ the\ number\ of\ sold\ cars}{change\ in\ years} = \frac{67-47}{2020-2015} = 4.$

2020 to 2022: $\frac{change\ in\ the\ number\ of\ sold\ cars}{change\ in\ years} = \frac{85-67}{2022-2020} = 9.$

Car sales have been at their greatest rate from 2022 to 2020. The slope of the line is positive because as time increases, the amount of car sales also increases.

✑ Solve.

47) Average food preparation time in a restaurant was tracked daily as part of an efficiency improvement program. According to the table, what was the rate of change between Tuesday and Wednesday?

Day	Time
Tuesday	45
Wednesday	49
Thursday	32
Friday	15
Saturday	25

Complete a Function Table from an Equation

A function table is a useful tool to demonstrate the relationship between input and output values in a mathematical equation. To complete a function table:

Step 1: Create a table with columns for the input variable (x) and the output variable (y).

Step 2: Fill in the input values in the column x.

Step 3: Substitute the input values into the equation.

Step 4: Evaluate the equation to find the corresponding output values and fill them in the column y.

Here is an example of how to complete a function table from an equation:

Complete the function table for the equation $y = 2x + 3$.

$f(x) = 2x + 3$	
x	$f(x)$
0	
1	
2	

Write down the equation $y = 2x + 3$.

Step 1: Write down a table with two columns, one for x and one for y.

Step 2: Insert a set of values for x in the x column of the table.

Step 3: Substitute each x value into the equation and solve for y.

$f(x) = 2x + 3$	
x	$f(x)$
0	3
1	5
2	7

Step 4: Insert the corresponding y values into the column y of the table.

Check if the input x value correctly corresponds to the output y value.

By following these steps, you can complete a function table from an equation and check if the relationship between x and y is correct.

Let's review an example:

Complete the table.

$f(x) = x^2 + 1$	
x	$f(x)$
−2	
0	
1	

Look at the function table. Clearly, the first value of the input in the table is −2. Evaluate $f(x) = x^2 + 1$ for $x = -2$.

$f(-2) = (-2)^2 + 1 = 4 + 1 = 5$.

When $x = -2$, then $f(-2) = 5$. Complete the first row of the table.

$f(x) = x^2 + 1$	
x	$f(x)$
−2	5
0	
1	

Similarly, evaluate $f(x) = x^2 + 1$ for $x = 0$ and $x = 1$, respectively. So,

$f(0) = (0)^2 + 1 = 0 + 1 = 1$,

$f(1) = (1)^2 + 1 = 1 + 1 = 2$.

Enter the obtained values in the table.

$f(x) = x^2 + 1$	
x	$f(x)$
−2	5
0	1
1	2

✎ Complete the tables.

48)

$f(x) = 3x - 2$	
x	$f(x)$
−3	
0	
2	

49)

$f(x) = 2x$	
x	$f(x)$
1	
2	
3	

Chapter 8: Answers

1) -3

2) 10

3) -10

4) 3

5) 37

6) -1

7) $8n^2 - 8n$

8) $-108a^3 - 10$

9) 13

10) 0

11) 16

12) 29

13) $3x^2 - 12x + 22$

14) $-6a^2 - 33$

15) -30

16) $\frac{1}{2}$

17) $\frac{14}{3}$

18) 49

19) -160

20) -4

21) 10

22) -5

23) 16

24) 6

25) 8

26) 19

27) $\frac{1}{3}$

28) 2

29) -6

30) $-\frac{5}{2}$

31) $\frac{1}{2}$

32) 2^{2a-3}

33) $\frac{3}{32}$

34) $\frac{3}{256}$

35) $-\frac{1}{x+9}$

36) $x^2 + 4x + 4$

37) $-\frac{5}{x} - 3$

38) $\frac{x-6}{6}$

39) $D = (1, 2, 0, -1),$
$R = (-1, -4, 5, 6)$

40) $D = (10, -16, -4, 16, 6),$
$R = (-5, -8, 19, 7, -14)$

41) $D = (4, -15, -20, 13, 7),$
$R = (7, 6, 9, 8, 5)$

42) $(-1, 1]$

43) $[3, +\infty)$

44) $[-2, -1] \cup (1, 4)$

45) $(-\infty, +\infty)$

46) $(-\infty, +\infty)$

47) 4

48)

$f(x) = 3x - 2$	
x	$f(x)$
-3	-11
0	-2
2	4

49)

$f(x) = 2x$	
x	$f(x)$
1	2
2	4
3	6

Effortless
Math
Education

CHAPTER

9 Radical Expressions

Math topics that you'll learn in this chapter:

- ☑ Simplifying Radical Expressions
- ☑ Adding and Subtracting Radical Expressions
- ☑ Multiplying Radical Expressions
- ☑ Rationalizing Radical Expressions
- ☑ Radical Equations
- ☑ Domain and Range of Radical Functions
- ☑ Simplify Radicals with Fractions

215

Simplifying Radical Expressions

Here are some steps to simplify radical expressions:

Step 1: Factor the radicand (the number or expression inside the radical symbol) as much as possible.

Step 2: Identify any perfect square factors (such as 4, 9, 16, etc.) in the radicand. The square root of a perfect square is the number itself.

Step 3: Use the product property of square roots, which states that the square root of a product is equal to the product of the square roots.

$$\sqrt[n]{xy} = \sqrt[n]{x} \times \sqrt[n]{y}$$

Step 4: Use the quotient property of square roots, which states that the square root of a quotient is equal to the quotient of the square roots.

$$\sqrt[n]{\frac{x}{y}} = \frac{\sqrt[n]{x}}{\sqrt[n]{y}}$$

Step 5: Simplify any radicals that have the same radicand by adding or subtracting them.

Step 6: Simplify any radicals that have the same index by multiplying or dividing them.

Note: When simplifying radical expressions, pay attention to converting radical expressions to exponential expressions, and vice versa:

$$\sqrt[n]{x^a} = x^{\frac{a}{n}}$$

By following these steps, you can simplify radical expressions and make them easier to work with and understand.

Let's review an example:

Find the square root of $\sqrt{144x^2}$.

Find the factor of the expression $144x^2$: $144 = 12 \times 12$ and

$x^2 = x \times x$, now use radical rule: $\sqrt[n]{a^n} = a$.

Then: $\sqrt{12^2} = 12$ and $\sqrt{x^2} = x$.

Finally: $\sqrt{144x^2} = \sqrt{12^2} \times \sqrt{x^2} = 12 \times x = 12x$.

Another example:

Write this radical in exponential form: $\sqrt[3]{x^4}$.

To write a radical in exponential form, use this rule: $\sqrt[n]{x^a} = x^{\frac{a}{n}}$.

Then: $\sqrt[3]{x^4} = x^{\frac{4}{3}}$.

One more example:

Simplify: $\sqrt{8x^3}$.

First, factor the expression $8x^3$: $8x^3 = 2^3 \times x \times x \times x$.

We need to find perfect squares: $8x^3 = 2^2 \times 2 \times x^2 \times x = 2^2 \times x^2 \times 2x$.

Then: $\sqrt{8x^3} = \sqrt{2^2 \times x^2} \times \sqrt{2x}$.

Now, use the radical rule: $\sqrt[n]{a^n} = a$.

Then: $\sqrt{2^2 \times x^2} \times \sqrt{(2x)} = 2x \times \sqrt{2x} = 2x\sqrt{2x}$.

✎ Evaluate.

1) $\sqrt{49} = $ ____

2) $\sqrt{4} \times \sqrt{81} = $ ____

3) $\sqrt{16} \times \sqrt{4x^2} = $ ____

4) $\sqrt{289} = $ ____

5) $\sqrt{25b^4} = $ ____

6) $\sqrt{9} \times \sqrt{x^2} = $ ____

Adding and Subtracting Radical Expressions

When adding or subtracting radical expressions, it's important to remember the following rules:

1. The radicand (the expression inside the radical symbol) must be the same to combine them.

2. To add or subtract radical expressions, simply add or subtract the numerical coefficients in front of each radical. For example:

$$\sqrt{9x^2} + 2\sqrt{9x^2} = (1 + 2)\sqrt{9x^2} = 3\sqrt{9x^2} = 9x.$$

3. When the radicand is not the same it is not possible to combine them, leaving the radical expressions as they are. For example: $\sqrt{5x^2} + 2\sqrt{3x}$, cannot be combined.

Here are a few more examples of adding and subtracting radical expressions:

Simplify: $\sqrt{48} + 2\sqrt{48}$.

In this example, the radicand is the same $\sqrt{48}$. So, we can add the numerical coefficients in front of the radical $(1 + 2)$ to get 3 and combine them.

Therefore, we get:

$$\sqrt{48} + 2\sqrt{48} = (1 + 2)\sqrt{48} = 3\sqrt{48}.$$

Note that the number of 48 can be written as the following product:

$$48 = 4^2 \times 3.$$

Next, we have: $\sqrt{48} = \sqrt{4^2 \times 3} = 4\sqrt{3}$. Therefore, substitute:

$$\sqrt{48} + 2\sqrt{48} = 3\sqrt{48} = 3 \times 4\sqrt{3} = 12\sqrt{3}.$$

Another example:

Simplify: $2\sqrt[3]{3x^2} - 3\sqrt[3]{3x^2}$.

In this example, the radicand is the same $3x^2$. So, we can add the numerical coefficients in front of the radical $(2 - 3)$ to get -1 and combine them.

Therefore, we have: $2\sqrt[3]{3x^2} - 3\sqrt[3]{3x^2} = (2 - 3)\sqrt[3]{3x^2} = -\sqrt[3]{3x^2}$.

Some other examples:

Simplify: $\sqrt{27x} + 2\sqrt{3x}$.

The two radical parts are not the same. Then, rewrite the expression as:

$\sqrt{27x} + 2\sqrt{3x} = \sqrt{(9 \times 3)x} + 2\sqrt{3x} = 3\sqrt{3x} + 2\sqrt{3x}$

Since we have the same radical parts, then we can add these two radicals.

Add like terms: $3\sqrt{3x} + 2\sqrt{3x} = (3 + 2)\sqrt{3x} = 5\sqrt{3x}$.

Simplify: $2\sqrt{8} - 2\sqrt{2}$.

The two radical parts are not the same.

First, we need to simplify the $2\sqrt{8}$. Then: $2\sqrt{8} = 2\sqrt{4 \times 2} = 2(\sqrt{4})(\sqrt{2}) = 4\sqrt{2}$.

Now, combine like terms: $2\sqrt{8} - 2\sqrt{2} = 4\sqrt{2} - 2\sqrt{2} = 2\sqrt{2}$.

Simplify: $8\sqrt{27} + 5\sqrt{3}$.

The two radical parts are not the same.

First, we need to simplify the $8\sqrt{27}$. Then: $8\sqrt{27} = 8\sqrt{9 \times 3} = 8(\sqrt{9})(\sqrt{3}) = 24\sqrt{3}$.

Now, add: $8\sqrt{27} + 5\sqrt{3} = 24\sqrt{3} + 5\sqrt{3} = 29\sqrt{3}$.

✎ Simplify.

7) $\sqrt{6} + 6\sqrt{6} =$

8) $9\sqrt{8} - 6\sqrt{2} =$

9) $-\sqrt{7} - 5\sqrt{7} =$

10) $10\sqrt{2} + 3\sqrt{18} =$

11) $\sqrt{12} - 6\sqrt{3} =$

12) $-2\sqrt{x} + 6\sqrt{x} =$

Multiplying Radical Expressions

When multiplying radical expressions, it's important to remember the following rules:

1. To multiply radical expressions, multiply the numerical coefficients in front of the radical and multiply the radicands (the expressions inside the radical symbol), separately.

2. When there are radicals with the same radicand, we can simplify the radical by adding the indices (the number written just outside or on the radical symbol).

Here are a few examples of multiplying radical expressions:

Evaluate: $2\sqrt{3x} \times 3\sqrt{5x}$.

In this example, we multiply the numerical coefficients in front of the radical (2×3) and multiply the radicands $(3x \times 5x)$, separately to get:

$2\sqrt{3x} \times 3\sqrt{5x} = 6\sqrt{15x^2} = 6x\sqrt{15}$.

Evaluate. $2\sqrt{5} \times \sqrt{3}$

Multiply the numbers outside of the radicals (2×1) and the radical parts (5×3).

Then: $2\sqrt{5} \times \sqrt{3} = (2 \times 1) \times (\sqrt{5} \times \sqrt{3}) = 2\sqrt{15}$.

Simplify: $3\sqrt{2x} \times 4\sqrt{2x}$.

For this purpose, we multiply the numerical coefficients in front of the radical (3×4) and multiply the radicands $(2x \times 2x)$, separately to get:

$3\sqrt{2x} \times 4\sqrt{2x} = (3 \times 4)\sqrt{2x \times 2x} = 12\sqrt{4x^2} = 24x$.

Simplify: $3x\sqrt{3} \times 4\sqrt{x}$.

Multiply the numbers outside of the radicals $(3x \times 4)$ and the radical parts $(3 \times x)$. Then, substitute and simplify:

$3x\sqrt{3} \times 4\sqrt{x} = (3x \times 4) \times (\sqrt{3} \times \sqrt{x}) = (12x)(\sqrt{3 \times x}) = 12x\sqrt{3x}$.

Evaluate the product of the radical expression: $\left(2\sqrt{5}\right)^3 =$.

Raise the coefficient of the radical to power 3 and multiply it with the radicand raised to power 3: $\left(2\sqrt{5}\right)^3 = (2)^3 \times \left(\sqrt{5}\right)^3$. So, we have: $(2 \times 2 \times 2)\sqrt{5 \times 5 \times 5} = 8\sqrt{125}$

Next, simplify: $8\sqrt{125} = 8 \times 5\sqrt{5} = 40\sqrt{5}$.

Therefore, the product of this expression is $\left(2\sqrt{5}\right)^3 = 40\sqrt{5}$.

Evaluate: $\left(2\sqrt{4x}\right)^2$.

We raise coefficient of the radical to the power 2 and multiply it with the radicand raised to power 2. So, we get:

$\left(2\sqrt{4x}\right)^2 = (2)^2 \times \left(\sqrt{4x}\right)^2 = 4\sqrt{(4x)^2} = 4\sqrt{16x^2} = 4 \times 4x = 16x$.

Multiply $6a\sqrt{7b}$ to $3\sqrt{2b}$ and simplify.

Multiply the numbers outside of the radicals $(6a \times 3)$ and the radical parts $(7b \times 2b)$. Then: $6a\sqrt{7b} \times 3\sqrt{2b} = (6a \times 3) \times \sqrt{7b \times 2b} = 18a\sqrt{14b^2}$.

Next, simplify: $18a\sqrt{14b^2} = 18a \times \sqrt{14} \times \sqrt{b^2} = 18ab\sqrt{14}$.

Simplify: $9\sqrt{9x} \times 5\sqrt{4x}$.

Multiply the numbers outside of the radicals (9 and 5), and the radical parts ($9x$ and $4x$). Then, substitute and simplify:

$9\sqrt{9x} \times 5\sqrt{4x} = (9 \times 5) \times \left(\sqrt{9x \times 4x}\right) = (45)\left(\sqrt{36x^2}\right) = 45\sqrt{36x^2}$.

$\sqrt{36x^2} = 6x$, then: $45\sqrt{36x^2} = 45 \times 6x = 270x$.

✎ Evaluate.

13) $\sqrt{4} \times 2\sqrt{9} =$

14) $\sqrt{5y} \times 3\sqrt{20y} =$

15) $-6\sqrt{4} \times 3\sqrt{4} =$

16) $-9\sqrt{3b^2} \times \left(-\sqrt{6}\right) =$

bit.ly/3ri1RqN

Find more at

Rationalizing Radical Expressions

Rationalizing radical expressions is the process of eliminating a radical in the denominator of a fraction. In other words, it's a way to convert an expression with a radical in the denominator into an equivalent expression that does not have a radical in the denominator. This is done by multiplying the numerator and denominator by some expression that will eliminate the radical in the denominator.

To rationalize a denominator that contains a radical, we can use the conjugate of the denominator. The conjugate of a binomial is the binomial with the same signs between the two terms but with the opposite sign on the radical. For example, the conjugate of $\sqrt{2} - 2$ is $\sqrt{2} + 2$. The product of the original binomial and its conjugate is a perfect square.

For example, simplify: $\frac{x}{\sqrt{2}-2}$.

To rationalize the denominator $\sqrt{2} - 2$, you can multiply the numerator and denominator by the conjugate of the denominator, which is $\sqrt{2} + 2$. The result is:

$$\frac{x}{\sqrt{2}-2} \times \frac{\sqrt{2}+2}{\sqrt{2}+2} = \frac{x(\sqrt{2}+2)}{(\sqrt{2}-2)(\sqrt{2}+2)} = \frac{x\sqrt{2}+2x}{2-4} = \frac{2x+x\sqrt{2}}{-2} = -\frac{2x+x\sqrt{2}}{2}.$$

In the same way, you can rationalize any denominator containing radicals, it's just about multiplying the numerator and denominator by the conjugate of the denominator to eliminate the radical in the denominator.

- Radical expressions cannot be in the denominator. (Number in the bottom)

- To get rid of the radical in the denominator, multiply both the numerator and denominator by the radical in the denominator.

- If there is a radical and another integer in the denominator, multiply both the numerator and denominator by the conjugate of the denominator.

- The conjugate of $(a + b)$ is $(a - b)$ and vice versa.

- Rationalizing radical expressions is the process of eliminating a radical in the denominator of a fraction.

Here are a few examples of how to rationalize radical expressions:

Simplify: $\frac{9}{\sqrt{3}}$.

Multiply both the numerator and denominator by $\sqrt{3}$. Then: $\frac{9}{\sqrt{3}} \times \frac{\sqrt{3}}{\sqrt{3}} = \frac{9\sqrt{3}}{\sqrt{9}} = \frac{9\sqrt{3}}{3}$.

Now, simplify: $\frac{9\sqrt{3}}{3} = 3\sqrt{3}$.

Simplify $\frac{5}{\sqrt{6}-4}$.

Multiply by the conjugate: $\frac{\sqrt{6}+4}{\sqrt{6}+4} \rightarrow \frac{5}{\sqrt{6}-4} \times \frac{\sqrt{6}+4}{\sqrt{6}+4}$. That is, $(\sqrt{6} - 4)(\sqrt{6} + 4) = -10$.

Then: $\frac{5}{\sqrt{6}-4} \times \frac{\sqrt{6}+4}{\sqrt{6}+4} = \frac{5(\sqrt{6}+4)}{-10}$.

Use the fraction rule: $\frac{a}{-b} = -\frac{a}{b} \rightarrow \frac{5(\sqrt{6}+4)}{-10} = -\frac{5(\sqrt{6}+4)}{10} = -\frac{1}{2}(\sqrt{6} + 4)$.

Simplify $\frac{2}{\sqrt{3}-1}$.

Multiply by the conjugate: $\frac{\sqrt{3}+1}{\sqrt{3}+1}$. So, $\frac{2}{\sqrt{3}-1} \times \frac{\sqrt{3}+1}{\sqrt{3}+1} = \frac{2(\sqrt{3}+1)}{2} = (\sqrt{3} + 1)$.

✎ Simplify.

17) $\frac{1}{\sqrt{2}} =$

18) $\frac{1+\sqrt{5}}{1-\sqrt{3}} =$

19) $\frac{2+\sqrt{6}}{\sqrt{2}-\sqrt{5}} =$

20) $\frac{4}{\sqrt{8}} =$

21) $\frac{\sqrt{7}}{\sqrt{6}-\sqrt{3}} =$

22) $\frac{\sqrt{8a}}{\sqrt{a^5}} =$

bit.ly/3vKudGO

Find more at

Radical Equations

A radical equation is an equation in which the independent variable is under the radical. For example:

$$\sqrt{x-1} = 2, \sqrt[3]{x} - \sqrt{2x+3} = 0, \text{ and } \ldots$$

To solve a radical equation, follow the steps below:

Step 1: Isolate the radical on one side of the equation. If more than one radical expression involves the variable, then isolate one of them.

Step 2: Square both sides of the equation to remove the radical.

Step 3: Solve the equation for the variable.

Step 4: Plug the answer (answers) into the original equation to avoid extraneous values.

Let's review some examples:

Solve: $\sqrt{x} - 5 = 15$.

Add 5 to both sides:

$$\sqrt{x} - 5 = 15 \rightarrow \left(\sqrt{x} - 5\right) + 5 = 15 + 5 \rightarrow \sqrt{x} = 20.$$

Square both sides: $\left(\sqrt{x}\right)^2 = 20^2 \rightarrow x = 400$.

Plugin the value of 400 for x in the original equation and check the answer:

$$x = 400 \rightarrow \sqrt{x} - 5 = \sqrt{400} - 5 = 20 - 5 = 15.$$

So, the value of 400 for x is correct.

Another example:

What is the value of x in this equation? $2\sqrt{x+1} = 4$

Divide both sides by 2. Then:

$$2\sqrt{x+1} = 4 \rightarrow \frac{2\sqrt{x+1}}{2} = \frac{4}{2} \rightarrow \sqrt{x+1} = 2.$$

Square both sides: $\left(\sqrt{x+1}\right)^2 = 2^2$.

Then, $x + 1 = 4 \rightarrow x = 3$.

Substitute x by 3 in the original equation and check the answer:

$x = 3 \rightarrow 2\sqrt{x+1} = 2\sqrt{3+1} = 2\sqrt{4} = 2(2) = 4$.

So, the value of 3 for x is correct.

One more example:

Solve: $\sqrt{x+3} - x = 1$.

First, isolate the radical expression on one side of the equation:

$\sqrt{x+3} - x = 1 \rightarrow \sqrt{x+3} = x + 1$.

Next, square both sides and simplify:

$\left(\sqrt{x+3}\right)^2 = (x+1)^2 \rightarrow x + 3 = x^2 + 2x + 1 \rightarrow x^2 + x - 2 = 0$

Now, Solve for x. Find the factors of the quadratic equation:

$x^2 + x - 2 = 0 \rightarrow (x-1)(x+2) = 0$

Then, the value of x is 1 or -2.

Check the answers by substituting in the original equation to confirm:

$x = 1 \rightarrow \sqrt{x+3} - x = \sqrt{1+3} - 1 = \sqrt{4} - 1 = 2 - 1 = 1$

$x = -2 \rightarrow \sqrt{x+3} - x = \sqrt{(-2)+3} - (-2) = \sqrt{1} + 2 = 1 + 3 = 4 \neq 1$.

Therefore, only the value $x = 1$ is the correct answer.

✍ Solve for x in each equation.

23) $2\sqrt{2x-4} = 8$

24) $9 = \sqrt{4x-1}$

25) $\sqrt{x} + 6 = 11$

26) $\sqrt{5x} = \sqrt{x+3}$

27) $\sqrt[3]{3x+2} = 2$

28) $\sqrt{1-2x} - 2\sqrt{x} = 0$

Domain and Range of Radical Functions

To find the domain of the radical function, find all possible values of the variable inside the radical.

Remember that having a negative number under the square root symbol is not possible. (For cubic roots, we can have negative numbers.)

To find the range, plugin the minimum and maximum values of the variable inside radical.

In order to find the domain and range of a radical function in the form,

$$f(x) = c\sqrt[m]{g(x)} + k$$

Where m is a positive integer and $g(x)$ is a function. $c \neq 0$ and k are constant number. Go through the following steps:

Step 1: Determine whether the radical index is even or odd.

Step 2: To find the domain of the radical function, we evaluate the possible values for the input x as follows:

If m is even, then the domain can be identified by finding the values of x satisfying $g(x) \geq 0$.

If m is odd, then the domain can be identified by finding the values of x for which $g(x)$ is defined.

Step 3: The range of the function f is the intersection of the set of all possible values for g with:

For m is even. Since $\sqrt[m]{g(x)} \geq 0$, then:

$$c > 0: c\sqrt[m]{g(x)} \geq 0 \rightarrow c\sqrt[m]{g(x)} + k \geq k \rightarrow f(x) \geq k$$

$$c < 0: c\sqrt[m]{g(x)} \leq 0 \rightarrow c\sqrt[m]{g(x)} + k \leq k \rightarrow f(x) \leq k$$

For m is odd. The expression $\sqrt[m]{g(x)}$ can be any real number for all the possible values of x, then $f(x) \in \mathbb{R}$.

Step 4: Write the final answer in inequality notation or interval notation.

Let's review an example:

Find the domain and range of the radical function. $y = \sqrt{x-3}$

Since the radical index is even (2).

Then the domain is the values of x such that: $x - 3 \geq 0 \rightarrow x \geq 3$.

It means that the domain is the interval $[3, +\infty)$.

For the range of the function, we know that $\sqrt{x-3} \geq 0$. So, $y \geq 0$. Therefore, the range is the interval $[0, +\infty)$.

Another example:

Find the domain and range of the radical function. $y = -6\sqrt{4x+8} + 5$

For the domain, find non-negative values for radicals: $4x + 8 \geq 0$.

Therefore, $4x + 8 \geq 0 \rightarrow 4x \geq -8 \rightarrow x \geq -2$.

The domain of the function $y = 6\sqrt{4x+8} + 5$ is all values of real numbers that are satisfied in the inequality $x \geq -2$. Equivalent to the interval $[-2, +\infty)$.

For range, we know that $\sqrt{4x+8} \geq 0$. Then,

$-6\sqrt{4x+8} \leq 0 \rightarrow -6\sqrt{4x+8} + 5 \leq 5 \rightarrow y \leq 5$.

The range of the function $y = -6\sqrt{4x+8} + 5$ is $y \leq 5$. Equivalent to the interval $(-\infty, 5]$.

✍ Identify the domain and range of each function.

29) $y = \sqrt{x+1}$

30) $y = \sqrt{x-2} + 6$

31) $y = \sqrt{x} - 1$

32) $y = \sqrt{x-4}$

bit.ly/2Pn4vIj
Find more at

Simplify Radicals with Fractions

To simplify radicals with fractions:

- Rewrite the numerator and denominator of the fraction as the product of the prime factorizations. (Write in the product of prime numbers.)

  For example, the number 19 is a prime number (factors of 19 are 1 and 19). The factors of the number 21 are 1, 3, 7 and 21.

$$21 = 3 \times 7$$

- Apply the multiplication and division properties of radical expressions.

  For $x, y \geq 0$:

$$\sqrt[n]{x \times y} = \sqrt[n]{x} \times \sqrt[n]{y}$$

  And $x \geq 0, y > 0$:

$$\sqrt[n]{\frac{x}{y}} = \frac{\sqrt[n]{x}}{\sqrt[n]{y}}$$

- Group the factors that form a perfect square, perfect cube, etc.

  For example, the factors of the number 360 can be grouped as follows:

$$360 = 2 \times 2 \times 2 \times 5 \times 3 \times 3 = 2^3 \times 5 \times 3^2$$

- Simplify.

Let's review some examples to further explanation:

Simplify: $\sqrt{\frac{9}{25}}$.

To simplify the radical fraction, rewrite the numerator and denominator as the product of the prime factorizations.

The product of the factors of 9 is 3×3.

The product of the factors of 25 is 5×5.

So, $\sqrt{\dfrac{9}{25}} = \sqrt{\dfrac{3\times3}{5\times5}}$.

Since the index of the given radical is 2. You can take one term out of radical for every two same terms multiplied inside the radical sign (perfect square): $9 = 3^2$, and $25 = 5^2$. Then: $\sqrt{\dfrac{9}{25}} = \sqrt{\dfrac{3^2}{5^2}} = \dfrac{3}{5}$.

Simplify the following radical fraction: $\sqrt{\dfrac{44}{16}}$.

Rewrite the numerator and denominator of the fraction as follow: $\sqrt{\dfrac{44}{16}} = \sqrt{\dfrac{2\times2\times11}{2\times2\times2\times2}}$

Consider the index of the given radical, take out one term of radical for every term that is repeated in an even number inside the radical sign. So,

$\sqrt{\dfrac{2\times2\times11}{2\times2\times2\times2}} = \sqrt{\dfrac{2^2\times11}{2^4}} = \dfrac{2\sqrt{11}}{2^2}$.

Simplify, $\dfrac{2\sqrt{11}}{2^2} = \dfrac{\sqrt{11}}{2}$.

Write the expression in the simplest radical form: $\sqrt{\dfrac{242}{45}}$.

Rewrite this radical fraction as the product of the prime factorizations:

$\sqrt{\dfrac{242}{45}} = \sqrt{\dfrac{2\times11\times11}{3\times3\times5}}$.

Now, take out the terms that are perfect squares, so, $\sqrt{\dfrac{2\times11\times11}{3\times3\times5}} = \sqrt{\dfrac{2\times11^2}{3^2\times5}} = \dfrac{11}{3}\sqrt{\dfrac{2}{5}}$.

✍ Solve.

33) $\sqrt{\dfrac{625}{36}}$

34) $\sqrt{\dfrac{1296}{25}}$

35) $\sqrt{\dfrac{147}{64}}$

36) $\sqrt{\dfrac{98}{18}}$

bit.ly/3j0dbUb

Find more at

Chapter 9: Answers

1) 7

2) 18

3) $8x$

4) 17

5) $5b^2$

6) $3x$

7) $7\sqrt{6}$

8) $12\sqrt{2}$

9) $-6\sqrt{7}$

10) $19\sqrt{2}$

11) $-4\sqrt{3}$

12) $4\sqrt{x}$

13) 12

14) $30y$

15) -72

16) $27b\sqrt{2}$

17) $\frac{\sqrt{2}}{2}$

18) $-\frac{(1+\sqrt{5})(1+\sqrt{3})}{2}$

19) $-\frac{2\sqrt{2}+2\sqrt{5}+2\sqrt{3}+\sqrt{30}}{3}$

20) $\sqrt{2}$

21) $\frac{\sqrt{7}(\sqrt{6}+\sqrt{3})}{3}$

22) $\frac{2\sqrt{2}}{a^2}$

23) $x = 10$

24) $x = 20.5$

25) $x = 25$

26) $x = \frac{3}{4}$

27) $x = 2$

28) $x = \frac{1}{6}$

29) $x \geq -1, y \geq 0$

30) $x \geq 2, y \geq 6$

31) $x \geq 0, y \geq -1$

32) $x \geq 4, y \geq 0$

33) $\frac{25}{6}$

34) $\frac{36}{5}$

35) $\frac{7\sqrt{3}}{8}$

36) $\frac{7}{3}$

Effortless
Math
Education

CHAPTER

10 Rational Expressions

Math topics that you'll learn in this chapter:

- ☑ Simplifying Complex Fractions
- ☑ Graphing Rational Functions
- ☑ Adding and Subtracting Rational Expressions
- ☑ Multiplying Rational Expressions
- ☑ Dividing Rational Expressions
- ☑ Evaluate Integers Raised to Rational Exponents

231

Simplifying Complex Fractions

A complex fraction is a fraction that contains one or more other fractions in either the numerator or denominator. To simplify a complex fraction, the first step is to find a common denominator for all the fractions involved. A common denominator is a number that is a multiple of all the denominators of the fractions. Once you have a common denominator, you can add or subtract the numerators as appropriate, and then simplify the resulting fraction if possible.

For example, consider the complex fraction $\frac{2}{3} + \frac{4}{5}$.

To simplify this fraction, we first need to find a common denominator. In this case, a common denominator would be 15. Since 15 is a multiple of both 3 and 5. Once we have a common denominator, we can rewrite the fractions. So, that they have the same denominator.

In this case, we would have $\frac{2}{3} = \frac{10}{15}$ and $\frac{4}{5} = \frac{12}{15}$. With these equivalent fractions, we can add the numerators: $10 + 12 = 22$, and the resulting fraction is $\frac{22}{15}$.

$$\frac{2}{3} + \frac{4}{5} = \frac{10}{15} + \frac{12}{15} = \frac{10 + 12}{15} = \frac{22}{15}$$

It's important to note that simplifying complex fractions doesn't always result in a fraction with a smaller numerator and denominator. The resulting fraction may have the same numerator and denominator or even greater numerator and denominator.

Let's review an example:

Simplify: $\frac{\frac{3}{5}}{\frac{3}{5} - \frac{5}{8}} =$.

To simplify the complex fraction $\frac{\frac{3}{5}}{\frac{3}{5} - \frac{5}{8}}$, we will first simplify each fraction within the complex fraction. First, we simplify the denominator of the complex fraction:

$$\frac{3}{5} - \frac{5}{8} = \frac{3\times8}{5\times8} - \frac{5\times5}{8\times5} = \frac{24}{40} - \frac{25}{40} = -\frac{1}{40}.$$

Now, substitute this simplified denominator into the original complex fraction:

$$\frac{\frac{3}{5}}{-\frac{1}{40}} = \left(\frac{3}{5}\right) \times \left(-\frac{40}{1}\right) = -\frac{120}{5}.$$

And we can simplify further if we want to, we can divide both the numerator and denominator by a common factor of 5: $-\frac{120}{5} = -24$.

So, the simplified form of the complex fraction is -24.

Simplify: $\frac{\frac{2}{7} \div \frac{1}{4}}{\frac{7}{8} + \frac{1}{4}}$.

First, simplify the numerator: $\frac{2}{7} \div \frac{1}{4} = \frac{8}{7}$.

Then, simplify the denominator: $\frac{7}{8} + \frac{1}{4} = \frac{9}{8}$.

Now, write the complex fraction using the division sign ($\div$):

$$\frac{\frac{2}{7} \div \frac{1}{4}}{\frac{7}{8} + \frac{1}{4}} = \frac{\frac{8}{7}}{\frac{9}{8}} = \frac{8}{7} \div \frac{9}{8}.$$

Use the dividing fractions rule: (Keep, Change, Flip: Keep the first fraction, Change the division sign to multiplication, Flip the second fraction)

$$\frac{8}{7} \div \frac{9}{8} = \frac{8}{7} \times \frac{8}{9} = \frac{64}{63} = 1\frac{1}{63}.$$

✎ Simplify each expression.

1) $\dfrac{\frac{2}{5}}{\frac{4}{3} + \frac{6}{5}} =$

2) $\dfrac{3}{\frac{1}{4} - \frac{3}{5}} =$

3) $\dfrac{\frac{3}{4} - \frac{2}{9}}{\frac{3}{8} + \frac{5}{9}} =$

4) $\dfrac{\frac{5}{21} - \frac{2}{3}}{\frac{6}{7} + \frac{4}{5}} =$

5) $\dfrac{\frac{18}{32}}{6} =$

6) $\dfrac{\frac{9}{15} + \frac{4}{5}}{\frac{36}{25}} =$

7) $\dfrac{\frac{8}{3}}{\frac{2}{5}} =$

8) $\dfrac{\frac{x}{3} + \frac{x}{8}}{\frac{1}{4}} =$

9) $\dfrac{\frac{x+3}{x-2}}{2} =$

10) $\dfrac{1 + \frac{x}{4}}{x} =$

Graphing Rational Functions

Graphing rational functions, which are functions of the form $f(x) = \frac{P(x)}{Q(x)}$, where $P(x)$ and $Q(x)$ are polynomials, can be done by following these steps:

Step 1: Find the asymptotes: Determine each of the types of asymptotes. There are three types of asymptotes for rational functions:

- Vertical asymptotes: These are the x−values at which the denominator of the function is equal to zero.

- Horizontal asymptotes: These are the y−values that the graph approaches as x approaches positive or negative infinity.

- Slanting asymptote: It is a slanted line with the equation of the form $y = mx + b$.

Step 2: Find the x−intercepts: These are the x−coordinates of the points where the graph crosses the x−axis.

Step 3: Find the y−intercept: This is the y−coordinate of the point where the graph crosses the y−axis.

Step 4: Find the values of y for several different values of x.

Step 5: Plot the points found in steps 2, 3, and 4.

Step 6: Draw the graph: Draw a smooth curve to connect the points.

Step 7: Identify any holes, or points where the graph is not defined, which occur at the x−coordinates where the denominator is zero and the numerator is not.

It's important to note that the degree of the numerator should be less than the degree of the denominator for the function to be defined for all x, except for the values that make the denominator zero. Also, the asymptotes of the graph are the vertical lines corresponding to the roots of the denominator.

Note: Rational functions can have some interesting properties, such as slant asymptotes, which occur when the degree of the denominator is one less than the degree of the numerator, and cusp, which occur when the numerator and denominator share a common root.

Let's review an example:

Graph the rational function: $f(x) = \frac{x^2-x+2}{x-1}$.

First, notice that the graph is in two pieces. Most rational functions have graphs in multiple pieces. Since the polynomial of the numerator of the function does not have a real root, therefore the original function is also rootless.

Find the $y-$intercept by substituting zero for x and solving for y, $f(x)$:

$$x = 0 \rightarrow y = \frac{x^2-x+2}{x-1} = \frac{0^2-0+2}{0-1} = -2,$$

the $y-$intercept is the point of the coordinate $(0, -2)$.

Find the asymptotes of $\frac{x^2-x+2}{x-1}$:

Find the zeros of the function for the vertical asymptote as: $x - 1 = 0 \rightarrow x = 1$,

Divide the numerator by the denominator to find the slant asymptote: $\frac{x^2-x+2}{x-1} = x + \frac{2}{x-1}$.

So, the slant asymptote is the line $y = x$ (Exactly the divisor of this division).

After finding the asymptotes, you can plug in some values for x and solve for y.

Here is the sketch for this function.

Note: When drawing the graph, make sure that the function graph does not intersect the asymptotes.

✎ Graph rational expressions.

11) $y = -\frac{1}{x}$

12) $y = \frac{x^2-4x+3}{x+1}$

13) $f(x) = \frac{x^2-2x}{x-3}$

14) $f(x) = \frac{6x+1}{x^2-4x}$

Adding and Subtracting Rational Expressions

When adding or subtracting rational expressions, it's important to first find a common denominator. A common denominator is a denominator that both rational expressions can be expressed with. Once a common denominator is found, you can add or subtract the numerators of the rational expressions, while keeping the common denominator.

Here's an example:

Solve: $\frac{3x+2}{x^2-1} + \frac{5x-4}{x^2-1} =$.

To add the rational expressions $\frac{3x+2}{x^2-1}$ and $\frac{5x-4}{x^2-1}$, we first find a common denominator which is $x^2 - 1$.

We can then add the numerators of the rational expressions while keeping the common denominator: $(3x + 2) + (5x - 4) = 8x$- 2.

So, the sum of the rational expressions is $\frac{8x-2}{x^2-1}$.

$$\frac{3x+2}{x^2-1} + \frac{5x-4}{x^2-1} = \frac{(3x+2)+(5x-4)}{x^2-1} = \frac{8x-2}{x^2-1}.$$

Another example:

Solve: $\frac{3x+2}{x^2-1} - \frac{5x-4}{x^2-1} =$.

To subtract the rational expressions $\frac{3x+2}{x^2-1}$ and $\frac{5x-4}{x^2-1}$, we again use the common denominator $x^2 - 1$: $(3x + 2) - (5x - 4) = 3x + 2 - 5x + 4 = -2x + 6$.

So, the difference of the rational expressions is $\frac{-2x+6}{x^2-1}$.

$$\frac{3x+2}{x^2-1} - \frac{5x-4}{x^2-1} = \frac{(3x+2)-(5x-4)}{x^2-1} = \frac{-2x+6}{x^2-1}.$$

It's important to simplify the resulting expression after adding or subtracting, by canceling out common factors between numerator and denominator or using other methods of simplification.

It's also important to note that when the denominators are not the same, we need to find a common denominator to add or subtract the

bit.ly/3d305j2

Find more at

expressions. Also, when the numerator and denominator share a common factor, we should cancel it out to get the simplified form of the expression.

Let's review an example:

Solve: $\frac{x+4}{x-5} + \frac{x-4}{x+6} =$.

Find the least common denominator of $(x-5)$ and $(x+6)$:

$$(x-5)(x+6) = x^2 + x - 30.$$

Then: $\frac{x+4}{x-5} + \frac{x-4}{x+6} = \frac{(x+4)(x+6)}{(x-5)(x+6)} + \frac{(x-4)(x-5)}{(x+6)(x-5)} = \frac{(x+4)(x+6)+(x-4)(x-5)}{(x+6)(x-5)}$.

Expand: $(x+4)(x+6) + (x-4)(x-5) = 2x^2 + x + 44$.

Then: $\frac{(x+4)(x+6)+(x-4)(x-5)}{(x+6)(x-5)} = \frac{2x^2+x+44}{(x+6)(x-5)} = \frac{2x^2+x+44}{x^2+x-30}$.

One more example:

Solve and simplify: $\frac{4}{2x+3} + \frac{x-2}{2x^2+x-3} =$.

To solve the equation, we need to first find a common denominator, which is in this case $2x^2 + x - 3$. Because $2x^2 + x - 3$ can be written as the product of two factors $2x + 3$ and $x - 1$, in which the denominator of the first part of the original expression is also present $2x + 3$. So,

$$\frac{4}{2x+3} + \frac{x-2}{2x^2+x-3} = \frac{4(x-1)}{2x^2+x-3} + \frac{x-2}{2x^2+x-3}$$

$$= \frac{4x-4+x-2}{2x^2+x-3}$$

$$= \frac{5x-6}{2x^2+x-3}.$$

🖋 Simplify each expression.

15) $\frac{x+6}{x+1} - \frac{x+9}{x+1} =$

16) $\frac{2x+1}{x+3} + \frac{2}{x+4} =$

17) $\frac{14}{x+4} + \frac{6}{x^2-16} =$

18) $\frac{2}{x} + \frac{x-1}{x+1} - 1 =$

19) $\frac{x+2}{x+8} - \frac{2x}{x-8} =$

20) $\frac{x}{3x^2-x+1} + \frac{1}{3x^2-x+1} =$

bit.ly/3d305i2

Find more at

Multiplying Rational Expressions

When multiplying rational expressions, we can multiply the numerators and denominators, separately. For example, to multiply the rational expressions $\frac{2x+3}{x-1}$ and $\frac{x+4}{x+2}$, we can use the following steps:

Step 1: Multiply the numerators:

$$(2x + 3) \times (x + 4) = 2x^2 + 8x + 3x + 12 = 2x^2 + 11x + 12.$$

Step 2: Multiply the denominators:

$$(x - 1) \times (x + 2) = x^2 + 2x - x - 2 = x^2 + x - 2.$$

Step 3: Write the product as the numerator over the denominator:

$$\frac{2x+3}{x-1} \times \frac{x+4}{x+2} = \frac{2x^2+11x+12}{x^2+x-2}.$$

Let's review an example:

Solve: $\frac{1}{x+3} \times \frac{x^2+x-2}{3x} =$.

Since the numerator and denominator polynomials of the fraction do not have a common factor, the product of this multiplication is obtained by multiplying the numerators and denominators, separately. So,

Multiply the numerators: $1 \times (x^2 + x - 2) = x^2 + x - 2$.

Multiply the denominators: $(x + 3) \times (3x) = 3x^2 + 9x$.

Write the product as the numerator over the denominator:

$$\frac{1}{x+3} \times \frac{x^2+x-2}{3x} = \frac{x^2+x-2}{3x^2+9x}.$$

It's also important to simplify the resulting expression, if possible, by canceling out common factors between the numerator and denominator or using other methods of simplification.

It's important to note that when we multiply fractions, we multiply the numerators and denominators separately, and then we simplify the result if possible.

Let's review another example:

Solve: $\frac{x^2+x}{x-1} \times \frac{2-2x}{x^3-4x^2+4x} =$.

Check the numerator and denominator polynomials to find the common factor.

For this purpose, rewrite each of the polynomials as a product of factors. Then:

$$\frac{x^2+x}{x-1} \times \frac{2-2x}{x^3-4x^2+4x} = \frac{x(x+1)}{x-1} \times \frac{-2(x-1)}{x(x-2)^2}.$$

Now, cancel the common factors: $\frac{x(x+1)}{x-1} \times \frac{-2(x-1)}{x(x-2)^2} = (x+1) \times \frac{-2}{(x-2)^2}$.

Next, multiply the numerator of the fractions together and the denominator of

the fractions together: $\frac{x^2+x}{x-1} \times \frac{2-2x}{x^3-4x^2+4x} = (x+1) \times \frac{-2}{(x-2)^2} = \frac{-2x-2}{(x-2)^2}$.

One more example:

Solve: $\frac{x-2}{x+3} \times \frac{2x+6}{x-2} =$.

First, we need to multiply the numerators and denominators, separately:

Multiply the numerators: $(x-2) \times (2x+6)$.

Multiply the denominators: $(x+3) \times (x-2)$.

Write the product as the numerator over the denominator:

$$\frac{x-2}{x+3} \times \frac{2x+6}{x-2} = \frac{(x-2)\times(2x+6)}{(x+3)\times(x-2)}.$$

Next, cancel the common factor: $\frac{(x-2)\times(2x+6)}{(x+3)\times(x-2)} = \frac{2x+6}{x+3}$.

Factor $(2x+6) = 2(x+3)$. Then: $\frac{2x+6}{x+3} = \frac{2(x+3)}{x+3} = 2$.

Therefore, the product of the multiplication is, $\frac{x-2}{x+3} \times \frac{2x+6}{x-2} = 2$.

✎ Simplify.

21) $\frac{20x^3}{3} \times \frac{15}{4x} =$

22) $\frac{x+6}{4} \times \frac{16}{x+6} =$

23) $\frac{x+10}{4x} \times \frac{3x}{7x+70} =$

24) $\frac{x+8}{x+6} \times \frac{x-6}{4x+32} =$

25) $\frac{x^2+1}{x^2-x} \times x =$

26) $\frac{x^2-2x}{x^3-1} \times \frac{x^2-1}{2x} =$

bit.ly/3fcliIU

Find more at

Dividing Rational Expressions

When dividing rational expressions, we can use the property that division is the same as multiplication by the reciprocal.

For example, to divide the rational expressions $\frac{2x+3}{x-1}$ by $\frac{x+4}{x+2}$, we can use the following steps:

Step 1: Flip the second fraction $\frac{x+4}{x+2}$:

$$\frac{x+2}{x+4}$$

Step 2: Multiply the first fraction $\frac{2x+3}{x-1}$ by the reciprocal of the second fraction:

$$\frac{2x+3}{x-1} \times \frac{x+2}{x+4}$$

Step 3: Simplify the resulting expression if possible by canceling out common factors between the numerator and denominator or using other methods of simplification.

So, the division is:

$$\frac{\frac{2x+3}{x-1}}{\frac{x+4}{x+2}} = \frac{2x+3}{x-1} \times \frac{x+2}{x+4} = \frac{(2x+3)(x+2)}{(x-1)(x+4)} = \frac{2x^2+4x+3x+6}{x^2+4x-x-4} = \frac{2x^2+7x+6}{x^2+3x-4}.$$

It's important to note that when we divide fractions, we flip the second fraction, then we multiply the numerators and denominators, separately, and then we simplify the result if possible.

Also, it's important to check the solutions in the original equation to make sure that they satisfy the equation.

Solve: $\frac{5x}{x+3} \div \frac{x}{2x+6} =$.

To solve this, we can use the following steps:

Step 1: Flip the second fraction $\frac{x}{2x+6}$ as: $\frac{2x+6}{x}$.

Step 2: Multiply the first fraction $\frac{5x}{x+3}$ by the reciprocal of the second fraction $\frac{2x+6}{x}$: $\frac{5x}{x+3} \times \frac{2x+6}{x}$.

Step 3: Simplify the resulting expression if possible, by canceling out common factors between the numerator and denominator or using other methods of simplification.

So, the division is: $\frac{5x}{x+3} \div \frac{x}{2x+6} = \frac{5x}{x+3} \times \frac{2x+6}{x} = \frac{5x(2x+6)}{(x+3)x}$.

Now, cancel the common factor: $\frac{5x(2x+6)}{(x+3)x} = 10$.

So, the division is: $\frac{5x}{x+3} \div \frac{x}{2x+6} = 10$.

Another example:

Simplify the fraction: $\frac{\frac{x^2+x-6}{3x-3}}{\frac{x+3}{x^2-1}} =$.

To simplify, rewrite the fraction in the form:

$$\frac{\frac{x^2+x-6}{3x-3}}{\frac{x+3}{x^2-1}} = \frac{x^2+x-6}{3x-3} \div \frac{x+3}{x^2-1}.$$

Now, flip the second fraction and multiply by the first fraction as follows:

$$\frac{x^2+x-6}{3x-3} \div \frac{x+3}{x^2-1} = \frac{x^2+x-6}{3x-3} \times \frac{x^2-1}{x+3}.$$

Next, by finding the common factor from the denominator and numerator of the fraction, cancel the common factors and multiply the remaining expressions:

$$\frac{x^2+x-6}{3x-3} \times \frac{x^2-1}{x+3} = \frac{(x-2)(x+3)(x-1)(x+1)}{3(x-1)(x+3)} = \frac{(x-2)(x+1)}{3} = \frac{x^2-x-2}{3}.$$

✍ Simplify.

27) $\frac{10x}{x+2} \div \frac{x}{60x+120} =$

29) $\frac{x-6}{x+3} \div \frac{4}{x+3} =$

28) $\frac{5}{4} \div \frac{45}{8x} =$

30) $\frac{7x^3}{x^2-64} \div \frac{x^3}{x^2+x-56} =$

Evaluate Integers Raised to Rational Exponents

Integers raised to rational exponents can be evaluated using the properties of exponents. A rational exponent is a fraction with a numerator and denominator that are integers.

For example, to evaluate $2^{\frac{3}{4}}$, we can use the following steps:

Step 1: Rewrite the exponent as a fraction with a numerator and denominator. In this case, $\frac{3}{4}$ is already in fraction form.

Step 2: Write the base number (in this case, 2) as the numerator of a fraction with a denominator of 1.

Step 3: Raise the base number to the power of the numerator of the exponent, and take the reciprocal of the base number to the power of the denominator of the exponent.

So, in this case: $2^{\frac{3}{4}} = (2^3)^{\frac{1}{4}} = 8^{\frac{1}{4}}$.

The result of this is the fourth root of 8.

It's important to note that these steps are valid as long as the denominator of the exponent is a positive integer, and the base is a positive real number.

Also, it's important to note that these steps are valid for integers, as well as real numbers.

If the base is a negative number, the exponent should be an even number, otherwise, the result will be a complex number.

Let's review a few examples:

Simplify: $(-32)^{-\frac{1}{5}}$.

To simplify $(-32)^{-\frac{1}{5}}$, we can use the properties of exponents. The negative exponent means that we need to find the reciprocal of the original expression.

That is, use this formula $a^{-b} = \frac{1}{a^b}$, so: $(-32)^{-\frac{1}{5}} = \frac{1}{(-32)^{\frac{1}{5}}}$.

Now, we need to find the fifth root of 32. Write the base in exponential notation, $32 = 2^5$. It's important to note that the base number -32 is negative and the exponent is a rational number, this means that the result will be a complex number. But we know that the expression inside the radical with an odd index can also be negative and $\sqrt[m]{a} = a^{\frac{1}{m}}$. That is, the value $(-32)^{\frac{1}{5}}$ is defined and is a real value. Then:

$$(-32)^{\frac{1}{5}} = ((-1) \times (32))^{\frac{1}{5}} = ((-1)^5 \times 2^5)^{\frac{1}{5}} = (-1)^{\frac{5}{5}} \times 2^{\frac{5}{5}} = -1 \times 2 = -2.$$

Now, we can find the reciprocal of this expression: $(-32)^{-\frac{1}{5}} = \dfrac{1}{(-32)^{\frac{1}{5}}} = \dfrac{1}{-2} = -\dfrac{1}{2}$.

Evaluate: $81^{\frac{3}{2}}$.

First, rewrite the base as exponential form $81 = 3^4$. Now, we have: $81^{\frac{3}{2}} = (3^4)^{\frac{3}{2}}$.
So, multiply two exponents, $(3^4)^{\frac{3}{2}} = 3^{4 \times \frac{3}{2}} = 3^6 = 729$.

Calculate the value of $\sqrt[3]{121^{\frac{3}{2}}}$.

Use this formula $\sqrt[n]{a} = a^{\frac{1}{n}}$. Then: $\sqrt[3]{121^{\frac{3}{2}}} = \left(121^{\frac{3}{2}}\right)^{\frac{1}{3}}$.

Now, by using $(a^n)^m = a^{nm}$. So, we have: $\left(121^{\frac{3}{2}}\right)^{\frac{1}{3}} = 121^{\frac{3}{2} \times \frac{1}{3}} = 121^{\frac{1}{2}}$.

Write the base in exponential notation, $121^{\frac{1}{2}} = (11^2)^{\frac{1}{2}}$.

Multiply the exponents and simplify: $(11^2)^{\frac{1}{2}} = 11^{2 \times \frac{1}{2}} = 11$.

✎ Evaluate.

31) $(121x^6)^{\frac{1}{2}}$

32) $(64x^{12})^{\frac{1}{6}}$

33) $(32)^{-\frac{1}{5}}$

34) $(-27)^{\frac{1}{3}}$

35) $\left(\sqrt{256a^2}\right)^{-\frac{3}{2}}$

36) $\sqrt{64^{\frac{5}{3}}}$

Chapter 10: Answers

1) $\frac{3}{19}$

2) $-\frac{60}{7}$

3) $\frac{38}{67}$

4) $-\frac{15}{58}$

5) $\frac{3}{32}$

6) $\frac{35}{36}$

7) $\frac{20}{3}$

8) $\frac{11x}{6}$

9) $\frac{2x+6}{3x-6}$

10) $\frac{4+x}{4x}$

11) $y = -\frac{1}{x}$

13) $f(x) = \frac{x^2-2x}{x-3}$

12) $y = \frac{x^2-4x+3}{x+1}$

14) $f(x) = \frac{6x+1}{x^2-4x}$

15) $-\frac{3}{x+1}$

16) $\frac{2x^2+11x+10}{(x+3)(x+4)}$

17) $\frac{14x-50}{(x+4)(x-4)}$

18) $\frac{2}{x^2+x}$

19) $\frac{-x^2-22x-16}{(x+8)(x-8)}$

20) $\frac{x+1}{3x^2-x+1}$

21) $25x^2$

22) 4

23) $\frac{3}{28}$

24) $\frac{x-6}{4(x+6)}$

25) $\frac{x^2+1}{x-1}$

26) $\frac{(x-2)(x+1)}{2(x^2+x+1)}$

27) 600

28) $\frac{2x}{9}$

29) $\frac{x-6}{4}$

30) $\frac{7(x-7)}{x-8}$

31) $11x^3$

32) $2x^2$

33) $\frac{1}{2}$

34) -3

35) $\frac{1}{2^6 a^3}$

36) 32

Effortless
Math
Education

CHAPTER

11 Statistics and Probabilities

Math topics that you'll learn in this chapter:

- ☑ Mean, Median, Mode, and Range of the Given Data
- ☑ Pie Graph
- ☑ Scatter Plots
- ☑ Probability Problems
- ☑ Permutations and Combinations
- ☑ Calculate and Interpret Correlation Coefficients
- ☑ Find the Equation of a Regression Line and Interpret Regression Lines
- ☑ Correlation and Causation

247

Mean, Median, Mode, and Range of the Given Data

Mean, median, mode, and range are four common measures of central tendency and variability in statistics.

Mean: The mean is the average of a set of data. It is calculated by adding all the values in the set and dividing the sum by the number of values. The formula for the mean is:

$$mean = \frac{sum\ of\ values}{number\ of\ values}$$

Median: The median is the middle value when a set of data is arranged in numerical order. If there is an even number of values, the median is the average of the two middle values.

Mode: The mode is the most frequently occurring value in a set of data. A set of data can have one mode, more than one mode, or no mode at all.

Range: The range is the difference between the highest and lowest values in a set of data. It is a measure of variability in the set. The formula for the range is:

$$range = highest\ value - lowest\ value$$

It's important to note that these measures are not always sufficient to describe the data, and in some cases, we may need to use other measures such as variance, standard deviation, etc. Also, it's important to note that the data should be numerical to be able to calculate these measures.

Let's review an example:

Find the mean, median, mode, and range of the following numbers:

$$5, 6, 8, 6, 8, 5, 3, 6$$

Mean: To find the mean, add up all the values and divide by the number of values. Therefore, the mean is equal to $\frac{5+6+8+6+8+5+3+6}{8} = 5.87$.

Median: To find the median, arrange the values in numerical order and find the middle value. 3, 5, 5, 6, 6, 6, 8, 8

In this case, since there is an even number of values, the median is the average of the two middle values: $\frac{6+6}{2} = 6$.

Mode: To find the mode, find the most frequently occurring value. In this case, the mode is 6, which occurs 3 times.

Range: To find the range, subtract the lowest value from the highest value: $8 - 3 = 5$.

Some other examples:

What is the mode of these numbers? 5, 6, 8, 6, 8, 5, 3, 5

Mode: the value in the list that appears most often.

Therefore, the mode is number 5. There are three number 5 in the data.

What is the median of these numbers? 6, 11, 15, 10, 17, 20, 7

Write the numbers in order: 6, 7, 10, 11, 15, 17, 20

The median is the number in the middle. Therefore, the median is 11.

What is the mean of these numbers? 7, 2, 3, 2, 4, 8, 7, 5

Use this formula: Mean: $\frac{sum\ of\ values}{number\ of\ values}$.

Therefore: Mean: $\frac{7+2+3+2+4+8+7+5}{8} = \frac{38}{8} = 4.75$.

What is the range in this list? 3, 7, 12, 6, 15, 20, 8

The range is the difference between the largest value and the smallest value in the list. The largest value is 20 and the smallest value is 3. Then: $20 - 3 = 17$.

✎ Find the mean, median, mode, and range of the following.

1) 6, 11, 5, 3, 6

2) 4, 9, 1, 9, 6, 7

3) 10, 3, 6, 10, 4, 15

4) 12, 4, 8, 9, 3, 12, 15

Pie Graph

A pie chart, also known as a pie graph or a circle graph, is a type of chart used to represent data as a proportion of the whole. It is useful for showing the relative sizes of different categories or parts of a whole.

A pie chart is made up of a circular area divided into wedges, with each wedge representing a proportion of the whole. The size of each wedge is determined by the proportion of the category it represents to the whole. The wedges are usually labeled with the category name and the percentage of the whole that the category represents.

To create a pie chart, you will need data that can be divided into categories or parts. Each category or part will be represented by a wedge in the chart. The total of the categories should equal 100%.

You can create a pie chart using charting software, spreadsheet software, or an online chart-making tool.

It's important to note that a pie chart is best used when there are few categories (less than 6) and the categories are not too close in size, otherwise, it's hard to compare the sizes of the wedges.

Let's review an example:

A library has 750 books that include Mathematics, Physics, Chemistry, English and History. Use the following graph to answer the questions.

What is the number of Mathematics books?

    Number of total books = 750.

Library Books

Percent of Mathematics books = 28%.

Then, the number of Mathematics books: $28\% \times 750 = 0.28 \times 750 = 210$.

What is the number of History books?

Number of total books = 750.

Percent of History books = 12%.

Then: $0.12 \times 750 = 90$.

What is the number of Chemistry books in the library?

Number of total books = 750.

Percent of Chemistry books = 22%.

Then: $0.22 \times 750 = 165$.

✎ **The pie chart shown below shows the percentages of types of transportation used by 800 students to come to school. With this given information, answer the following questions:**

5) How much did Bob's total expenses last month? _____

6) How much did Bob spend on food last month? _____

7) How much did Bob spend on his bills last month? _____

8) How much did Bob spend on his car last month? _____

Bpb's last month expenses

Scatter Plots

A scatter plot, also known as a scatter graph or scatter chart, is a type of plot used to show the relationship between two quantitative variables. It is a way to represent the data in the form of points on a two-dimensional graph, with one variable on the x −axis and the other variable on the y −axis. Each point on the scatter plot represents a single observation in the data set, with the x −coordinate representing the value of one variable and the y −coordinate representing the value of the other variable.

Scatter plots are useful for visualizing patterns in data, such as correlation, clustering, and outliers. A scatter plot can show a positive correlation, a negative correlation, or no correlation at all between the two variables. If the points on the plot tend to fall along a straight line, then there is likely a strong correlation between the two variables.

Scatter plots can be created using spreadsheet software, charting software, or online chart-making tools. When creating a scatter plot, it is important to label the axes and provide a title that describes the variables being plotted.

In some cases, Scatter plots can be useful to detect outliers, which are data points that are significantly different from the other points in the dataset.

It's important to note that scatter plots are best used when there is more than one observation, and the data is numerical.

Let's review an example:

The following table shows the number of people in a family and the amount of money they spend on movie tickets.

Number of People	1	2	3	4	5	6	7
Money ($)	13	14	17	15	28	18	16

a) Make a scatter plot to represent the data.

b) Does this scatter plot show a positive trend, a negative trend, or no trend?

c) Find the outlier on the scatter plot.

Write the ordered pairs. Number of people goes on the x −axis, so put the number of people first. The amount of money goes on the y −axis, so put the amount of money second. $(1,13)$, $(2,14)$, $(3,17)$, $(4,15)$, $(5,28)$, $(6,18)$, $(7,16)$.

Now, graph the ordered pairs.

y tends to increase as x increases. So, this scatter plot shows a positive trend.

$(5,28)$ is the outlier because this point is separated from all other points in the data set.

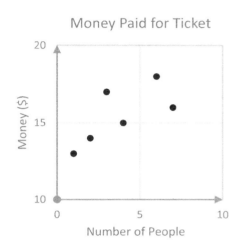

✎ **In the scatterplots below, determine which is a positive trend, negative or no trend, and find the outlier if there is one.**

9)

Day	Money ($)
1	$12
2	$8
3	$14
4	$5
5	$7
6	$10
7	$4
8	$12

10)

bit.ly/3EKozdu

Find more at

Probability Problems

Probability problems involve using mathematical concepts and techniques to determine the likelihood of certain events occurring. These types of problems can involve a wide range of scenarios, from simple coin flips and dice rolls to more complex real-world situations.

For example, if you flip a coin 10 times and it lands on heads 6 times, the experimental probability of flipping heads on the next flip would be $\frac{6}{10}$ or $\frac{3}{5}$.

Probability theory provides the foundation for many concepts and techniques used in data analysis and decision-making, and it is an important area of study for anyone interested in the mathematical and scientific foundations of these fields.

There are several ways to solve probability problems, but the general process involves the following steps:

Step 1: Define the sample space: The sample space is the set of all possible outcomes of the experiment or event being considered.

Step 2: Define the event: The event is the specific outcome or set of outcomes that we are interested in finding the probability of.

Step 3: Use the formula for probability: The probability of an event is the number of favorable outcomes (the outcomes that make up the event) divided by the total number of possible outcomes in the sample space. This is represented by the formula: $P(E) = \frac{n(E)}{n(S)}$, where $P(E)$ is the probability of the event E, $n(E)$ is the number of favorable outcomes and, $n(S)$ is the total number of possible outcomes in the sample space S.

Step 4: Check for the probability of the event to be: $0 \leq P(E) \leq 1$.

Step 5: Find the complementary probability if necessary. The complementary probability is the probability that the event will not happen and it's represented by the formula $P(E') = 1 - P(E)$.

It's important to note that the sample space should be exhaustive, meaning that should include all possible outcomes, and mutually exclusive, meaning that the sample space should not contain overlapping outcomes.

Probability problems can be tricky, but with practice and understanding of the concepts, you'll be able to solve them with ease.

Probability can be expressed as a fraction, a decimal, or a percent.

Let's review an example:

Anita's trick–or–treat bag contains 10 pieces of chocolate, 16 suckers, 16 pieces of gum, 22 pieces of licorice. If she randomly pulls a piece of candy from her bag, what is the probability of her pulling out a piece of sucker?

Use this formula: $P(E) = \frac{n(E)}{n(S)} = \frac{number\ of\ favorable\ outcomes}{the\ total\ number\ of\ possible\ outcomes}$.

Probability of pulling out a piece of sucker $= \frac{16}{10+16+16+22} = \frac{16}{64} = \frac{1}{4}$.

One more example:

A bag contains 20 balls: four green, five black, eight blue, a brown, a red and one white. If 19 balls are removed from the bag at random, what is the probability that a brown ball has been removed?

If 19 balls are removed from the bag at random, there will be one ball in the bag. The probability of choosing a brown ball is 1 out of 20. Therefore, the probability of not choosing a brown ball is 19 out of 20 and the probability of having not a brown ball after removing 19 balls is the same. The answer is: $\frac{19}{20}$.

✎ Solve.

11) Bag *A* contains 8 red marbles and 6 green marbles. Bag *B* contains 5 black marbles and 7 orange marbles. What is the probability of selecting a green marble at random from bag *A*? What is the probability of selecting a black marble at random from Bag *B*?

bit.ly/3phwk1p

Find more at

Permutations and Combinations

Permutations and combinations are two related concepts in combinatorics, the branch of mathematics that deals with counting and arranging objects in different ways.

Permutations refer to the number of ways in which a set of objects can be arranged in a specific order. For example, if you have 3 objects: A, B, and C, there are 3! (3 factorial) or 6 possible permutations: ABC, ACB, BAC, BCA, CAB, CBA.

Combinations, on the other hand, refer to the number of ways in which a set of objects can be chosen without regard to order. For example, if you have 3 objects: A, B, and C, there are 3 choose 2 or 3 possible combinations: AB, AC, BC.

The formula for permutations of n objects taken r at a time is $\frac{n!}{(n-r)!}$, and the formula for combinations of n objects taken r at a time is $nCr = \frac{n!}{r!(n-r)!}$.

Permutations and combinations are used in a variety of fields such as combinatorial game theory, coding theory, cryptography, statistics, and probability.

It's important to note that the order of the elements matter when it comes to permutations while it doesn't matter in combinations.

In addition, Permutations are used when the order of elements matters, like arranging people in a line, while combinations are used when the order doesn't matter, like choosing a committee. In summary:

- **Factorials** are products, indicated by an exclamation mark. For example, $4! = 4 \times 3 \times 2 \times 1$. (Remember that 0! Is defined to be equal to 1.)

- **Permutations:** The number of ways to choose a sample of k elements from a set of n distinct objects where order does matter, and replacements are not allowed. For a permutation problem, use this formula: $nPk = \frac{n!}{(n-k)!}$.

- **Combination:** The number of ways to choose a sample of r elements from a set of n distinct objects where order does not matter, and replacements are not allowed. For a combination problem, use this formula: $nCr = \frac{n!}{r!(n-r)!}$.

Let's review an example:

How many ways can the first and second place be awarded to 7 people?

Since the order matters, (The first and second places are different!) we need to use permutation formula where n is 7 and k is 2. Then: $\frac{n!}{(n-k)!} = \frac{7!}{(7-2)!} = \frac{7!}{5!} = \frac{7\times6\times5!}{5!}$, remove 5! From both sides of the fraction. Then: $\frac{7\times6\times5!}{5!} = 7 \times 6 = 42$.

How many ways can we pick a team of 3 people from a group of 8?

Since the order doesn't matter, we need to use a combination formula where n is 8 and r is 3. Then: $\frac{n!}{r!(n-r)!} = \frac{8!}{3!(8-3)!} = \frac{8!}{3!(5)!} = \frac{8\times7\times6\times5!}{3!(5)!} = \frac{8\times7\times6}{3\times2\times1} = \frac{336}{6} = 56$.

✎ Determine whether each situation involves a permutation or a combination.

12) Susan is baking cookies. She uses sugar, flour, butter, and eggs. How many different orders of ingredients can she try?

13) Jason is planning for his vacation. He wants to go to a museum, go to the beach, and play volleyball. How many different ways of ordering are there for him?

14) In how many ways can a team of 6 basketball players choose a captain and co-captain?

15) How many ways can you give 5 balls to your 8 friends?

16) A professor is going to arrange her 5 students in a straight line. In how many ways can she do this?

17) In how many ways can a teacher choose 12 out of 15 students?

Calculate and Interpret Correlation Coefficients

A correlation coefficient is a statistical measure that describes the strength and direction of a linear relationship between two variables. The correlation coefficient is used for a set of n data points, (x_i, y_i), where $1 \leq i \leq n$. The most commonly used correlation coefficient is the Pearson correlation coefficient, denoted by r.

The Pearson correlation coefficient can range from -1 to 1, where -1 indicates a perfect negative linear relationship, 0 indicates no linear relationship, and 1 indicates a perfect positive linear relationship. A positive value of r indicates that as one variable increases, the other variable also increases, while a negative value of r indicates that as one variable increases, the other variable decreases. The formula for the Pearson correlation coefficient is:

$$r = \frac{\sum (x_i - \bar{x})(y_i - \bar{y})}{\sqrt{\sum (x_i - \bar{x})^2 \sum (y_i - \bar{y})^2}}$$

where x_i and y_i are the values of the two variables for the i−th observation, n is the total number of observations, $\sum$ (Sigma) denotes the sum of the values, and $\bar{x}$ and $\bar{y}$ are the mean of the variables.

A correlation coefficient of 0.8 or higher is considered strong, a coefficient between 0.5 and 0.8 is moderate, and a coefficient below 0.5 is weak. However, it's important to note that correlation doesn't imply causation, it only implies a relationship.

The correlation coefficient is a useful tool for identifying patterns in data, but it is important to remember that it does not indicate causality and should not be used to infer cause-and-effect relationships between variables. Also, it's important to note that the correlation coefficient only measures linear relationships, so if there's a non-linear relationship between variables, the correlation coefficient would not be an appropriate measure.

bit.ly/3QWsz0c

Find more at

Let's review an example:

Find the correlation coefficient of the following data and then interpret the answer. Round your answer to the nearest thousandth.

Arthur plans to improve his studies. In order to achieve this goal, he has written down the number of pages read daily and the hours of daily reading in the table below. He records the hours of daily reading, x, and the number of pages read daily, y.

Hours of Daily Reading	Number of Pages Read Daily
3	60
4	75
6	82
7	90
8	105

Each row in the above table shows a data point (x_i, y_i). x_i is the number of hours Arthur reads per day and y_i is the number of pages Arthur reads per day. You can simply use your calculator to find the above data set's correlation coefficient: $r = 0.968971 \approx 0.969$. The correlation coefficient is positive. So, the data points have a positive trend or increasing trend. The correlation coefficient is so close to 1, So the data set has a strong linear correlation.

✍ Find the correlation coefficient of the following data.

18)

x	50	51	52	53	54
y	4.1	4.2	4.3	4.4	4.5

19)

x	12	14	18	21	28
y	2	4	6	8	12

Find the Equation of a Regression Line and Interpret Regression Lines

A regression line is a line that is used to model the relationship between two variables. The equation of a regression line is typically represented in the form of the equation $y = bx + a$, where y is the dependent, x is the independent variable, a is the y −intercept (the point at which the line crosses the y −axis), and b is the slope of the line (the rate of change of y with respect to x).

The slope of line, b, can be calculated using the following formula:

$$b = \frac{n \sum (x_i y_i) - \sum x_i \sum y_i}{n \sum x_i^2 - (\sum x_i)^2}$$

The y −intercept, a, can be calculated using the following formula:

$$a = \frac{\sum y_i - b \sum x_i}{n}$$

where x_i and y_i are the values of the two variables for the i −th observation, n is the total number of observations, and $\sum$ (Sigma) denotes the sum of the values. Once the slope and y −intercept are calculated, the equation of the regression line can be written as:

$$y = a + bx$$

The slope of the line, b, can be interpreted as the rate of change of y with respect to x , and the y −intercept, a, can be interpreted as the expected value of y when $x = 0$.

The equation of the regression line can be used to make predictions about the value of the dependent variable (y) based on the value of the independent variable (x). For example, if the equation of the regression line is $y = 2 + 3x$, then a value of $x = 2$ would correspond to a predicted value of $y = 8$.

It's important to note that a regression line is a model, and it's always going to have some error. The error can be measured by the coefficient of determination (R^2), which is a number between 0 and 1 that indicates how well the line fits the data. An $R^2 = 0$, indicates that the line fits the data perfectly, while an $R^2 = 1$, indicates that the line does not fit the data at all.

$$y = a + bx + R^2$$

Let's review an example:

Find the equation for the least squares regression line of the following data set. Round your answers to the nearest hundredth. Then interpret the regression line.

Use a calculator to find the least squares regression line's equation for the above data set: $y = -0.15875x + 22.53709$.

Round your answers to the nearest hundredth:

$$y = -0.16x + 22.54.$$

x_i	y_i
9	24
15	20
23	17
32	13
45	9

The slope is negative so, there is a negative linear relationship. It means when one variable increases the other variable decreases.

✎ Determine the linear regression equation from the given set of data.

20)

x	2	3	5	8
y	3	6	4	13

21)

x	2	4	6	8
y	4	7	10	12

bit.ly/3wnRS1O

Find more at

Correlation and Causation

Correlation and causation are two related but distinct concepts in statistics. Correlation refers to a statistical relationship between two variables, where the values of one variable tend to change in a predictable way in relation to the values of the other variable. A correlation coefficient (such as Pearson's r) is a numerical measure of the strength and direction of this relationship.

Causation, on the other hand, refers to the relationship between an event (the cause) and a second event (the effect), where the second event is a result of the first event. In other words, causation implies that one variable causes the other variable to change.

It's important to note that correlation does not imply causation. Just because two variables are correlated, it does not mean that one variable causes the other. For example, ice cream sales and crime rates are positively correlated, but it doesn't mean that ice cream causes crime. The reason for the correlation is that both ice cream sales and crime rates increase during the summer months.

To establish causation, it's important to use experimental methods, such as randomized controlled trials, where the effect of the independent variable on the dependent variable can be established. Additionally, it's important to consider other factors that might be influencing the relationship between the two variables and controlling for any potential confounding variables.

One example of correlation not implying causation is the relationship between the number of fire trucks in a city and the number of fires in that city. There is likely a positive correlation between the number of fire trucks and the number of fires - as the number of fire trucks increases, the number of fires also increases. However, it doesn't mean that having more fire trucks causes more fires.

The reason for the correlation is that both the number of fire trucks and the number of fires are related to the population size of the city. As the population of the city grows, the number of fire trucks and the number of fires also increases. Therefore, we cannot conclude that the number of fire trucks causes the number of fires, instead, the relationship is due to another variable (population size) that influences both.

It's important to note that correlation is just a statistical relationship between two variables and it should be interpreted with caution. It's necessary to use other methods to establish the causal relationship between variables.

Keep in mind a correlation does not signify causation, but causation always signifies correlation. There are 2 situations when a correlation isn't causation:

The third variable problem happens when a confounded variable affects two other variables and makes them seem causally linked when they are not.

The directionality problem happens when 2 variables have a correlation connection and might really have a causal link, but it isn't possible to determine which variable is the reason for changing in the other.

✍ Determine whether the following relationships reflect both correlation and causation or not.

22) The number of cold and snowy days and the amount of coffee at the ski resort.

23) The number of miles traveled and the gas used.

Chapter 11: Answers

1) Mode: 6, Range: 8,

   Mean: 6.2, Median: 6

2) Mode: 9, Range: 8,

   Mean: 6, Median: 6.5

3) Mode: 10, Range: 12,

   Mean: 8, Median: 8

4) Mode: 12, Range: 12,

   Mean: 9, Median: 9

5) $1,975

6) $158

7) $730.75

8) $197.5

9) No trend

10) Negative trend

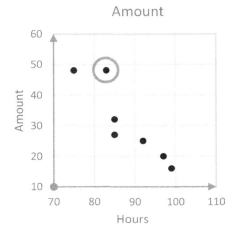

11) $\frac{3}{7}, \frac{5}{12}$

12) 24 (It's a permutation problem.)

13) 6 (It's a permutation problem.)

14) 30 (It's a permutation problem.)

15) 792 (It's a combination problem.)

16) 120 (It's a permutation problem.)

17) 455 (It's a combination problem.)

18) 1

19) 0.9971

20) $y = 1.476x - 0.142$

21) $y = 1.35x + 1.5$

22) Correlation no causation

23) Correlation and causation

Effortless
Math
Education

CHAPTER

12 Direct and Inverse Variation

Math topics that you'll learn in this chapter:

- ☑ Find the Constant of Variation
- ☑ Model Inverse Variation
- ☑ Write and Solve Direct Variation Equations

265

Find the Constant of Variation

A constant of variation is a relationship between two variables that can be expressed as a constant multiplied by one of the variables. The constant of variation is also known as the proportionality constant or the coefficient of proportionality.

Constant variation is usually seen in one of these two types of formats: direct variation or inverse variation. In both of these formats, k is considered the constant of variation. If you have an equation in one of these two formats, you can easily find the constant of variation.

$$Direct\ Variation \rightarrow y = kx \qquad\qquad Inverse\ Variation \rightarrow y = \frac{k}{x}$$

Where k is a non-zero constant, x and y are variables.

The most common form of constant variation is direct variation, where the two variables y and x are directly proportional to each other. The value of k represents how much y changes for a unit change in x.

In contrast, inverse variation is also another form of constant variation, where the two variables y and x are inversely proportional. This equation shows that as the value of x increases, the value of y decreases and vice versa.

It's important to note that in both cases, the constant of variation is a fixed value that doesn't change, regardless of the specific values of x and y.

Note that all equations don't have a constant of variation and they can't be written this way.

An example of a direct variation is the relationship between distance and the time it takes to travel that distance at a certain speed. Let's say you're driving on a highway at a constant speed of 60 miles per hour. The distance you travel is directly proportional to the time it takes to travel that distance. If you drive for 1 hour, you will travel 60 miles ($1\ hour \times 60\ \frac{miles}{hour} = 60\ miles$). If you drive for 2 hours, you will travel 120 miles ($2\ hours \times 60\frac{miles}{hour} = 120\ miles$). The equation that represents this relationship is: $Distance = Speed \times Time$.

In this case, the constant of variation (k) is equal to the speed of 60 miles per hour.

An example of an inverse variation is the relationship between the weight of an object and the gravitational force acting on it. The force of gravity acting on an object is inversely proportional to the distance between the object and the center of the Earth. The equation that represents this relationship is:

$$F = \frac{G(m_1 \times m_2)}{d^2}$$

Where F is the force of gravity, G is the gravitational constant, m_1 and m_2 are the masses of the objects and d is the distance between the objects.

In this case, the constant of variation k is equal to $G(m_1 \times m_2)$ and as the distance between the objects increases, the force of gravity decreases and vice versa.

One more example:

If y varies directly as x, and $x = 24$ when $y = 21$, what is the direct variation equation?

First, put x and y values in the *Direct Variation* $\rightarrow y = kx$ to find the constant of variation: $y = kx \rightarrow k = \frac{y}{x} = \frac{21}{24} \rightarrow k = \frac{7}{8}$.

Now using the constant of variation, write the direct variation equation: $y = \frac{7}{8}x$.

✎ Find the constant of variation in each case.

1) Let x and y be in direct variation, $x = 6$ and $y = 22$. Then find the direct variation equation.

2) If $x = 15$ and $y = 30$ follow a direct variation then find the constant of proportionality.

3) If y varies inversely as x, and $x = 5$ when $y = 7$, what is the inverse variation equation?

Model Inverse Variation

An inverse variation is a relationship between two variables which is shown by the following equation:

Sample Graph of
Inverse Variation

$$y = \frac{k}{x}$$

Where k is a non-zero constant, x and y are variables.
This equation shows that as the value of x increases, the value of y decreases, and vice versa.

To model inverse variation, you can use the equation to find the value of k and then use it to find the value of y for a given value of x or vice versa.

For example, let's say we have an inverse variation between the distance of a planet from the sun and its orbital period. The data shows that when a planet is 4 million miles from the sun, its orbital period is 365 days and when a planet is 40 million miles from the sun, its orbital period is 10,000 days. We can use this data to find k and then use it to find the orbital period of a planet that is 20 million miles from the sun.

$$y = \frac{k}{x} \rightarrow k = xy \rightarrow k = 365 \times 4 = 1460$$

So, the equation becomes: $y = \frac{1460}{x}$

To find the orbital period of a planet that is 20 million miles from the sun, we can substitute $x = 20$ million miles into the equation: $y = \frac{1460}{20} = 73$

So, the orbital period of a planet that is 20 million miles from the sun is 73 days.

In general, when modeling inverse variation, you can use any given pair of x and y values to find k, and then use the resulting equation to find the value of the other variable for a given value of x or y.

bit.ly/3luhUYw

Find more at

Another example:

According to the following table, determine if y values change inversely with x.

x	3	4	6	8
y	16	12	8	6

If yes, write an equation for the inverse variation and show it in a graph.

In a table with inverse changes, the product of all x and y pairs of its data are the same value. You can see that the product of any pair of x and y is equal to 48, so: $k = 48$. write an equation for the inverse variation: $y = \frac{k}{x} \rightarrow y = \frac{48}{x}$.

You can make a graph of the equation $y = \frac{48}{x}$ with points from the table as follows.

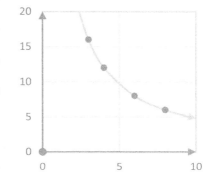

✍ In each case, state the constant of variation and graph the model.

4)

x	y
2	12
4	6
6	4
8	3

5)

x	y
2	15
3	10
5	6
6	5

Write and Solve Direct Variation Equations

Direct variation is a mathematical relationship that exists between two variables, where one variable is directly proportional to the other. In other words, as the value of one variable increases, the value of the other variable also increases in a consistent manner, and vice versa. The ratio between the two variables always remains the same in a direct variation.

The equation of a direct variation can be written as $y = kx$, where y and x are the two variables in question, and k is the constant of variation. The constant of variation is a value that remains the same throughout the equation and represents the ratio between the two variables.

To solve a direct variation equation, we can use the given values of the variables and the constant of variation to find the unknown variable.

For example, if we are given $y = 3x$ and $x = 4$, we can substitute the value of x into the equation to find the value of y: $y = 3x \rightarrow y = 3(4) \rightarrow y = 12$.

Therefore, the value of y in this example is 12.

Another example, if we are given the equation $y = 2x$ and $y = 7$. We can substitute the value of y into the equation and solve for x:

$$y = 2x \rightarrow 7 = 2x \rightarrow x = 3.5$$

Therefore, the value of x in this example is 2.

It's worth noting that the graph of a direct variation is always a straight line, with the constant of variation represented by the slope of the line. Considering the last issue, the following method can be used to write and solve the equation of a direct variation.

A two-variables linear equation's slope-intercept form is as follows: $y = mx + b$. Now, if you consider the $y-$intercept occurs at the point of $(0,0)$ and substitute the slope (m) with the constant of variation (k), you get a direct variation equation: $y = kx$, where k is the constant of variation and it's a value that always remains with no changes.

In the direct variation, the proportion between the variables stays the same, therefore the direct variation graph always makes a straight line.

Let's review some examples:

If y varies directly with x and $y = 21$ when $x = 7$, find y when $x = 8$.

First, you should find the constant of variation. Put $x = 3$ and $y = 21$ into the direct variation equation to find the value of k:

$$y = kx \rightarrow 21 = k \times 7 \rightarrow k = \frac{21}{7} = 3 \rightarrow k = 3.$$

Now, use $k = 3$ to find y when $x = 8$: $y = kx \rightarrow y = 3 \times 8 = 24 \rightarrow y = 24$.

If y varies directly with x and $y = 16$ when $x = 4$, find x when $y = 32$.

First, you should find the constant of variation. Put $x = 4$ and $y = 16$ into the direct variation equation to find the value of k:

$$y = kx \rightarrow 16 = k \times 4 \rightarrow k = \frac{16}{4} = 4 \rightarrow k = 4.$$

Now, use $k = 4$ to find x when $y = 32$: $y = kx \rightarrow 32 = 4 \times x = x = \frac{32}{4} = 8 \rightarrow x = 8$.

If y varies directly with x and $y = 42$ when $x = 6$, find y when $x = 11$.

First, you should find the constant of variation. Put $x = 6$ and $y = 42$ into the direct variation equation to find the value of k:

$$y = kx \rightarrow 42 = k \times 6 \rightarrow k = \frac{42}{6} = 7 \rightarrow k = 7.$$

Now, use $k = 7$ to find y when $x = 11$: $y = kx \rightarrow y = 7 \times 11 = 77 \rightarrow y = 77$.

✍ Solve.

6) If y varies directly with x and $y = 8$ when $x = 12$, find y when $x = -6$.

7) If y varies directly with x, find the missing value of x in $(-3, 27)$ and $(x, -27)$.

8) If y varies directly with x and $y = 12$ when $x = 2$, find y when $x = 7$.

bit.ly/3EQww1p

Find more at

Chapter 12: Answers

1) $y = \frac{11}{3}x$

2) $k = 2$

3) $y = \frac{35}{x}$

4) $y = \frac{24}{x}$

5) $y = \frac{30}{x}$

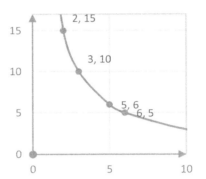

6) $y = -4$

7) $x = 3$

8) $y = 42$

CHAPTER

13 Number Sequences

Math topics that you'll learn in this chapter:

- ☑ Evaluate Recursive Formulas for Sequences
- ☑ Evaluate Variable Expressions for Number Sequences
- ☑ Write Variable Expressions for Arithmetic Sequences
- ☑ Write Variable Expressions for Geometric Sequences
- ☑ Write a Formula for a Recursive Sequence

273

Evaluate Recursive Formulas for Sequences

A sequence is an ordered list of numbers, where each number is called a term. The terms of a sequence are usually represented by the notation $T_1, T_2, \cdots, T_n, \cdots$, where T_n denotes the nth term of the sequence. The position of the term in the sequence is called an index and is represented by the subscript n. Sequences can be defined in different ways, such as an explicit formula, a recursion formula, or a set of given terms.

A recursive sequence is a sequence whose general term defines each term of the sequence using a previous term or terms. The general formula for a recursive sequence is $T_{n+1} = f(T_n)$, where T_n represents the nth term of the sequence, and f is a function that relates the nth term to one or more previous terms. To find the terms of a recursive sequence, it is necessary to know several previous terms of the sequence and use the recursive formula to find the next term.

Let's review an example:

Find a_2 and a_3, where the first term is $a_1 = -1$, and the general term is:

$$a_n = 2a_{n-1} - 1$$

Use the recursive sequence $a_n = 2a_{n-1} - 1$.

To find a_2, plug $n = 2$ in $a_n = 2a_{n-1} - 1$. So, $a_2 = 2a_{2-1} - 1 \rightarrow a_2 = 2a_1 - 1$. Now, substitute $a_1 = -1$ into the obtained formula $a_2 = 2a_1 - 1$.

Therefore, $a_2 = 2(-1) - 1 = -3$.

In the same way, plug in $n = 3$. Then, $a_3 = 2a_{3-1} - 1 \rightarrow a_3 = 2a_2 - 1$.

To find the value of a_3, put the obtained value for a_2 in this relation $a_3 = 2a_2 - 1$.

Therefore, $a_2 = -3 \rightarrow a_3 = 2(-3) - 1 = -7$.

The terms are $a_2 = -3$ and $a_3 = -7$.

Another example:

Write the first five terms of the sequence $T_n = T_{n-1} + T_{n-2}$, where $n \geq 3$, $T_1 = 1$ and $T_2 = 3$.

Recall that the recursive formula defines each term of a sequence using a previous term or terms.

Then by looking at the recursive formula $T_{n+1} = T_n + T_{n-1}$, you notice that to generate the terms of the sequence, you need the previous two terms of the sequence.

Here you are given the first two terms $T_1 = 1$ and $T_2 = 3$ together with the recursive formula $T_n = T_{n-1} + T_{n-2}$. To find the third term which is T_3, plug in $n = 3$. So, $T_3 = T_{3-1} + T_{3-2} \rightarrow T_3 = T_2 + T_1$.

Now, substitute the previous terms into the obtained expression.

That is $T_3 = 3 + 1 = 4$. Similarly, by substituting $n = 4$ and $n = 5$ into the given recursive formula, you get:

$$T_4 = T_{4-1} + T_{4-2} \rightarrow T_4 = T_3 + T_2 \rightarrow T_4 = 4 + 3 = 7,$$
$$T_5 = T_{5-1} + T_{5-2} \rightarrow T_5 = T_4 + T_3 \rightarrow T_5 = 7 + 4 = 11.$$

The first five terms of the sequence are 1, 3, 4, 7, and 11.

✍ Solve.

1) Find the first five terms of the sequence with the general term
$$a_n = 2a_{n-1} + a_{n-2}; n \geq 3, a_1 = 5 \text{ and } a_2 = -1$$

2) The nth term in a sequence is given by $a_n = 3a_{n-1} + n$ Find the first six terms of this sequence, given that $a_1 = -1$.

3) Find a recursive formula for the sequence $a_n = 1 + 2^n$.

4) Find the 7th term of the following recursive sequence.
$$x_{n+1} = (n - 3)x_n + 2; x_2 = 4$$

bit.ly/3H2uHzd

Find more at

Evaluate Variable Expressions for Number Sequences

An example of a sequence that has a general term dependent on the index value is an arithmetic sequence. In an arithmetic sequence, the difference between any two consecutive terms is always the same. To find the general term of an arithmetic sequence, we can use the following formula: $x_i = a + (i - 1)d$, where a is the first term of the sequence, d is the common difference, and i is the index of the term. By plugging in different values for i, we can find the specific values of the terms in the sequence.

For example, given the sequence 2, 6, 10, 14, 18, $\cdots$, we can see that the common difference is 4. Using the formula above, we can find that the general term of this sequence is $x_i = 2 + (i - 1)4$. By plugging in different values for i, such as $i = 1, 2, 3, 4, 5$, and 6 we can find that the first term is 2, the second term is 6, the third term is 10, the fourth term is 14, and the fifth term is 18, respectively. Similarly, we can also find the general term of a geometric sequence. In a geometric sequence, the ratio of any two consecutive terms is always the same. To find the general term of a geometric sequence, we can use the formula $x_i = ar^{i-1}$, where a is the first term of the sequence, r is the common ratio, and i is the index of the term. By plugging in different values for i, we can find the specific values of the terms in the sequence.

In this way we can easily find the terms of the sequence by plugging in different values for the index value in the general term, making it easy to understand and work with sequences.

Let's review an example:

Find the first three terms of the sequence with the general term $a_n = (-1)^{n-1}n$, where n represents the position of a term in the sequence and $n \geq 1$.

Since $n \geq 1$, the sequence starts at one. So, to find the first term, plug-in $n = 1$.

Then: $a_1 = (-1)^{1-1} \times 1 = 1$.

In a similar way, enter the natural numbers in order to find the other terms of the sequence. Therefore,

Plug in $n = 2$ as $a_2 = (-1)^{2-1} \times 2 = -2$.

Plug in $n = 3$ as $a_3 = (-1)^{3-1} \times 3 = 3$.

The first three terms of the sequence are $1, -2$, and 3.

Find the first five terms of the sequence with the general term $x_k = \left(-\frac{1}{2}\right)^k$, where k represents the position of a term in the sequence and starts with $k = 1$.

To find the first term, plug-in $k = 1$. Then: $x_1 = \left(-\frac{1}{2}\right)^1 = -\frac{1}{2}$.

In the same way, to find the 2nd term, plug-in $k = 2$. So, $x_2 = \left(-\frac{1}{2}\right)^2 = \frac{1}{4}$.

To find the 3rd term, plug-in $k = 3 \rightarrow x_3 = \left(-\frac{1}{2}\right)^3 = -\frac{1}{8}$.

Finally, $k = 4 \rightarrow x_3 = \left(-\frac{1}{2}\right)^4 = \frac{1}{16}$, and $k = 5 \rightarrow x_3 = \left(-\frac{1}{2}\right)^5 = -\frac{1}{32}$.

The first five terms of the sequence are $-\frac{1}{2}, \frac{1}{4}, -\frac{1}{8}, \frac{1}{16}$, and $-\frac{1}{32}$.

✎ Given two terms in an arithmetic sequence find the term named in the problem.

5) $a_{12} = 75$ and $a_7 = 40$
   Find a_{10}

6) $a_{10} = 36$ and $a_{20} = 156$
   Find a_{16}

✎ Given two terms in a geometric sequence find the term named.

7) $a_3 = -24$ and $a_7 = -384$
   Find a_5

8) $a_5 = 2$ and $a_7 = \frac{1}{2}$
   Find a_2

✎ Given the explicit formula. Find the first four terms and the 7th term.

9) $a_n = 2 + 3n$

10) $a_n = 2 \cdot a_{n-1}; a_1 = -3$

11) $a_n = (-3)^n + 1$

12) $a_n = a_{n-1} \cdot a_{n-2}; a_1 = -1, a_2 = 2$

13) $a_n = 81 \cdot \left(\frac{1}{3}\right)^{n+1}$

Find more at

Write Variable Expressions for Arithmetic Sequences

A sequence where the difference between consecutive terms is constant is known as an arithmetic sequence. To write the variable expression for an arithmetic sequence, the following steps should be taken:

Step 1: Identify the initial value, such as $x_1 = a$. This initial value is the first term of the sequence and is usually given in the problem, but if it is not, you will need to find it by observing the first term of the sequence.

Step 2: Determine the common difference, represented as d, between the terms. The common difference is the value that is added or subtracted to each term to get the next term in the sequence.

For example, if the sequence is 2, 5, 8, and 11, the common difference is 3, since each term is increased by 3 to get the next term.

Step 3: Add the first term to the product of the common difference multiplied by the position of the term in the sequence. The position of the term in the sequence is represented by the index of the term, starting from 1.

For example, the first term has an index of 1, the second term has an index of 2, and so on.

So, the variable expression for the nth term of an arithmetic sequence is:

$$x_n = a + (n-1)d.$$

It's important to note that this method will only work if the sequence is arithmetic in nature, if not the sequence is not arithmetic.

For example, if the sequence is 2, 4, 6, 8, 10, 12, $\cdots$, the initial value $a = 2$, and the common difference $d = 2$, and the variable expression for the nth term of the sequence is $x_n = 2 + (n-1)2 = 2n$.

Let's review an example:

Write the variable expression for the following sequence 3, 6, 9, 12, 15, $\cdots$.

According to the sequence, the common difference between the consecutive terms is $d = 3$. By dividing the terms by 3, obtains the sequence as 1, 2, 3, 4, 5, $\cdots$. Actually, the variable expression of this sequence is $a_n = 3n$. Since the first term is $a_1 = 3$, so, the expression $a_n = 3n$ is defined for $n \geq 1$.

Write the general formula for the following sequence 5, 6, 7, 8, 9, $\cdots$ in terms of variable k.

See that, the common difference between the consecutive terms is $d = 1$.

Subtract 4 from the terms of the sequence, then the obtained the sequence as:

1, 2, 3, 4, 5, $\cdots$.

Therefore, the general formula of this sequence in terms of variable k is $a_k = 4 + k$ such that $k \geq 1$.

Find the variable expression corresponding to the following sequence.

$$3, 7, 11, 15, 19, \cdots$$

Let $x_1, x_2, x_3, \cdots$ equivalent to the sequence of the content question. So, the first term is $x_1 = 3$. Look for the difference between consecutive terms.

Since the difference of the consecutive terms is the same value equal to $d = 4$.

The sequence is arithmetic and it can be rewritten as follows:

$$3, 3 + 4, 3 + 2 \times 4, 3 + 3 \times 4, 3 + 4 \times 4, \cdots.$$

It seems that the general rule is $x_n = 3 + 4n$. Since the first term in the sequence is 3, the term x_n is not defined for $n \leq 1$.

✎ Determine if the sequence is arithmetic. If it is, find the common difference.

14) 11, 15, 19, 23, $\cdots$ 16) 19, 14, 10, 7, $\cdots$

15) $-9, -7, -5, -3, \cdots$ 17) 5, 8, 11, 14, $\cdots$

✎ Solve.

18) An arithmetic sequence has an 8th term of 25 and an 11th term of 34. Find the common difference.

bit.ly/3Gmpz8K

Find more at

Write Variable Expressions for Geometric Sequences

A sequence where the ratio of consecutive terms is constant is known as a geometric sequence. To write the variable expression for a geometric sequence, the following steps should be taken:

Step 1: Identify the initial value, such as $x_1 = a$. This initial value is the first term of the sequence and is usually given in the problem, but if it is not, you will need to find it by observing the first term of the sequence.

Step 2: Determine the common ratio, represented as r, for the consecutive terms. The common ratio is the value that the terms are multiplied by to get the next term in the sequence.

For example, if the sequence is 2, 4, 8, and 16, the common ratio is 2, since each term is multiplied by 2 to get the next term.

Step 3: Multiply the first term by the product of the common ratio raised to the power of the position of the term in the sequence. The position of the term in the sequence is represented by the index of the term, starting from 1.

For example, the first term has an index of 1, the second term has an index of 2, and so on. So, the variable expression for the nth term of a geometric sequence is $x_n = ar^{n-1}$.

It's important to note that this method will only work if the sequence is geometric in nature, if not the sequence is not geometric.

Let's review some examples:

Write an equation to describe the following sequence 2, 4, 8, 16, 32, $\cdots$.

The given sequence is a geometric sequence since the ratio of consecutive terms is constant. To write the equation that describes this sequence, we can use the variable expression for the nth term of a geometric sequence: $x_n = ar^{n-1}$.

Here: $x_1 = 2$, $a = 2$, and the common ratio $r = 2$, since each term is multiplied by 2 to get the next term. So, the equation that describes this sequence is

$$x_n = 2(2)^{n-1} = 2^n.$$

So, the equation that describes the given sequence is $x_n = 2^n$.

In summary:

- The given recursive sequence x_1, x_2, x_3, $\cdots$ such that the ratio of the consecutive terms is equal to the same value, is called a geometric sequence.

- To write the variable expression for the geometric sequences, follow these steps:

    • Specify the initial values as $x_1 = a$.

    • Determine $r =$ the common ratio of the consecutive terms.

    • Multiply the first term by the product of the number of terms in the common ratio.

Write the general formula for the following sequence 6, 18, 54, 162, 486, $\cdots$ in terms of variable i.

By dividing the consecutive terms by previous terms, you notice that the common ratio is $r = 3$. According to the terms of the sequence, you can see that all terms have the common multiple of 2. Then the initial value is $x_1 = 2$. Therefore, by multiplying the first term by the common ratio, we get: $x_i = 2(3)^i$, where $i \geq 1$.

✎ Determine if the sequence is geometric. If it is, find the common ratio.

19) $-1, 6, 8, -36, 216, \cdots$

20) $-2, -2, -4, -8, -16, \cdots$

21) $1, 0.5, 0.25, 0.125, 0.625, \cdots$

22) $9, -3, 1, -\frac{1}{3}, \frac{1}{9}, \cdots$

Write a Formula for a Recursive Sequence

To determine the general formula for a recursive sequence, the following steps should be taken:

Step 1: Identify the initial values, such as a_1 or a_2. These initial values are usually given in the problem, but if they are not, you will need to find them by observing the first few terms of the sequence.

Step 2: Observe the relationship between the previous terms, such as a_{n-1} or a_{n-2}, that is consistent throughout the sequence by evaluating the differences and ratios of consecutive terms.

For example, you might notice that the nth term is always twice the $(n-1)$th term, or that the nth term is always the sum of the previous two terms.

Step 3: Express this relationship as a function of the previous term or terms.

For example, if you notice that the nth term is always twice the $(n-1)$th term, you would express this as a function as: $a_n = 2a_{n-1}$.

Step 4: You can then use this function to express the general formula of the recursive sequence which is $a_n = f(a_{n-1})$ or $a_n = f(a_{n-1}, a_{n-2})$, and so on.

It's important to note that this method will only work if the relationship between the terms is consistent throughout the sequence, if not the sequence is not recursive.

Let's review an example:

Find the recursive formula corresponding to the following sequence.

$$12, 17, 22, 27, 32, \cdots$$

The recursive formula can be found by observing the relationship between consecutive terms in the given sequence.

Notice that the difference between consecutive terms is 5.

So, the recursive formula could be $a_n = a_{n-1} + 5$.

To confirm that this is the correct recursive formula, we can substitute it back into the sequence:

$$a_1 = 12, a_2 = a_1 + 5 = 12 + 5 = 17, a_3 = a_2 + 5 = 17 + 5 = 22,$$

$$a_4 = a_3 + 5 = 22 + 5 = 27, a_5 = a_4 + 5 = 27 + 5 = 32.$$

We can see that this recursive formula generates the given sequence, so the recursive formula corresponding to the sequence is $a_n = a_{n-1} + 5$.

Find the recursive formula for the following sequence.

$$1, 3, 9, 27, 81, \cdots$$

Here, let the first term of this sequence $a_1 = 1$. Looking at the terms in this sequence, you can see that each term has an equal ratio to the previous term. Thus, the following relationship is obtained: $\frac{a_n}{a_{n-1}} = 3$. Now, rewrite this rule in terms of a_{n-1}. Therefore, $a_n = 3a_{n-1}$. You know that $a_1 = 1$. It means that the terms a_{n-1} define for $n \geq 2$.

Find the recursive formula corresponding to the following sequence.

$$1, 3, 2, -1, -3, -4, \cdots$$

Here, after evaluating the terms in the sequence, since the differences and ratios of consecutive terms are not the same value, therefore, look for another relationship between the previous term or even terms of the sequence. However, by evaluating the difference between the terms of the sequence, you can see that the difference of each term from the previous term makes the following sequence: $2, -1, -3, -4, \cdots$. Actually, the term of the last sequence has the formula as $a_n - a_{n-1}$. Therefore, the obtained formula is the recursive formula of the content of question $a_{n+1} = a_n - a_{n-1}$, where $n \geq 2$ $a_1 = 1$, and $a_2 = 3$.

✐ Solve.

23) Write a recursive formula for the following sequence that is valid for $n \geq 2$: $1, 3, 5, 11, 21, 43, \cdots$.

bit.ly/3WqJYPT

Chapter 13: Answers

1) $5, -1, 3, 5, 13$

2) $-1, -1, 0, 4, 17, 57$

3) $x_n = 2x_{n-1} - 1; x_1 = 3$

4) 32

5) 61

6) 108

7) -96

8) 16

9) $5, 8, 11, 14$ and $x_7 = 23$

10) $-3, -6, -12, -24$ and $x_7 = -192$

11) $-2, 10, -26, 82$ and $x_7 = -2{,}186$

12) $-1, 2, -2, -4$ and $x_7 = -256$

13) $9, 3, 1, \frac{1}{3}$ and $x_7 = \frac{1}{81}$

14) It's an arithmetic sequence with difference $d = 4$.

15) It's an arithmetic sequence with common $d = 2$.

16) It's not an arithmetic sequence.

17) It's an arithmetic sequence with common $d = 3$.

18) $d = 3$

19) It's not a geometric sequence.

20) It's not a geometric sequence.

21) It's a geometric sequence with common ratio $r = 0.5$.

22) It's a geometric sequence with common ratio $r = -\frac{1}{3}$.

23) $a_n = a_{n-1} + 2a_{n-2}; a_1 = 1, a_2 = 3$ and $n \geq 3$

Time to Test

Time to refine your algebra skills with a practice test

Take an Algebra I test to simulate the test day experience. After you've finished, score your test using the answer keys.

Before You Start

- You'll need a pencil and a calculator to take the test.

- For multiple questions, there are five possible answers. Choose which one is best.

- It's okay to guess. There is no penalty for wrong answers.

- Use the answer sheet provided to record your answers.

- **Scientific calculator is permitted for Algebra I Test.**

- After you've finished the test, review the answer key to see where you went wrong.

Good Luck!

North Carolina Algebra I Practice Test 1

2024

Total number of questions: 50

Total time: No time limit

Calculator is permitted for North Carolina Algebra I Test.

287

North Carolina Algebra I Practice Test Answer Sheet
Remove (or photocopy) this answer sheet and use it to complete the practice test.

North Carolina Algebra I Practice Test 1 Answer Sheet

1	Ⓐ Ⓑ Ⓒ Ⓓ	21	Ⓐ Ⓑ Ⓒ Ⓓ	41	Ⓐ Ⓑ Ⓒ Ⓓ	
2	Ⓐ Ⓑ Ⓒ Ⓓ	22	Ⓐ Ⓑ Ⓒ Ⓓ	42		
3	Ⓐ Ⓑ Ⓒ Ⓓ	23	Ⓐ Ⓑ Ⓒ Ⓓ	43	Ⓐ Ⓑ Ⓒ Ⓓ	
4	Ⓐ Ⓑ Ⓒ Ⓓ	24	Ⓐ Ⓑ Ⓒ Ⓓ	44	Ⓐ Ⓑ Ⓒ Ⓓ	
5	Ⓐ Ⓑ Ⓒ Ⓓ	25	Ⓐ Ⓑ Ⓒ Ⓓ	45	Ⓐ Ⓑ Ⓒ Ⓓ	
6	Ⓐ Ⓑ Ⓒ Ⓓ	26	Ⓐ Ⓑ Ⓒ Ⓓ	46	Ⓐ Ⓑ Ⓒ Ⓓ	
7	Ⓐ Ⓑ Ⓒ Ⓓ	27		47	Ⓐ Ⓑ Ⓒ Ⓓ	
8	Ⓐ Ⓑ Ⓒ Ⓓ	28	Ⓐ Ⓑ Ⓒ Ⓓ	48	Ⓐ Ⓑ Ⓒ Ⓓ	
9	Ⓐ Ⓑ Ⓒ Ⓓ	29	Ⓐ Ⓑ Ⓒ Ⓓ	49	Ⓐ Ⓑ Ⓒ Ⓓ	
10	Ⓐ Ⓑ Ⓒ Ⓓ	30	Ⓐ Ⓑ Ⓒ Ⓓ	50	Ⓐ Ⓑ Ⓒ Ⓓ	
11	Ⓐ Ⓑ Ⓒ Ⓓ	31	Ⓐ Ⓑ Ⓒ Ⓓ			
12	Ⓐ Ⓑ Ⓒ Ⓓ	32	Ⓐ Ⓑ Ⓒ Ⓓ			
13	Ⓐ Ⓑ Ⓒ Ⓓ	33	Ⓐ Ⓑ Ⓒ Ⓓ			
14		34				
15	Ⓐ Ⓑ Ⓒ Ⓓ	35	Ⓐ Ⓑ Ⓒ Ⓓ			
16	Ⓐ Ⓑ Ⓒ Ⓓ	36	Ⓐ Ⓑ Ⓒ Ⓓ			
17	Ⓐ Ⓑ Ⓒ Ⓓ	37	Ⓐ Ⓑ Ⓒ Ⓓ			
18	Ⓐ Ⓑ Ⓒ Ⓓ	38	Ⓐ Ⓑ Ⓒ Ⓓ			
19	Ⓐ Ⓑ Ⓒ Ⓓ	39	Ⓐ Ⓑ Ⓒ Ⓓ			
20		40	Ⓐ Ⓑ Ⓒ Ⓓ			

1) The graph of quadratic function q is shown on the grid. Which answer choice best represents the intercepts of the graph of q?

A. $x -$intercept $(-6,0)$ and $(2,0)$
   $y -$ intercept $(0,5)$
B. $x -$ intercept $(0,5)$
   $y -$ intercept $(-6,0)$ and $(2,0)$
C. $x -$ intercept $(5,0)$
   $y -$ intercept $(0,-6)$ and $(0,2)$
D. $x -$ intercept $(0,5)$
   $y -$intercept $(6,0)$ and $(-2,0)$

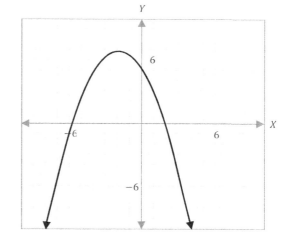

2) Which graph best represents $y = 8(0.75)^x$?

A.

B.

C.

D.

3) Which of the following is one solution to this equation?

$$x^2 + 2x - 5 = 0$$

    A. $\sqrt{2} + 1$

    B. $\sqrt{2} - 1$

    C. $\sqrt{6} + 1$

    D. $\sqrt{6} - 1$

4) Divide: $\frac{16n^6 - 32n^2 + 8n}{8n}$.

    A. $2n^5 - 4n$

    B. $2n^6 - 4n^2$

    C. $2n^5 - 4n + 1$

    D. $2n^6 - 4n^2 + 1$

$$4x^2 + 6x - 3, \; 3x^2 - 5x + 8$$

5) Which of the following is the sum of the two polynomials shown above?

    A. $x^2 + 5x + 4$

    B. $4x^2 - 6x + 3$

    C. $5x^2 + 3x + 4$

    D. $7x^2 + x + 5$

6) The table represents some points on the graph of linear function f. Which function represents f?

x	-1	0	3	4	7
$f(x)$	-48	-36	0	12	48

    A. $y = -12(x - 3)$

    B. $y = 2(12x - 1)$

    C. $y = -7(x - 4)$

    D. $y = 12(x - 3)$

7) The graph of the quadratic function is shown on the grid.
   Which function is best represented by this graph?

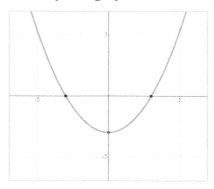

   A. $y = -3x^2 - 3$

   B. $y = -\frac{1}{3}x^2 - 3$

   C. $y = \frac{1}{3}x^2 - 3$

   D. $y = 3x^2 + 3$

8) The graph of $f(x) = x^2$ was translated as 1 unit to the left and 2 units up to create the graph of function n. Which function represents n?
   A. $n(x) = (x + 1)^2 - 2$
   B. $n(x) = (x - 1)^2 - 2$
   C. $n(x) = (x + 1)^2 + 2$
   D. $n(x) = (x - 1)^2 + 2$

9) The amount of water in an artificial lake decreases by 0.06% per day. The amount of water in the lake was initially 450,000 cubic meters. Which function models the amount of water in cubic meters remaining after a week?
   A. $f(w) = 1.03(450{,}000)^w$
   B. $f(w) = 450{,}000(0.93)^w$
   C. $f(w) = 450{,}000(1.03)^w$
   D. $f(w) = 0.93(450{,}000)^w$

10) Which expression is a factor of $15x^2 - 12x - 3$?
   A. $x + 1$
   B. $5x + 1$
   C. $5x - 1$
   D. $3x - 1$

11) Which inequality is best represented by the graph?

A. $3y + 2x < 2$

B. $3y + 2x \geq 2$

C. $3y - 2x \leq 2$

D. $3y - 2x > 2$

12) Which graph best represents $p(x) = (x - 2)(x + 3)$?

A.

B.

C.

D.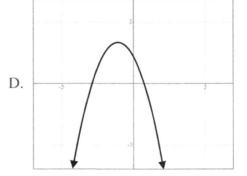

13) If $x \neq 0$ and $x = x^{-6}$, what is the value of x?

    A. 1

    B. 2

    C. -2

    D. 3

14) The expression $6x^2 + 4x - 10$ can be written in factored form as $(2x - m)(3x + 5)$, where m represents a number. What is the value of m?

15) Which of the following is the equation of a quadratic graph with a vertex $(3, -3)$?

    A. $y = 3x^2 - 3$

    B. $y = -3x^2 + 3$

    C. $y = x^2 + 3x - 3$

    D. $y = 4(x - 3)^2 - 3$

16) Which of the following is equal to $m^{\frac{1}{2}} n^{-2} m^4 n^{\frac{2}{3}}$?

    A. $m^2 n^{-\frac{4}{3}}$

    B. $\dfrac{1}{m^{\frac{9}{4}} n^{\frac{4}{3}}}$

    C. $\dfrac{m^{\frac{9}{4}}}{n^{\frac{4}{3}}}$

    D. $\dfrac{m^{\frac{9}{2}}}{n^{\frac{4}{3}}}$

17) An editor earns $400 per week for working 30 hours plus $15 per hour worked over 30 hours. She can work a maximum of 54 hours per week.

Which graph best represents the editor's weekly earnings in dollars for working h hours over 30?

A.

B.

C.

D.
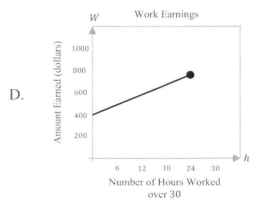

18) Which graph best represents a function with a range of all real numbers less than or equal to -1?

A.

B.

C.

D.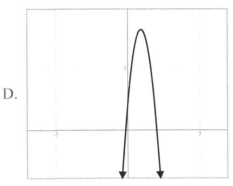

19) Which of the following is equal to the expression below?

$$\frac{8}{\sqrt{5} - 1}$$

A. $\sqrt{5} + 1$

B. $2(\sqrt{5} + 1)$

C. 1

D. $\sqrt{5}$

20) What is the negative solution to the equation $0 = \frac{2x^2}{5} - 10$?

21) The conversion of degrees to degrees Celsius can be represented by a linear relationship. The graph shows the linear relationship between y, the temperature in degrees Celsius, and x, the temperature in degrees Fahrenheit from the freezing point of water.

Temperatures

Which equation best represents this situation?

A. $y = \frac{5}{9}x$

B. $y = \frac{9}{5} + 32$

C. $y = \frac{5}{9}(x - 32)$

D. $y = \frac{9}{5}(x - 32)$

22) A football team had $20,000 to spend on supplies. The team spent $14,000 on new balls. New sports shoes cost $120 each. Which of the following inequalities represents the number of new shoes the team can purchase?

A. $120x - 14{,}000 \leq 20{,}000$

B. $120x + 14{,}000 \leq 20{,}000$

C. $120x + 14{,}000 \geq 20{,}000$

D. $14{,}000x + 120 \leq 20{,}000$

23) Jack earns $616 for his first 44 hours of work in a week and is then paid 1.5 times his regular hourly rate for any additional hours. This week, Jack needs $826 to pay his rent, bills, and other expenses. How many hours must he work to make enough money this week?

A. 54

B. 43

C. 48

D. 52

24) Which expression is equivalent to $35r^2 - 28r$?

A. $7r(5r - 4)$

B. $7r(5r + 4)$

C. $7(5r + 4)$

D. $7(5r - 4)$

25) A rocket is launched into the air from the ground. The table shows the height of the rocket, $h(x)$ at different times.

Time (seconds)	Height (meters)
5	748
10	1289
15	1621
20	1743
25	1651
30	1351
35	839

Based on the table, which function can best be used to model this situation?

A. $y = 12t^2 + 374$

B. $y = -4.2t^2 + 171t$

C. $y = -4.2t^2 + 165t - 30$

D. $y = 12t^2 - 218t + 1742$

26) The table represents some points on the graph of an exponential function.

x	$f(x)$
-1	13.5
0	18
1	24
2	32

Which function represents the same relationship?

A. $f(x) = 18 \left(\frac{4}{3}\right)^x$

B. $f(x) = 24 \left(\frac{4}{3}\right)^x$

C. $f(x) = 18 \left(\frac{3}{4}\right)^x$

D. $f(x) = 24 \left(\frac{3}{4}\right)^x$

27) Given $f(x^3) = 2x - 5$, for all values of x, what is the value of $f(8)$?

28) Which of the following is the same as: $0.000,000,000,000,042,121$?

A. 4.2121×10^{-14}

B. 42.121×10^{-12}

C. 4.2121×10^{-13}

D. 4.2121×10^{14}

29) Solve for x: $2 + \frac{3x}{x-5} = \frac{3}{5-x}$.

A. $\frac{4}{5}$

B. $\frac{6}{5}$

C. $\frac{7}{5}$

D. $\frac{8}{5}$

30) Which expression is equivalent to a factor of $3n^2 + 5n - (n+3)(3n-5)$?

    A. $3n - 5$

    B. $n + 3$

    C. $n + 15$

    D. $n + 5$

31) A salesman's total earnings from a job include a fixed amount plus an amount based on the number of hours worked. The values in the table represent the linear relationship between the number of hours worked and the salesman's total earnings in dollars.
What is the rate of change of the salesman's total earnings in dollars with respect to the number of hours worked?

Number of Hours Worked	Total Earnings
0	$35
4	$69
8	$103
12	$137
16	$171
20	$205

    A. 8.5

    B. 9.75

    C. 10

    D. 12

32) The following table represents the value of x and function $f(x)$. Which of the following could be the equation of the function $f(x)$?

    A. $f(x) = x^2 - 5$

    B. $f(x) = x^2 - 1$

    C. $f(x) = \sqrt{x+2}$

    D. $f(x) = \sqrt{x} + 4$

x	$f(x)$
1	5
4	6
9	7
16	8

33) The graph of $2y - 5x = 5$ is shown on the grid.

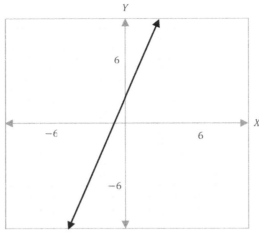

Which ordered pair is in the solution set of $2y - 5x \geq 5$?

A. $(1,1)$

B. $(0,1)$

C. $(1,0)$

D. $(-1,1)$

34) What is the positive value of x in solution set of this equation? $2 = \dfrac{3x}{2-x} - x$

35) Which graph shows a non-proportional linear relationship between x and y?

A.

B.

C.

D.

36) If $4x + y = 25$ and $x - 2z = 24$, what is the value of x?

A. 0

B. 4

C. 5

D. It cannot be determined from the information given.

37) Given the equation $4x - 2y = 18$, find the missing value in the ordered pair (__, -3).

A. -2

B. 2

C. 3

D. 6

38) Create a cubic function that has roots at $x = -1, 1, 3$.

A. $f(x) = x^3 + 3x^2 + x + 3$

B. $f(x) = x^3 - 3x^2 - x - 3$

C. $f(x) = x^3 - 3x^2 - x + 3$

D. $f(x) = x^3 - 6x^2 - 2x - 3$

39) If $(ax + 4)(bx + 3) = 10x^2 + cx + 12$ for all values of x and $a + b = 7$, what are the two possible values for c?

   A. $20, 22$

   B. $22, 21$

   C. $23, 26$

   D. $24, 23$

40) Which expression is a factor of $25x^2 + 5x + 1$?

   A. $5x + 1$

   B. $x - 1$

   C. $25x + 1$

   D. There are no real factors.

41) Which of the lines in the following figure is the graph of $x = -3$?

   A. A

   B. B

   C. C

   D. D

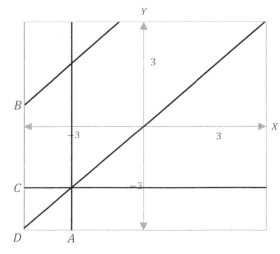

42) What is the value of the $y-$intercept of the graph of $f(x) = \frac{3}{4}(2)^x$?

43) If $9x + 3y = 69$, what is $3x + y + 22$?

    A. 45

    B. 43

    C. 23

    D. Cannot be determined

44) Which graph represents y as a function of x?

A.

B.

C.

D.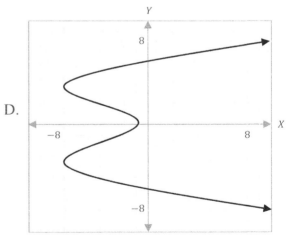

45) What appears to be the domain of the part of the exponential function graphed on the grid?

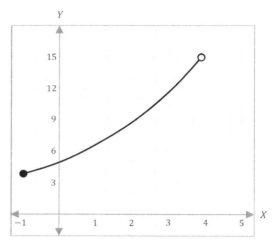

A. $-1 \leq x < 3.8$

B. $-1 < y \leq 3.8$

C. $3.75 \leq x < 15$

D. $3.75 < y \leq 15$

46) What are all real values of a in the following equation?

$$\frac{a}{4} + \frac{1}{2} = \frac{3}{a-2}$$

A. $a = 4$

B. $a = 2, a = 4$

C. $a = 2, a = 6$

D. $a = -4, a = 4$

47) The graph of $y = f(x)$ is shown in the xy−plane below. Which of the following equations could define $f(x)$?

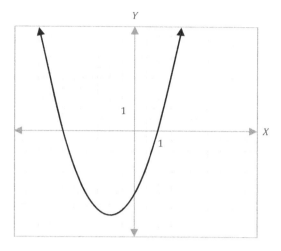

A. $x^2 + 2x - 3$

B. $-x^2 - 2x + 3$

C. $(x - 2)(x + 3)$

D. $(x - 1)^2 + 3$

48) In the xy−plane, the line determined by the points $(6, m)$ and $(m, 12)$ passes through the origin. Which of the following could be the value of m?

A. 6

B. 9

C. $6\sqrt{2}$

D. $\sqrt{6}$

49) The shaded region in the figure below represents the intersection of the graphs of $x \geq 0$, $y \geq 0$, and which of the following inequalities?

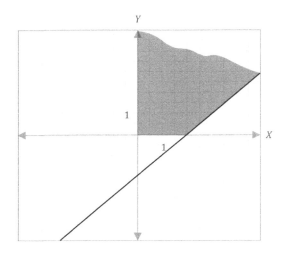

A. $y \geq 2x - 1$

B. $y \leq x + 2$

C. $y \geq x + 2$

D. $y \geq x - 2$

50) Which of the following is not an equivalent statement?

A. $x^{-2} = \frac{1}{x^2}$

B. $(x^2)^3 = x^6$

C. $x^6 - 5x^2 = x^2(x^4 - 5)$

D. $4x^2 - 16x + 8 = (2x - 4)^2$

End of North Carolina Algebra I Practice Test 1

North Carolina
Algebra I
Practice Test 2

2024

Total number of questions: 50

Total time: No time limit

Calculator is permitted for North Carolina Algebra I Test.

307

North Carolina Algebra I Practice Test Answer Sheet

Remove (or photocopy) this answer sheet and use it to complete the practice test.

North Carolina Algebra I Practice Test 2 Answer Sheet

1	Ⓐ Ⓑ Ⓒ Ⓓ	21	Ⓐ Ⓑ Ⓒ Ⓓ	41	Ⓐ Ⓑ Ⓒ Ⓓ
2	Ⓐ Ⓑ Ⓒ Ⓓ	22	Ⓐ Ⓑ Ⓒ Ⓓ	42	
3	Ⓐ Ⓑ Ⓒ Ⓓ	23	Ⓐ Ⓑ Ⓒ Ⓓ	43	Ⓐ Ⓑ Ⓒ Ⓓ
4	Ⓐ Ⓑ Ⓒ Ⓓ	24	Ⓐ Ⓑ Ⓒ Ⓓ	44	Ⓐ Ⓑ Ⓒ Ⓓ
5	Ⓐ Ⓑ Ⓒ Ⓓ	25	Ⓐ Ⓑ Ⓒ Ⓓ	45	Ⓐ Ⓑ Ⓒ Ⓓ
6	Ⓐ Ⓑ Ⓒ Ⓓ	26	Ⓐ Ⓑ Ⓒ Ⓓ	46	Ⓐ Ⓑ Ⓒ Ⓓ
7	Ⓐ Ⓑ Ⓒ Ⓓ	27		47	Ⓐ Ⓑ Ⓒ Ⓓ
8	Ⓐ Ⓑ Ⓒ Ⓓ	28	Ⓐ Ⓑ Ⓒ Ⓓ	48	Ⓐ Ⓑ Ⓒ Ⓓ
9	Ⓐ Ⓑ Ⓒ Ⓓ	29	Ⓐ Ⓑ Ⓒ Ⓓ	49	Ⓐ Ⓑ Ⓒ Ⓓ
10	Ⓐ Ⓑ Ⓒ Ⓓ	30	Ⓐ Ⓑ Ⓒ Ⓓ	50	Ⓐ Ⓑ Ⓒ Ⓓ
11	Ⓐ Ⓑ Ⓒ Ⓓ	31	Ⓐ Ⓑ Ⓒ Ⓓ		
12	Ⓐ Ⓑ Ⓒ Ⓓ	32	Ⓐ Ⓑ Ⓒ Ⓓ		
13	Ⓐ Ⓑ Ⓒ Ⓓ	33	Ⓐ Ⓑ Ⓒ Ⓓ		
14		34			
15	Ⓐ Ⓑ Ⓒ Ⓓ	35	Ⓐ Ⓑ Ⓒ Ⓓ		
16	Ⓐ Ⓑ Ⓒ Ⓓ	36	Ⓐ Ⓑ Ⓒ Ⓓ		
17	Ⓐ Ⓑ Ⓒ Ⓓ	37	Ⓐ Ⓑ Ⓒ Ⓓ		
18	Ⓐ Ⓑ Ⓒ Ⓓ	38	Ⓐ Ⓑ Ⓒ Ⓓ		
19	Ⓐ Ⓑ Ⓒ Ⓓ	39	Ⓐ Ⓑ Ⓒ Ⓓ		
20		40	Ⓐ Ⓑ Ⓒ Ⓓ		

1) The graph of quadratic function f was transformed to create the graph of

$g(x) = f(x + 3) + 2.$

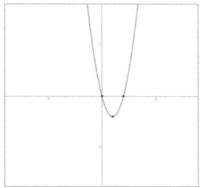

Which graph best represents g?

A.

B.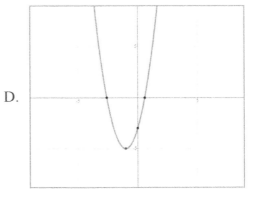

C.

D.

2) Which of the following is a factor of $6x^2 - 4x - 10$?
   A. $x - 1$
   B. $3x - 2$
   C. $3x - 5$
   D. $4x - 2$

3) The table shows the heights and the lengths of several rectangles.

Height (cm)	36	70	16	30	10	87	53	28	9	39
Length (cm)	21	20	32	11	18	45	38	23	42	39

What does the correlation coefficient for the data indicate about the strength of the linear association between the height and the length of these rectangles?
A. Weak positive correction

B. Weak negative correction

C. Strong negative correction

D. Strong positive correction

4) The graph of an exponential function is shown on the grid.

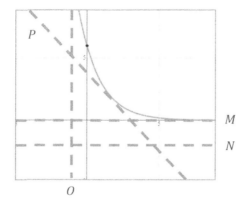

Which dashed line is an asymptote for the graph?
A. Line M

B. Line N

C. Line O

D. Line P

5) The graph of $f(x) = x^2$ was transformed to create the graph of $g(x) = f\left(-\frac{x}{2}\right) - 4$.

Which of the following statements is true about the graphs of f and g?
A. The graph of g is a reflection of the graph of f across the x −axis.

B. The vertex of the graph of g is 4 units to the right of the vertex of the graph of f.

C. The graph of g is a reflection of the graph of f across the y −axis.

D. The y −intercept of the graph of g is 4 units above the y −intercept of the graph of f.

6) Which of the following is equal to x^{yz} for all values of x, y, and z?

A. $x^{(y+z)}$

B. $x^y z$

C. $x^y x^z$

D. $(x^y)^z$

7) Simplify $-15a(a+b)^2 + 23a(a+b)^2 =$.

A. $8a(a+b)^2$

B. $8a$

C. $8(a+b)$

D. $8(a+b)^2$

8) Which graph best represents the solution set of $y > -3x$?

A.

B.

C.

D.

9) Which statement about the graph of $f(x) = 4(1.25)^x$ is true?

   A. The graph includes the point $(-1,2)$.

   B. There is an asymptote to the equation of $x = 0$.

   C. The x −intercept is 4.

   D. It is an increasing function.

10) The graph of a function is shown on the grid.

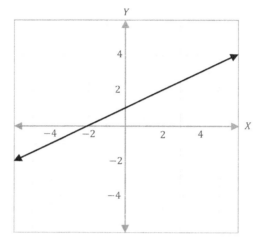

   Which ordered pair best represents the location of the y −intercept?

   A. $(0,1)$

   B. $(-2,0)$

   C. $(0,-2)$

   D. $(1,0)$

11) The graph below represents part of an exponential function.

   Which statement is best supported by the graph?

   A. The y −intercept is -1.

   B. The domain of the function is $(-\infty, 1]$.

   C. The range of the function is $(-1,3)$.

   D. The x −intercept is 1.

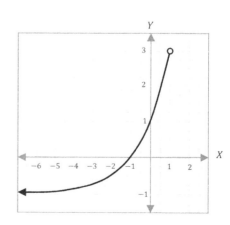

12) If $f(x^2) = 3x + 4$, for all positive values of x, what is the value of $f(121)$?

    A. 29

    B. -29

    C. -33

    D. 37

13) If a and b are solutions of the following equation, which of the following is the ratio $\frac{a}{b}$?

    $(a > b)$ $2x^2 - 11x + 8 = -3x + 18$

    A. $\frac{1}{5}$

    B. $-\frac{1}{5}$

    C. 5

    D. -5

14) The table shows the linear relationship between the distance in feet above the ground level and the time in seconds traveled by a dirigible.

    What is the rate of change of the distance in feet above the ground level with respect to the time that the dirigible traveled?

Dirigible

Time (seconds)	Distance Below See Level (feet)
0	72
14	198
27	315
49	513
91	891
103	999
146	1,386

15) What is the parent graph of the following function and what transformations have taken place on it? $y = x^2 - 2$

    A. The parent graph is $y = x^2$, which is shifted 2 units up.

    B. The parent graph is $y = x^2$, which is shifted 2 units down.

    C. The parent graph is $y = x^2$, which is shifted 2 units left.

    D. The parent graph is $y = x^2$, which is shifted 2 units right.

16) Which of the following is the expansion of $(3x + 2)^3$?

    A. $27x^3 + 54x^2 + 36x + 8$

    B. $3x^3 + 18x^2 + 18x + 8$

    C. $3x^3 + 12x^2 + 18x + 8$

    D. $27x^3 + 18x^2 + 12x + 8$

17) If a quadratic function with equation $y = ax^2 + 5x + 10$, where a is constant, passes through the point $(2, 12)$, what is the value of a^2?

    A. 2

    B. -2

    C. 4

    D. -4

18) A graph of a quadratic function is shown on the grid.
Which coordinates best represent the vertex of the graph?

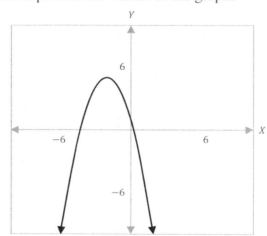

    A. $(0,1)$

    B. $(-2,5)$

    C. $(0.2,0)$

    D. $(-4.2,0)$

19) Which function is equivalent to $f(x) = 2(2 - 3x)^2 - 7$?

    A. $f(x) = 18x^2 - 24x + 1$

    B. $f(x) = 18x^2 + 1$

    C. $f(x) = -18x^2 - 24x + 1$

    D. $f(x) = 18x^2 + 24x + 1$

20) The graph of linear function g is shown on the grid.

   What is the zero of g?

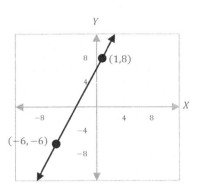

21) What is the solution to the following system of equations? $\begin{cases} \frac{-x}{2} + \frac{y}{4} = 1 \\ \frac{-5y}{6} + 2x = 4 \end{cases}$

   A. $x = 20, y = 50$

   B. $x = 20, y = 48$

   C. $x = 22, y = 48$

   D. $x = 48, y = 22$

22) If $8 + 2x$ is 16 more than 20, what is the value of $6x$?

   A. 40

   B. 55

   C. 62

   D. 84

23) Which graph corresponds to the following inequalities?

$$y \leq x + 4$$
$$2x + y \leq -4$$

A.

B.

C.

D.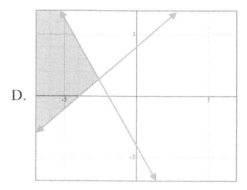

24) Which statement about $p(x) = 4x^2 - 81$ is true?

A. The factors of p are $(x - 4.5)$ and $(x - 4.5)$.

B. The factors of p are $(x + 9)$ and $(x - 4.5)$.

C. The factors of p are $(x - 4.5)$ and $(x - 9)$.

D. The factors of p are $(x + 4.5)$ and $(x - 4.5)$.

25) Which of the following points lies on line $2x + 4y = 6$?

A. $(2, 1)$

B. $(-1, 2)$

C. $(-2, 2)$

D. $(2, 2)$

26) Simplify $(3x - 5)^2$.

 A. $9x^2 + 30x + 25$

 B. $9x^2 - 30x + 25$

 C. $9x^2 + 25$

 D. $9x^2 - 25$

27) The value of a is directly proportional to the value of b. When $a = 2.5$, the value of b is 7. What is the value of b when $a = 15$?

28) A kingfisher jumps into a pond to hunt. The table shows the depth in feet of the kingfisher from the surface of the water after x seconds. The data can be shown by a quadratic function.

Pool

Time, x (seconds)	Depth of Kingfisher from Surface of Water, $j(x)$ (meter)
1	-2.5
3	-5
4	-5.1
5.5	-3.7
6	-2.9
6.5	-1.85

Which function best models the data?

 A. $y = 0.4x^2 - 2.88x$

 B. $y = 0.4x^2 - 2.88x + 2$

 C. $y = 0.075x^2 - 1.11x$

 D. $y = 0.075x^2 - 1.11x + 18.7$

29) Which of the following expression is equivalent to $16x^2 + 24$?

    A. $-8x(2x^2 + 3)$

    B. $(4x + 6)(4x - 6)$

    C. $8(2x^2 + 3)$

    D. $(4x + 6)(4x + 6)$

30) The table represents different values of function $g(x)$. What is the value of the expression $3g(-2) - 2g(3)$?

x	$g(x)$
-2	3
-1	2
0	1
1	0
2	-1
3	-2

    A. -2

    B. 3

    C. -12

    D. 13

31) A baker is buying barley flour and wheat flour and can spend no more than $630. Each kilogram of wheat flour costs $3, and each kilogram of barley flour costs $5. The inequality $3x + 5y \leq 630$ represents all possible combinations of x, the amount of wheat flour, and y, the amount of barley flours the customer can buy.

Which graph best represents the solution set for this inequality?

A.   B.

C.   D.

32) Point A lies on the line with equation $y - 3 = 2(x + 5)$. If the x-coordinate of A is 8, what is the y −coordinate of A?

A. 14

B. 16

C. 22

D. 29

33) What is the sum of $\sqrt{x-7}$ and $\sqrt{x}-7$ when $\sqrt{x}=4$?

A. 0

B. -1

C. 3

D. -3

34) The graph of quadratic function f is shown on the grid.
If $g(x)=x^2$ and $f(x)=g(x)+k$, what is the value of k?

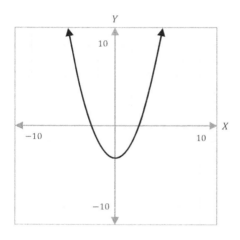

35) If $(x-2)^2+1>3x-1$, then x can equal which of the following?

A. 3

B. 4

C. 6

D. 8

36) Which of the following is equal to the expression below?
$$(3x-y)(2x+2y)$$

A. $6x^2-2y^2$

B. $4x^2+6xy-2y^2$

C. $6x^2+4xy-2y^2$

D. $6x^2+4xy+2y^2$

37) What is the solution of the equation $81 = 3^{2x}$?

    A. 2

    B. $\dfrac{3}{2}$

    C. $\dfrac{5}{2}$

    D. 1

38) The table shows the net revenue in thousands of dollars of a broker every month for nine months. An exponential function can be used to show the data.

Brokerage

Time, x (months)	Net Revenue, $r(x)$ (thousands of dollars)
1	247
2	276
3	311
4	347
5	393
6	426
7	488
8	548
9	617

Which function best models the data?

A. $r(x) = 1.12(246.7)^x$

B. $r(x) = 246.7(1.12)^x$

C. $r(x) = 1,423.9(0.83)^x$

D. $r(x) = 0.83(1,423.9)^x$

39) The graph models the linear relationship between the temperature of the air conditioner and the power consumption per hour.

Which of the following expressions best represents the rate of change of the temperature with respect to the power consumption?

A. $-\dfrac{200}{3}\,°C/KW$

B. $-\dfrac{3}{200}\,°C/KW$

C. $-\dfrac{100}{7}\,°C/KW$

D. $\dfrac{3}{200}\,°C/KW$

40) In an archery school, the coach has 107 arrows for the players. The coach will give each player on the team 9 arrows. The graph shows the linear relationship between y, the number of arrows of players, and x, the number of players.

The coach will use no more than 9 players for the team. Which set best represents the domain of the function for this situation?

A. {9,18,27,36,45,54,63,72,81}

B. {107,98,89,80,71,62,53,44,35}

C. {0,1,2,3,4,5,6,7,8,9}

D. {1,2,3,4,5,6,7,8,9,10}

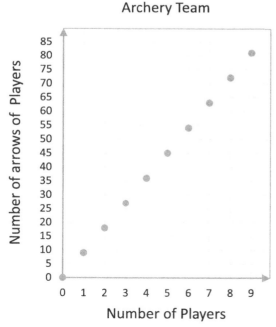

41) Find the solution (x, y) to the following system of equations.

$$-3x - y = 6$$
$$6x + 4y = 10$$

A. $(14, 5)$

B. $(6, 8)$

C. $(11, 17)$

D. $(-\frac{17}{3}, 11)$

42) What is the solution to $2(n - 1) = 3(n + 2) - 10$? _____

43) What is the sum of all values of n that satisfies $2n^2 + 16n + 24 = 0$?

A. 4

B. -4

C. 8

D. -8

44) Which graph best represents the solution set for this system of inequalities?

$$2x + y > -2$$
$$x + y \leq 1$$

A.

B.

C.

D.

45) Which graph best represents $y = 2\left(\frac{2}{3}\right)^x$?

A.

B.

C.

D.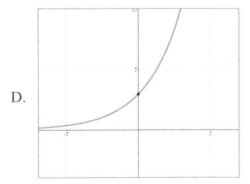

46) In an arithmetic sequence, the 4th term is 15, and the 9th term is 35. What is the sum of the first 10 terms of this series?

A. 171

B. 210

C. 308

D. 265

47) If $2x - 5y = 10$, what is x in terms of y?

A. $x = \frac{5}{2}y + 5$

B. $x = \frac{2}{5}y + 10$

C. $x = -\frac{5}{2}y - 5$

D. $x = -\frac{5}{2}y + 5$

48) Which of the following is equivalent to $\frac{x+(5x)^2+(3x)^3}{x}$?

    A. $27x^2 + 25x + 1$

    B. $16x^3 - 16x^2 + 1$

    C. $16x^2 + 25x + 1$

    D. $27x^3 + 16x^2 + 1$

49) What is the range of the function shown below?

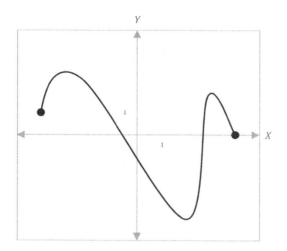

    A. $-4 \leq x \leq 3$

    B. $-4 \leq y \leq 3$

    C. $-4 \leq x \leq 4$

    D. $-4 \leq y \leq 4$

50) Sara opened a bank account that earns 2 percent interest compounded annually. Her initial deposit was $150, and she uses the expression $150(x)^n$ to find account's value after n years. What is the value of x in the expression?

    A. 0.02

    B. 0.20

    C. 20%

    D. 1.02

End of North Carolina Algebra I Practice Test 2

North Carolina Algebra I Practice Tests Answer Keys

Now, it's time to review your results to see where you went wrong and what areas you need to improve.

Algebra I Practice Test 1						Algebra I Practice Test 2					
1	A	21	C	41	A	1	C	21	C	41	D
2	D	22	B	42	$\frac{3}{4}$	2	C	22	D	42	2
3	D	23	A	43	A	3	A	23	B	43	D
4	C	24	A	44	C	4	A	24	D	44	C
5	D	25	B	45	A	5	A	25	B	45	C
6	D	26	A	46	D	6	D	26	B	46	B
7	C	27	−1	47	A	7	A	27	42	47	A
8	C	28	A	48	C	8	C	28	A	48	A
9	B	29	C	49	D	9	D	29	C	49	B
10	B	30	C	50	D	10	A	30	D	50	D
11	C	31	A			11	C	31	C		
12	A	32	D			12	D	32	D		
13	A	33	D			13	D	33	A		
14	2	34	1			14	9	34	−2		
15	D	35	B			15	B	35	D		
16	D	36	D			16	A	36	C		
17	D	37	C			17	C	37	A		
18	C	38	C			18	B	38	B		
19	B	39	C			19	A	39	B		
20	−5	40	D			20	−3	40	C		

EffortlessMath.com

North Carolina Algebra I Practice Test 1 Answers and Explanations

Algebra I Practice Tests 1 Explanations

1) Choice A is correct

The x −intercept of a graph is the point where the graph intersects the x −axis. For the given graph in the question, the points marked in the figure below are x −intercepts.

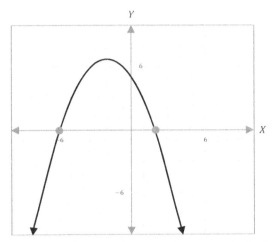

You see that the y −coordinate of these points on the x −axis is 0. So, the coordinate of the x −intercepts are $(-6,0)$ and $(2,0)$. Similarly, we know for y −intercept of a graph that it is the point where the graph intersects the y −axis. We know that the x −coordinate of any point on the y −axis is 0. Therefore,

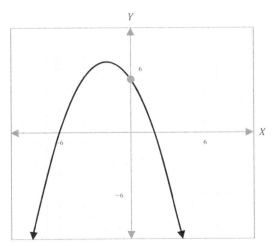

The y −intercept is one point with coordinates $(0,5)$. This information corresponds to choice A.

2) Choice D is correct

To find the graph of the exponential function of the question content, considering that the base of the exponential equation is 0.75 and smaller than 1, we can understand that the function is going down. It means one of the graphs of either A or D is the correct answer. In this case, substitute a few points in the function and check to see if it's correct or not. Choose point 0 and plug it into the function as follow: $y = 8(0.75)^0 = 8$.

That is, the corresponding graph must pass through the ordered pair (0,8). Therefore, the correct answer is D.

3) Choice D is correct

$$x_{1,2} = \frac{-b \pm \sqrt{b^2 - 4ac}}{2a} \quad ax^2 + bx + c = 0$$

$x^2 + 2x - 5 = 0 \Rightarrow$ then: $a = 1, b = 2$ and $c = -5$

$$x = \frac{-2 + \sqrt{2^2 - 4(1)(-5)}}{2(1)} = \sqrt{6} - 1 \qquad x = \frac{-2 - \sqrt{2^2 - 4(1)(-5)}}{2(1)} = -1 - \sqrt{6}$$

4) Choice C is correct

$$\frac{16n^6 - 32n^2 + 8n}{8n} = \frac{16n^6}{8n} - \frac{32n^2}{8n} + \frac{8n}{8n} = 2n^5 - 4n + 1$$

5) Choice D is correct

The sum of the two polynomials is $(4x^2 + 6x - 3) + (3x^2 - 5x + 8)$

This can be rewritten by combining like terms:

$$(4x^2 + 6x - 3) + (3x^2 - 5x + 8) = (4x^2 + 3x^2) + (6x - 5x) + (-3 + 8)$$

$$= 7x^2 + x + 5$$

6) Choice D is correct

Given that the data is related to a linear function and $x = 3$ is the zero of the function, therefore it has a factor of $(x - 3)$. Now, substitute some points like 0 and 4 in choices A and D to determine the correct answer. So,

A. $x = 0 \rightarrow y = -12(0 - 3) = 36$, it's not true.

D. $x = 0 \rightarrow y = 12(0 - 3) = -36$, it's true and correct answer.

7) Choice C is correct

Since the function is quadratic and the graph is going upward, then one of the choices of either C or D is the answer. Because the corresponding function must satisfy all points on the graph. So, substitute a few points like $(0, -3)$ and $(-3, 0)$ on the graph in the remaining choices.

C. $(0, -3) \rightarrow \frac{1}{3}(0)^2 - 3 = -3$. It's true.

D. $(0, -3) \rightarrow 3(0)^2 + 3 = 3 \neq -3$. It's NOT true.

8) Choice C is correct

We know that the graph $y = f(x) + k$; $k > 0$, is shifted k units up of the graph $y = f(x)$, and if $k < 0$, it is shifted k units down. Then, $y = x^2 + 2$ is shifted 2 units up of the graph $y = x^2$. On the other hand, to shift 1 unit to the left, a negative number $k < 0$ must be substituted for k in the equation $y = f(x - k)$. Therefore,

$$n(x) = \left(x - (-1)\right)^2 + 2 \rightarrow n(x) = (x + 1)^2 + 2.$$

9) Choice B is correct

The amount of water in the lake was initially 450,000 cubic meters. It means that the value of f for $w = 0$ is $f(0) = 450,000$. Put $w = 0$ in the choices and compare with $f(0) = 450,000$.

A. $f(0) = 1.03(450,000)^0 = 1.03$

B. $f(0) = 450,000(0.93)^0 = 450,000$

C. $f(0) = 450,000(1.03)^0 450,000$

D. $f(0) = 0.93(450,000)^0 = 0.93$

Then, one of the choices B or C is the solution. Note that in a descending exponential function, the base is less than one. Therefore, choice B is correct.

10) Choice B is correct

Notice that $(bx - a)$ is a factor of an expression whenever $x = \frac{a}{b}$ is a zero of that expression. Check which of the choices is a zero of the expression.

A. $x + 1 = 0 \rightarrow x = -1 \rightarrow 15(-1)^2 - 12(-1) - 3 = 15 + 12 - 3 = 24 \neq 0$

B. $\qquad 5x + 1 = 0 \rightarrow x = -\frac{1}{5} \rightarrow 15\left(-\frac{1}{5}\right)^2 - 12\left(-\frac{1}{5}\right) - 3 = 15\left(\frac{1}{25}\right) + \frac{12}{5} - 3 =$
$\frac{15+60-75}{25} = 0$

C. $\qquad 5x - 1 = 0 \rightarrow x = \frac{1}{5} \rightarrow 15\left(\frac{1}{5}\right)^2 - 12\left(\frac{1}{5}\right) - 3 = 15\left(\frac{1}{25}\right) - \frac{12}{5} - 3 = \frac{15-60-75}{25} =$
$-\frac{24}{5} \neq 0$

D. $\qquad 3x - 1 = 0 \rightarrow x = \frac{1}{3} \rightarrow 15\left(\frac{1}{3}\right)^2 - 12\left(\frac{1}{3}\right) - 3 = 15\left(\frac{1}{9}\right) - \frac{12}{3} - 3 = \frac{15-36-27}{9} =$
$-\frac{16}{3} \neq 0$

Therefore, B is the correct answer.

11) Choice C is correct

Since the represented graph of the inequality is shown as a line, so, the sign of inequality is less than or equal to $\leq$ or greater than or equal to $\geq$. Now, to find the inequality of the given graph, substitute a number of points of the solution region into the given inequalities. Substitute $x = 0$, and $y = 0$ into the remaining inequalities, that is the choices of either B or C. Therefore,

B. $(0,0) \rightarrow 3(0) + 2(0) \geq 2 \rightarrow 0 \geq 2$, this is not true.

C. $(0,0) \rightarrow 3(0) - 2(0) \leq 2 \rightarrow 0 \leq 2$, this is true and the correct answer.

12) Choice A is correct

First, find the zeros of the function $p(x)$:

$$p(x) = 0 \rightarrow (x - 2)(x + 3) = 0 \rightarrow x - 2 = 0 \rightarrow x = 2, \text{ or } x + 3 = 0 \rightarrow x = -3$$

Graphs A and C have roots 2 and -3.

Now, simplify the equation of the function:

$$p(x) = (x - 2)(x + 3) = x^2 + x - 6.$$

The coefficient of the leading term in the polynomial function is positive, so the end behavior of the function is $+\infty$ when $x \rightarrow \pm\infty$. Graph A is upward and thus the best represents the polynomial $p(x)$.

13) Choice A is correct

The easiest way to solve this one is to plug the answers into the equation.

When you do this, you will see the only time $x = x^{-6}$ is when $x = 1$ or $x = 0$.

Only $x = 1$ is provided in the choices.

14) The value of m is 2

Let the equation be $P(x) = 6x^2 + 4x - 10$. Factor 2 from the equation: $6x^2 + 4x - 10 = 2(3x^2 + 2x - 5)$. We just need to factor the expression $Q(x) = 3x^2 + 2x - 5$. First, find the roots of the equation $3x^2 + 2x - 5 = 0$ by evaluating the discriminant expression $\Delta = b^2 - 4ac$ of the quadratic equation as $ax^2 + bx + c = 0$. So, we have:

$$\Delta = (2)^2 - 4(3)(-5) = 4 + 60 = 64 \rightarrow \Delta > 0$$

Use the quadratic formula: $x_{1,2} = \frac{-b \pm \sqrt{\Delta}}{2a}$. Therefore, the zeros of the equation $3x^2 + 2x - 5 = 0$ are $x_1 = \frac{-2+\sqrt{64}}{2(3)} = \frac{-2+8}{6} = 1$ or $x_2 = \frac{-2-\sqrt{64}}{2(3)} = \frac{-2-8}{6} = -\frac{10}{6} = -\frac{5}{3}$.

Then, the equation $Q(x) = 0$, can be written in factored form as

$$(x-1)\left(x + \frac{5}{3}\right) = 0$$

Multiply both sides of the equation by 3:

$$3 \times (x-1)\left(x + \frac{5}{3}\right) = 3 \times 0 \rightarrow (x-1)(3x + 5) = 0$$

It's equivalent to the equation $3x^2 + 2x - 5 = 0$. Now, to obtain the expression $P(x)$, multiply both sides of the expression $Q(x)$ by 2. Thus,

$$P(x) = 2Q(x) \rightarrow P(x) = 2(x-1)(3x+5) \rightarrow P(x) = (2x-2)(3x+5)$$

Compare the resulting factor with the factored expression in the content of the question:

$$(2x-2)(3x+5) = (2x-m)(3x+5)$$

You can see that the value of m is 2.

15) Choice D is correct

The value of x of the vertex in the equation of a quadratic in standard form is: $x = \frac{-b}{2a}$. (The standard equation of a quadratic is: $ax^2 + bx + c = 0$)
Let's find the vertex of each choice provided:

    A. $y = 3x^2 - 3$ The vertex is: $(0, -3)$

    B. $y = -3x^2 + 3$ The vertex is: $(0, 3)$

    C. $y = x^2 + 3x - 3$ The vertex is: $(\frac{-3}{2}, \frac{-21}{4})$

    D. $y = 4(x - 3)^2 - 3$

The vertex form of a parabola equation is in the form of $y = a(x - h)^2 + k$, where (h, k) is the vertex. Then $h = 3$ and $k = -3$. (This is the answer)

16) Choice D is correct

$$m^{\frac{1}{2}} n^{-2} m^4 n^{\frac{2}{3}} \rightarrow m^{\frac{1}{2}}. m^4 = m^{\frac{1}{2}+4} = m^{\frac{9}{2}}, \quad n^{-2}.n^{\frac{2}{3}} = n^{-2+\frac{2}{3}} = n^{-\frac{4}{3}} = \frac{1}{n^{\frac{4}{3}}},$$

$$m^{\frac{9}{2}}.\frac{1}{n^{\frac{4}{3}}} = \frac{m^{\frac{9}{2}}}{n^{\frac{4}{3}}}$$

17) Choice D is correct

From the content of the question, we know that the starting point is 0 with the value of $400 (Corresponds to the ordered pair $(0, 400)$.). So far, one of the choices of either A or D can be the correct answer. She can work a maximum of 54 hours per week. Then the endpoint of the domain is $54 - 30 = 24$. Because the editor earns $15 per hour worked over 30 hours, the final income is $15 \times 24 + 400 = 760$. It is the point at the coordinate $(24, 760)$. Therefore, choice D is the answer.

18) Choice C is correct

The choices are the graphs of quadratic functions. If the range of a quadratic function is less than a number, it means that the function has a maximum value. Then, either graph C or D is the answer. The maximum value is -1, then the graph C is the correct answer.

19) Choice B is correct

Multiply by the conjugate: $\frac{\sqrt{5}+1}{\sqrt{5}+1}$

$$\frac{8}{\sqrt{5}-1} \times \frac{\sqrt{5}+1}{\sqrt{5}+1} = \frac{8(\sqrt{5}+1)}{4} = 2(\sqrt{5} + 1)$$

20) The negative solution is -5

Simplify, $\frac{2x^2}{5} - 10 = 0$. First, multiply both sides of the equation by 5:

$$5 \times \left(\frac{2x^2}{5} - 10\right) = 5 \times 0 \rightarrow 5 \times \frac{2x^2}{5} - 5 \times 10 = 0 \rightarrow 2x^2 - 50 = 0.$$

Add 50 to both sides: $2x^2 - 50 + 50 = 0 + 50 \rightarrow 2x^2 = 50$. Now, divide both sides by 2. Then, $2x^2 \div 2 = 50 \div 2 \rightarrow x^2 = 25$. Therefore, $x = \pm 5$.

21) Choice C is correct

The $x-$intercept is equal to 32. Actually, 32 is the root of the equation corresponding to the graph. Evaluate the root of the equation of each choice.

A. $y = 0 \rightarrow \frac{5}{9}x = 0 \rightarrow x = 0$

B. $y = 0 \rightarrow \frac{9}{5}x + 32 = 0 \rightarrow \frac{9}{5}x = -32 \rightarrow x = -\frac{160}{9}$

C. $y = 0 \rightarrow \frac{5}{9}(x - 32) = 0 \rightarrow x - 32 = 0 \rightarrow x = 32$

D. $y = 0 \rightarrow \frac{9}{5}(x - 32) = 0 \rightarrow x - 32 = 0 \rightarrow x = 32$

Therefore, one of the choices C or D is the answer. To determine the correct model, substitute another point on the graph in the possible equations. For example, we check point $x = 104$. So,

C. $x = 104 \rightarrow \frac{5}{9}(104 - 32) = \frac{5}{9}(72) = 5(8) = 40$

D. $x = 104 \rightarrow \frac{9}{5}(104 - 32) = \frac{9}{5}(72) = \frac{648}{5} = 129.6$

Thus, the choice C is the best representation of the graph.

22) Choice B is correct

Let x be the number of new shoes the team can purchase. Therefore, the team can purchase $120x$. The team had \$20,000 and spent \$14,000. Now the team can spend on new shoes \$6,000 at most. Now, write the inequality: $120x + 14,000 \leq 20,000$

23) Choice A is correct

The amount of money that Jack earns for one hour: $\frac{\$616}{44} = \$14$

The number of additional hours that he works to make enough money is: $\frac{\$826 - \$616}{1.5 \times \$14} = 10$

The number of total hours is: $44 + 10 = 54$

24) Choice A is correct

First, determine the common factors from each part of the expression: $35r^2 = 7 \times 5 \times r \times r$ and $28r = 7 \times 2 \times 2 \times r$. The common factors are 7 and r. Now, Rewrite as follow:

$$35r^2 - 28r = 7r(5r) - 7r(4)$$

Factor in $7r$: It means that $7r(5r) - 7r(4) = 7r(5r - 4)$. Therefore,

$$35r^2 - 28r = 7r(5r - 4).$$

25) Choice B is correct

By looking at the choices, you can see that the expected model is a quadratic function. After the rocket is launched, the height first increases and then decreases. Therefore, the suitable model has a maximum value. So, the coefficient of the leading term is negative. Either choice B or C is true. Now, substitute some points of the left column on the functions of B and C, then compare the corresponding values to the value of the right column.

Time (seconds)	Height (meters) for Choice C, y	Height (meters) for Choice B, y
5	690	750
10	1200	1290
15	1500	1620
20	1590	1740
25	1470	1650
30	1140	1350
35	600	840

The choice B is the best answer.

26) Choice A is correct

For this purpose, all the points in the left column of the table must generate the corresponding value of the right column in the suitable function. So, we have:

$$A. \ x = -1 \rightarrow f(-1) = 18\left(\frac{4}{3}\right)^{-1} = 18\left(\frac{3}{4}\right) = 13.5$$

$$x = 0 \rightarrow f(0) = 18\left(\frac{4}{3}\right)^{0} = 18(1) = 18$$

$$x = 1 \rightarrow f(1) = 18\left(\frac{4}{3}\right)^{1} = 18\left(\frac{4}{3}\right) = 24$$

$x = 2 \rightarrow f(2) = 18\left(\frac{4}{3}\right)^2 = 18\left(\frac{16}{9}\right) = 32$, it's correct answer.

B. $x = -1 \rightarrow f(-1) = 24\left(\frac{4}{3}\right)^{-1} = 24\left(\frac{3}{4}\right) = 18$, it's NOT true!

C. $x = -1 \rightarrow f(-1) = 18\left(\frac{3}{4}\right)^{-1} = 18\left(\frac{4}{3}\right) = 24$, it's NOT true!

D. $x = -1 \rightarrow f(-1) = 24\left(\frac{3}{4}\right)^{-1} = 24\left(\frac{4}{3}\right) = 32$, it's NOT true!

27) The value of $f(8)$ is -1

To find the value of $f(8)$, make $x^3 = 8$. Then,

$$x^3 = 8 \rightarrow x = 2$$

Finally, $x = 2 \rightarrow f(2^3) = 2(2) - 5 = -1 \rightarrow f(8) = -1$.

28) Choice A is correct

In scientific notation, all numbers are written in the form of $m \times 10^n$, where m is between 1 and 10. To find an equivalent value of $0.000,000,000,000,042,121$, move the decimal point to the right so that you have a number that is between 1 and 10. Then: 4.2121. Now, determine how many places the decimal moved in step 1, then put it as the power of 10. We moved the decimal point 14 places. Then: 10^{-14} when the decimal moves to the right, the exponent is negative. Then: $0.000,000,000,000,042,121 = 4.2121 \times 10^{-14}$.

29) Choice C is correct

First, find a common denominator for 2 and $\frac{3x}{x-5}$. It's $x - 5$. Then:
$$2 + \frac{3x}{x-5} = \frac{2(x-5)}{x-5} + \frac{3x}{x-5} = \frac{2x-10+3x}{x-5} = \frac{5x-10}{x-5}.$$
Now, multiply the numerator and denominator of $\frac{3}{5-x}$ by -1. Then: $\frac{3\times(-1)}{(5-x)\times(-1)} = \frac{-3}{x-5}$. Rewrite the expression: $\frac{5x-10}{x-5} = \frac{-3}{x-5}$. Since the denominators of both fractions are equal, then, the numerators must be equal:
$$5x - 10 = -3 \rightarrow 5x = 7 \rightarrow x = \frac{7}{5}$$

30) Choice C is correct

First, calculate the product of the multiplication term: $(n + 3)(3n - 5) = 3n^2 + 4n - 15$. Substitute the obtained term and simplify $3n^2 + 5n - 3n^2 - 4n + 15 = n + 15$. Then:

$$3n^2 + 5n - (n + 3)(3n - 5) = n + 15.$$

31) Choice A is correct

The rate of change for a linear relationship is the slope of the line passing through two ordered pairs, where the first component of the ordered pair corresponds to the numbers in the left column of the table and the second component is the opposite number in the right column. Therefore, use the following formula:

Rate of Change $= \frac{y_2 - y_1}{x_2 - x_1}$,

So, for ordered pairs like (8,103) and (16,171), we get:

Rate of Change $= \frac{171 - 103}{16 - 8} = \frac{68}{8} = 8.5$.

32) Choice D is correct

Let's review the choices when $x = 1$.

     A. $f(x) = x^2 - 5$ if $x = 1 \rightarrow f(1) = (1)^2 - 5 = 1 - 5 = -4 \neq 5$

     B. $f(x) = x^2 - 1$ if $x = 1 \rightarrow f(1) = (1)^2 - 1 = 1 - 1 = 0 \neq 5$

     C. $f(x) = \sqrt{x + 2}$ if $x = 1 \rightarrow f(1) = \sqrt{1 + 2} = \sqrt{3} \neq 5$

     D. $f(x) = \sqrt{x} + 4$ if $x = 1 \rightarrow f(1) = \sqrt{1} + 4 = 5$

Only choice D provides a correct answer.

33) Choice D is correct

Put the given ordered pair into the inequality. Any ordered pair that applies to the inequality is the answer to the question. Therefore,

     A. $(1,1) \rightarrow 2(1) - 5(1) = 2 - 5 = -3 \ngeq 5$

     B. $(0,1) \rightarrow 2(1) - 5(0) = 2 - 0 = 2 \ngeq 5$

     C. $(1,0) \rightarrow 2(0) - 5(1) = 0 - 5 \ngeq 5$

     D. $(-1,1) \rightarrow 2(1) - 5(-1) = 2 + 5 = 7 \geq 5$

By checking the choices, we find that choice D is correct.

34) The correct answer is 1

First, find a common denominator for x and $\frac{3x}{2-x}$. It's $2 - x$. Then:

$$\frac{3x}{2-x} - x = \frac{3x}{2-x} - \frac{x(2-x)}{2-x} = \frac{3x-2x+x^2}{2-x} = \frac{x^2+x}{2-x}.$$

Now, multiply both sides of equation $1 = \frac{x^2+x}{2-x}$ by $2 - x$. Then:

$$(2 - x) \times 2 = (2 - x) \times \frac{x^2+x}{2-x}.$$

Rewrite the expression: $4 - 2x = x^2 + x$. Simplify as $x^2 + 3x - 4 = 0$.

Now, factor it. To factorize this quadratic equation, we need to find two numbers that multiply to -4 (the constant term) and add up to 3 (the coefficient of the x term).

These numbers are 4 and -1 because 4 multiplied by -1 equals -4 and 4 plus -1 equals 3.

So, the factored form of the equation is: $(x + 4)(x - 1) = 0$

Setting each factor equal to zero gives the solutions: $(x + 4) = 0 \Rightarrow x = -4$ and

$$(x - 1) = 0 \Rightarrow x = 1$$

So, the solutions to the equation are $x = -4$ and $x = 1$.

Only $x = 1$ is a positive solution.

35) Choice B is correct

A linear equation is a relationship between two variables, x, and y, and can be written in the form of $y = mx + b$. A non-proportional linear relationship takes on the form $y = mx + b$, where $b \neq 0$ and its graph is a line that does not cross through the origin. Only in graph B, the line does not pass through the origin.

36) Choice D is correct

We have two equations and three unknown variables, therefore x cannot be obtained.

37) Choice C is correct

Substitute -3 for y in the equation and solve for x.

$$4x - 2y = 18 \rightarrow 4x - 2(-3) = 18 \rightarrow 4x + 6 = 18 \rightarrow 4x = 12 \rightarrow x = \frac{12}{4} \rightarrow x$$
$$= 3$$

38) Choice C is correct

$-1, 1$ and 3 are the roots of the function so: $x = 1 \rightarrow x - 1 = 0$.

$$x = -1 \rightarrow x + 1 = 0$$

$$x = 3 \rightarrow x - 3 = 0$$

Multiply the terms together: $f(x) = (x - 1)(x + 1)(x - 3) \rightarrow : f(x) = (x^2 - 1)(x - 3)$

FOIL: $f(x) = (x^2 - 1)(x - 3) \rightarrow f(x) = x^3 - 3x^2 - x + 3$

39) Choice C is correct

You can find the possible values of a and b in $(ax + 4)(bx + 3)$ by using the given equation $a + b = 7$ and finding another equation that relates the variables a and b. Since $(ax + 4)(bx + 3) = 10x^2 + cx + 12$, expand the left side of the equation to obtain

$$abx^2 + 4bx + 3ax + 12 = 10x^2 + cx + 12$$

Since ab is the coefficient of x^2 on the left side of the equation and 10 is the coefficient of x^2 on the right side of the equation, it must be true that $ab = 10$

The coefficient of x on the left side is $4b + 3a$ and the coefficient of x on the right side is c. Then: $4b + 3a = c$, $a + b = 7$, then: $a = 7 - b$

Now, plug in the value of a in equation $ab = 10$. Then:

$$ab = 10 \rightarrow (7 - b)b = 10 \rightarrow 7b - b^2 = 10$$

Add $-7b + b^2$ on both sides. Then: $b^2 - 7b + 10 = 0$

Solve for b using the factoring method. $b^2 - 7b + 10 = 0 \rightarrow (b - 5)(b - 2) = 0$

Thus, either $b = 2$ and $a = 5$, or $b = 5$ and $a = 2$. If $b = 2$ and $a = 5$, then

$4b + 3a = c \rightarrow 4(2) + 3(5) = c \rightarrow c = 23$. If $b = 5$ and $a = 2$, then, $4b + 3a = c \rightarrow$

$4(5) + 3(2) = c \rightarrow c = 26$. Therefore, the two possible values for c are 23 and 26.

40) Choice D is correct

We know that the factors of an expression $p(x)$ are the zeros of the equation $p(x) = 0$. Find the zeros of the quadratic equation as follow. First, evaluate Δ from the formula $\Delta = b^2 - 4ac$ for the quadratic equation like $ax^2 + bx + c = 0$. Then:

$$\Delta = (5)^2 - 4(25)(1) = 25 - 100 = -75 < 0$$

There are no real solutions. Therefore, there are no real factors.

41) Choice A is correct

Line A is the graph of $x = -3$.

42) The value of the y-intercept of the graph is $\frac{3}{4}$

The y-intercept is a point with the coordinate $(0, f(0))$, where f is the equation of function y. So, by plugging $x = 0$, we get the y-intercept. Therefore,

$$x = 0 \rightarrow y = f(0) = \frac{3}{4}(2)^0 = \frac{3}{4}.$$

43) Choice A is correct

To solve this, we can write the given equation in the form of the equation we want to find:

$9x + 3y = 69$

Dividing the equation by 3, we get:

$3x + y = 23$

So, if we add 22 to the equation we get:

$3x + y + 22 = 23 + 22 = 45$

Therefore, the answer is 45.

44) Choice C is correct

In order to identify the function of a graph, the lines parallel to the axis corresponding to the outputs (here the y-axis) must intersect the graph in at most one point. Therefore, finding

A.   B.

C.   D.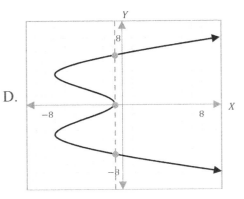

even one line with this property means that the given graph is not a function. As shown in the graphs below.

Graphs A, B, and D clearly do not represent a function. Since in graph C, each line parallel to the $y-$axis has at most one point of intersection, it can represent a function.

45) Choice A is correct

Since the domain of the graph of the function is the image of the graph on the $x-$axis. Draw the image of the graph on the $x-$axis.

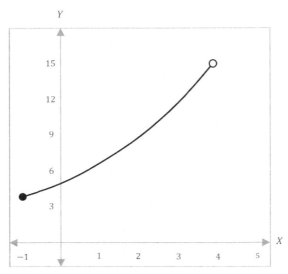

Therefore, the inequality $-1 \le x < 3.8$ is the solution set of the domain of the part of the graph.

46) Choice D is correct

To solve $\frac{a}{4} + \frac{1}{2} = \frac{3}{a-2}$, first, multiply by the least common multiplier $4(a-2)$. Then:

$\frac{a}{4}.4(a-2) + \frac{1}{2}.4(a-2) = \frac{3}{a-2}.4(a-2)$. Now, simplify: $a(a-2) + 2(a-2) = 12 \rightarrow$

$$a^2 - 2a + 2a - 4 = 12 \rightarrow a^2 = 16 \rightarrow a = \sqrt{16} \rightarrow a = -4 , a = 4.$$

47) Choice A is correct

The graph of $y = f(x)$ crosses the x-axis at $x = -3$ and $x = 1$, and crosses the y-axis at $y = -3$ and has its vertex at the point $(-1, -4)$. Therefore, the ordered pairs $(-3,0)$, $(1,0)$, $(0,-3)$, and $(-1,-4)$ must satisfy the equation for $f(x)$. Furthermore, because the graph opens upward, the equation defining $f(x)$ must have a positive leading coefficient. All of these conditions are met by the equation: $f(x) = x^2 + 2x - 3$

48) Choice C is correct

The line passes through the origin, $(6, m)$ and $(m, 12)$. Any two of these points can be used to find the slope of the line. Since the line passes through $(0, 0)$ and $(6, m)$, the slope of the line is equal to $\frac{m-0}{6-0} = \frac{m}{6}$. Similarly, since the line passes through $(0, 0)$ and $(m, 12)$, the slope of the line is equal to $\frac{12-0}{m-0} = \frac{12}{m}$. Since each expression gives the slope of the same line, it must be true that $\frac{m}{6} = \frac{12}{m}$, using cross multiplication gives

$$\frac{m}{6} = \frac{12}{m} \rightarrow m^2 = 72 \rightarrow m = \pm\sqrt{72} = \pm\sqrt{36 \times 2} = \pm\sqrt{36} \times \sqrt{2} = \pm6\sqrt{2}$$

49) Choice D is correct

First, find the equation of the line. Two points on the line are $(0, -2)$ and $(2, 0)$. The slope of the line is 1 and the equation of the line is: $y = x - 2$. Only choice D is similar to the equation of the line.

50) Choice D is correct

A. $x^{-2} = \frac{1}{x^2}$ This is true.

B. $(x^2)^3 = x^6$ This is true.

C. $x^6 - 5x^2 = x^2(x^4 - 5)$ This is true.

D. $4x^2 - 16x + 8 = (2x - 4)^2$ This is incorrect: $4x^2 - 16x + 16 = (2x - 4)^2$

Algebra I Practice Tests 2 Explanations

1) Choice C is correct

According to the given graph of the function f, first, the graph f goes 3 units to the left, and the graph of $k(x) = f(x + 3)$ is obtained as follows:

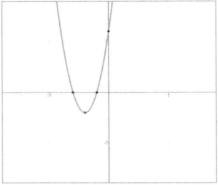

Now, by shifting 2 units to the up, the graph of $g(x) = f(x + 3) + 2$ is obtained.

2) Choice C is correct

$$6x^2 - 4x - 10 = 2(x + 1)(3x - 5)$$

3) Choice A is correct

Use the correlation coefficient formula:

$$r = \frac{\sum(x_i - \bar{x})(y_i - \bar{y})}{\sqrt{\sum(x_i - \bar{x})^2(y_i - \bar{y})^2}}$$

Where $\bar{x}$ and $\bar{y}$ are the means of the values of the x and y variables. Evaluate the mean of the heights, x_i, and the lengths, y_i. Then, the mean of the heights is $\bar{x} = 37.8$ and the lengths is $\bar{y} = 28.9$. According to the following table, we have:

$$r = \frac{\sum(x_i - \bar{x})(y_i - \bar{y})}{\sqrt{\sum(x_i - \bar{x})^2(y_i - \bar{y})^2}} = \frac{725.8}{\sqrt{7355558.84}} \cong 0.27$$

Height, x_i	36	70	16	30	10	87	53	28	9	39
Length, y_i	21	20	32	11	18	45	38	23	42	39
$x_i - \bar{x}$	−1.8	32.2	−21.8	−7.8	−27.8	49.2	15.2	−9.8	−28.8	1.2
$y_i - \bar{y}$	−7.9	−8.9	3.1	−17.9	−10.9	16.1	9.1	−5.9	13.1	10.1

The correlation coefficient is positive. So, it's a weak positive correction.

4) Choice A is correct

Remember that an exponential function has one horizontal asymptote. The horizontal asymptote of the exponential function is the horizontal line (the choices A or B can be the suitable answer) that becomes close to it for large negative or positive x. Clearly, the above exponential function graph gets close to the line M for the large positive x.

5) Choice A is correct

Check the transformation properties of the functions. The graph of function $k(x) = f(x) + (-4)$ shifted up by -4 units. Note that the graph of function $h(x) = f\left(\frac{1}{2}x\right)$, is stretched horizontally relate to $f(x)$, and the graph of $l(x) = f(-x)$, is symmetric to the function $f(x)$ with respect to the x −axis. The combination of these functions produces the function $g(x) = f\left(-\frac{x}{2}\right) - 4$.

A is true. The graph of g is a reflection of the graph of f across the x −axis. B, C, and D are not correct.

6) Choice D is correct

Choice D is the correct answer because $(x^y)^z$ is the same as $x^{y \times z}$.

7) Choice A is correct

Consider the variable part to be $a(a + b)^2$, then this expression has two like terms with coefficients -15 and 23. Then: $-15a(a + b)^2 + 23a(a + b)^2 = 8a(a + b)^2$.

8) Choice C is correct

First, graph the equation $y = -3x$. So, we have:

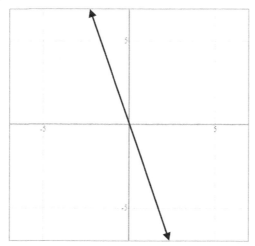

Since the sign of the inequality is greater than $>$, then the corresponding graph has a dashed line. That is, the choice B or C is the possible answer. Now, substitute an arbitrary point on the coordinate plane of one side of the graph in the given inequality like $(1,0)$. So,

$$(1,0) \rightarrow -3(1) = -3 < 0. \text{ It is true.}$$

Choice C is the correct answer.

9) Choice D is correct

Check the correctness of each statement:

A. Plug the point $(-1,2)$ in the function and evaluate: $f(-1) = 4(1.25)^{-1} = 3.2 \neq 2$.

B. Exponential functions in standard form $y = a(b)^x$ have a horizontal asymptote to the equation of $y = 0$.

C. The function $f(x)$ does not intersect the $x-$axis. Because the equation $f(x) = 0$ has no solution.

D. The base of the exponential function $f(x) = 4(1.25)^x$ is greater than 1, so it is increasing.

10) Choice A is correct

Remember that the $y-$intercept is the point where the graph intersects the $y-$axis. Then the first component of the ordered pair of corresponding to the $y-$intercept is zero. One of the choices is A or C. The graph intersects the $y-$axis on the upside of the $y-$axis. So, the second component of the ordered pair is positive. That is, the choice A is the answer.

11) Choice C is correct

A. The given graph cuts the y −axis in one point with the coordinate $(0,1)$, then the y −intercept is 1. Then, this choice is NOT true!

B. To find the domain of the graph of the function, draw the image of the graph on the x −axis.

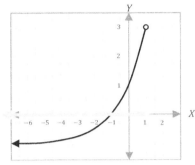

Therefore, the inequality $-\infty < x < 1$ is the solution set of the domain of the part of the graph. It means that the interval $(-\infty, 1)$. This interval is NOT equal to the interval $(-\infty, 1]$.

C. The image of the graph on the y −axis is as follows:

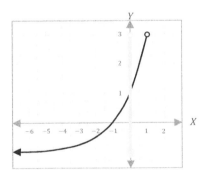

Therefore, the interval $(-1,3)$ is the range of the graph. It's the correct answer.

D. Choice D is NOT true! Because the graph cuts the x −axis in the point $(-1,0)$, then the x −intercept is -1.

12) Choice D is correct

$x^2 = 121 \rightarrow x = 11$ (Positive value)Or $x = -11$ (negative value)

Since x is positive, then: $f(121) = f(11^2) = 3(11) + 4 = 33 + 4 = 37$.

13) Choice D is correct

$2x^2 - 11x + 8 = -3x + 18 \rightarrow 2x^2 - 11x + 3x + 8 - 18 = 0 \rightarrow 2x^2 - 8x - 10 = 0$

$\rightarrow 2(x^2 - 4x - 5) = 0 \rightarrow$ Divide both sides by 2. Then: $x^2 - 4x - 5 = 0$, Find the factors of the quadratic equation. $\rightarrow (x - 5)(x + 1) = 0 \rightarrow x = 5$ or $\quad x = -1$

$a > b$, then: $a = 5$ and $b = -1 \qquad \frac{a}{b} = \frac{5}{-1} = -5$

14) The rate of change is 9

Since the relationship is linear, the rate of change is equal to the slope of the line passing through the table points. Use the slope formula of the line passing through two points (x_1, y_1) and (x_2, y_2) in the form of $m = \frac{y_2 - y_1}{x_2 - x_1}$. Consider arbitrary points like $(0, 72)$ and $(91, 891)$ from the given table. Therefore,

Rate of change $= \frac{891 - 72}{91 - 0} = \frac{819}{91} = 9$.

15) Choice B is correct

We know that the graph $y = f(x) + k$; $k > 0$, is shifted k units up of the graph $y = f(x)$, and if $k < 0$, is shifted k units down. Then, $y = x^2 - 2$ is shifted 2 units down of the graph $y = x^2$.

16) Choice A is correct

Perfect cube formula: $(a + b)^3 = a^3 + 3a^2b + 3ab^2 + b^3$. Then:
$(3x + 2)^3 = (3x)^3 + 3.(3x)^2.2 + 3.(3x).2^2 + 2^3 = 27x^3 + 54x^2 + 36x + 8$

17) Choice C is correct

Plug in the values of x and y of the point $(2, 12)$ in the equation of the quadratic function. Then:

$12 = a(2)^2 + 5(2) + 10 \rightarrow 12 = 4a + 10 + 10 \rightarrow 12 = 4a + 20$

$\rightarrow 4a = 12 - 20 = -8 \rightarrow a = \frac{-8}{4} = -2 \rightarrow a^2 = (-2)^2 = 4$

18) Choice B is correct

Since the vertex of a quadratic function is the highest/lowest point on the graph. So, the vertex of this quadratic function is clearly an ordered pair with coordinates $(-2,5)$. Indicated in the graph below.

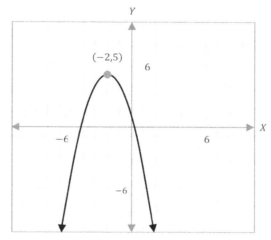

19) Choice A is correct

Use the polynomial identity: $(x - y)^2 = x^2 - 2xy + y^2$ for the part of the equation of function $(2 - 3x)^2$. Then:

$$(2 - 3x)^2 = (2)^2 - 2(2)(3x) + (3x)^2 = 4 - 12x + 9x^2.$$

Substitute the obtained expression in the equation of function and simplify.

$$2(2 - 3x)^2 - 7 = 2(4 - 12x + 9x^2) - 7 = 18x^2 - 24x + 1.$$

Therefore: $f(x) = 18x^2 - 24x + 1.$

20) The zeros of function g is -3

First, write the equation of the line passing through the two points (marked) on the graph. For the two points $(x_1 y_1)$ and $(x_2 y_2)$, use the formula

$$y - y_1 = m(x - x_1)$$

Where the slope is $m = \frac{y_2 - y_1}{x_2 - x_1}$. For two points $(-6, -6)$ and $(1,8)$ the slope is $m = \frac{8 - (-6)}{1 - (-6)} = \frac{14}{7} = 2$. Then:

$$y - 8 = 2(x - 1) \rightarrow y = 2x + 6$$

To find the zero of the function g put $y = 0$ and solve this equation

$$2x + 6 = 0 \rightarrow 2x = -6 \rightarrow x = -3$$

The zero of function g is -3.

21) Choice C is correct

$\begin{cases} \frac{-x}{2} + \frac{y}{4} = 1 \\ \frac{-5y}{6} + 2x = 4 \end{cases}$ $\rightarrow$ Multiply the top equation by 4. Then,

$\begin{cases} -2x + y = 4 \\ \frac{-5y}{6} + 2x = 4 \end{cases}$ $\rightarrow$ Add two equations. $\frac{1}{6}y = 8 \rightarrow y = 48$, plug in the value of y into the first

equation $x = 22$

22) Choice D is correct

The description $8 + 2x$ is 16 more than 20 can be written as the equation $8 + 2x = 16 + 20$, which is equivalent to $8 + 2x = 36$. Subtracting 8 from each side of $8 + 2x = 36$ gives $2x = 28$. Since $6x$ is 3 times $2x$, multiplying both sides of $2x = 28$ by 3 gives $6x = 84$.

23) Choice B is correct

For each option, choose a point in the solution part and check it on both inequalities.

$y \leq x + 4, 2x + y \leq -4$

A. Let's choose this point $(0, 5)$ $5 \leq 0 + 4$, That's not true.

B. Point $(-4, -4)$ is in the solution section. Let's check the point in both inequalities.

$-4 \leq -4 + 4$, It works

$2(-4) + (-4) \leq -4 \Rightarrow -12 \leq -4$, it works (this point works in both inequalities)

C. Let's choose this point $(0, 0)$ $0 \leq 0 + 4$, It works, $2(0) + (0) \leq -4$, That's not true!

D. Let's choose this point $(-5, 0)$, $0 \leq -5 + 4$, That's not true!

Only choice B represents both inequalities.

24) Choice D is correct

First, use this polynomial identity: $(x + y)(x - y) = x^2 - y^2$. Then:

$$4x^2 - 81 = (2x + 9)(2x - 9)$$

By factoring the value of 2 from each parenthesis as $(2x + 9) = 2(x + 4.5)$ and $(2x - 9) = 2(x - 4.5)$, we have:

$$4x^2 - 81 = 4(x + 4.5)(x - 4.5)$$

25) Choice B is correct

Plug in each pair of numbers in the equation:

    A. $(2, 1)$: $2(2) + 4(1) = 8$ This is NOT true.

    B. $(-1, 2)$: $2(-1) + 4(2) = 6$ This is true.

    C. $(-2, 2)$: $2(-2) + 4(2) = 4$ This is NOT true.

    D. $(2, 2)$: $2(2) + 4(2) = 12$ This is NOT true.

26) Choice B is correct

Use the FOIL (First-Out-In-Last) method to simplify the expression:
$(3x - 5)^2 = (3x - 5)(3x - 5) = 9x^2 - 15x - 15x + 25 = 9x^2 - 30x + 25$

27) The value of b is 42

Note that two variables are directly proportional whenever one amount increases, another amount increases at the same rate. First, evaluate the rate of b to a. So,

$$b = ra \rightarrow r = \frac{b}{a} \rightarrow r = \frac{7}{2.5} = 2.8$$

Now, put the rate of b to a equal to $r = 2.8$. Then, $b = 2.8a \rightarrow 2.8 \times 15 = 42$.

28) Choice A is correct

Consider the moment when the kingfisher enters the pond at zero time and the surface of the water depth is zero. In this case, one of the roots of the quadratic model is at zero seconds. Check which functions have zero roots $(t = 0)$.

    A. $j(0) = 0.4(0)^2 - 2.88(0) = 0$
    B. $j(0) = 0.4(0)^2 - 2.88(0) + 2 = 2 \neq 0$
    C. $j(0) = 0.075(0)^2 - 1.11(0) = 0$
    D. $j(0) = 0.075(0)^2 - 1.11(0) + 18.7 = 18.7 \neq 0$

So, the choice of A or C models is possible. Now, put some points on the left column of the table in the remaining models and compare the output values of each equation with the values of the right column of the table. First, check the point $x = 1$. Then,

A. $j(1) = 0.4(1)^2 - 2.88(1) = -2.48$
C. $j(1) = 0.075(1)^2 - 1.11(1) = -1.035$

The choice A is closer to the data in the right column of the table, so it is the best model to describe the given data.

29) Choice C is correct

Identify and factor in common factors:

$$16x^2 + 24 = 8 \times (2x^2) + 8 \times 3$$
$$= 8(2x^2 + 3)$$

30) Choice D is correct

Based on the table provided: $g(-2) = g(x = -2) = 3 \rightarrow g(3) = g(x = 3) = -2$

$$3g(-2) - 2g(3) = 3(3) - 2(-2) = 9 + 4 = 13.$$

31) Choice C is correct

The corresponding inequality to all possible combinations for purchase f has a sign less than or equal, so the graph for this model contains the line (One of the choices A or C). Now, by selecting and substituting a point from one side of the inequality graph, check whether the assumed point in the inequality is valid.

For example, we evaluate the marked point in the figure below.

Then,

$$(100,120) \to 3(100) + 5(120) = 300 + 600 = 900 \nleq 630$$

Because the marked point does not apply to t (100,120) ality, so this side of the line is not part of the answer set. Therefore, choice C is the correct answer.

32) Choice D is correct
Here we can substitute 8 for x in the equation. Thus, $y - 3 = 2(8 + 5)$, $\quad y - 3 = 26$.

Adding 3 to both sides of the equation: $y = 26 + 3$, $y = 29$.

33) Choice A is correct
$\sqrt{x} = 4 \to x = 16$, then; $\sqrt{x} - 7 = \sqrt{16} - 7 = 4 - 7 = -3$ and $\sqrt{x - 7} = \sqrt{16 - 7} = \sqrt{9} = 3$

Then: $\left(\sqrt{x - 7}\right) + \left(\sqrt{x} - 7\right) = 3 + (-3) = 0$

34) The value of k is -2
Notice that for the function $g(x)$, if $k > 0$ then $f(x) = g(x) + k$ shifted to the up by $|k|$ units, and if $k < 0$ the function $f(x) = g(x) + k$ shifted to the down by $|k|$ units. The graph of the function $g(x) = x^2$ is as follow:

If $g(x)$ is shifted down by 2 units, the graph of $f(x)$ is obtained. Therefore, the value of k is -2 and the corresponding equation is $f(x) = g(x) - 2 \to f(x) = x^2 - 2$.

35) Choice D is correct
Plug in the value of each choice in the inequality.

A. 3	$(3 - 2)^2 + 1 > 3(3) - 1 \to 2 > 8$	This is Not true.
B. 4	$(4 - 2)^2 + 1 > 3(4) - 1 \to 5 > 11$	This is Not true.
C. 6	$(6 - 2)^2 + 1 > 3(6) - 1 \to 17 > 17$	This is Not true.
D. 8	$(8 - 2)^2 + 1 > 3(8) - 1 \to 37 > 23$	This is true.

36) Choice C is correct
To solve use the FOIL method:

$$(3x - y)(2x + 2y) = 6x^2 + 6xy - 2xy - 2y^2 = 6x^2 + 4xy - 2y^2.$$

37) Choice A is correct

$81 = 3^{2x}$. Convert to base 3: $81 = 3^{2x} \rightarrow 3^4 = 3^{2x}$. If $a^{f(x)} = b^{g(x)}$, then $f(x) = g(x)$

Therefore: $4 = 2x \rightarrow x = \frac{4}{2} \rightarrow x = 2$

38) Choice B is correct

By checking the information in the table, we realize when the variable x increases, the values of $r(x)$ increase (The function is increasing). An exponential function is increasing if the base is greater than 1 (The choice C is certainly not the answer to the question). Now, put some values from the left column of the table into the remaining choices and check which values of each choice are closest to the values in the right column of the table. We start from point $x = 1$.

    A. $x = 1 \rightarrow r(1) = 1.12(246.7)^1 \cong 276$
    B. $x = 1 \rightarrow r(1) = 246.7(1.12)^1 \cong 276$
    D. $x = 1 \rightarrow r(1) = 0.83(1,423.9)^1 \cong 1182$. This is not a possible answer.

For the choice A and B, we continue with $x = 2$:

    A. $x = 2 \rightarrow r(2) = 1.12(246.7)^2 \cong 68164$
    B. $x = 2 \rightarrow r(2) = 246.7(1.12)^2 \cong 309$

Therefore, the function B is the best model.

39) Choice B is correct

The relationship is linear, then the rate of change is equal to the slope of the graph. Select two points (x_1, y_1) and (x_2, y_1) on the graph line passing through the two points using the formula:

$$m = \frac{y_2 - y_1}{x_2 - x_1}$$

For the points $(500,1)$ and $(700,-2)$, we have:

$$m = \frac{-2 - 1}{700 - 500} = -\frac{3}{200}$$

40) Choice C is correct

If you consider this linear relationship as a function of the number of players to find the number of arrows of players. The number of players is equivalent to the acceptable inputs of the function. In actuality, the domain is a part of the set $\{0,1,2,3,\cdots\}$. In addition, we know that the coach will use no more than 9 players on the school's team,
The number of players ≤ 9.
Therefore, these two sets of intersection is the suitable domain of this relationship.
Domain $= \{0,1,2,3,4,5,6,7,8,9\}$.

41) Choice D is correct

Multiplying each side of $-3x - y = 6$ by 2 gives $-6x - 2y = 12$. Adding each side of $-6x - 2y = 12$ to the corresponding side of $6x + 4y = 10$ gives $2y = 22$ or $y = 11$. Finally, substituting 11 for y in $6x + 4y = 10$ gives $6x + 4(11) = 10$ or $x = -\frac{17}{3}$.

42) The solution is $n = 2$

Simplify and solve for n in the equation.

$$2(n - 1) = 3(n + 2) - 10 \rightarrow 2n - 2 = 3n + 6 - 10 \rightarrow 2n - 2 = 3n - 4$$

Subtract $2n$ from both sides: $-2 = n - 4$, Add 4 to both sides: $n = 2$.

43) Choice D is correct

The problem asks for the sum of the roots of the quadratic equation $2n^2 + 16n + 24 = 0$. Dividing each side of the equation by 2 gives $n^2 + 8n + 12 = 0$. If the roots of $n^2 + 8n + 12 = 0$ are n_1 and n_2, then the equation can be factored as $n^2 + 8n + 12 = (n - n_1)(n - n_2) = 0$. Looking at the coefficient of n on each side of $n^2 + 8n + 12 = (n + 6)(n + 2)$ gives $n = -6$ or $n = -2$,   then, $-6 + (-2) = -8$

44) Choice C is correct

In the system of inequalities, the sign of one of the inequalities is greater and the sign of the other is less than or equal to. So, the corresponding graph consists of one line and one dashed line (B cannot be the correct choice).

Substitute some points of each graph that are specific to the same graph in the system of inequalities and check if it applies to the system of inequalities. For example, we check the origin (0,0) of the coordinates which include the answer set of choices A and C and does not include the answer set of choice D.

$$(0,0) \rightarrow \begin{array}{l} 2(0) + (0) = 0 > -2 \\ (0) + (0) = 0 \leq 1 \end{array}.$$

Then, the graph D is not the correct answer. In this step, we check the point with coordinate $(-3,3)$ of graph A.

$$(-3,3) \rightarrow \begin{array}{l} 2(-3) + (3) = -6 + 3 = -3 \not> -2 \\ (-3) + (3) = 0 \leq 1 \end{array}.$$

The only remaining choice is C.

45) Choice C is correct

To match the function to its corresponding graph, you will see that the function is going down Because the base value of the exponential equation is less than 1. Now, evaluate the functions at a few inputs to find some points on the graph. Choose points such as -1 and 0 to plug into the equation. Therefore, substitute 0 into $y = 2\left(\frac{2}{3}\right)^x$. So, $y = 2\left(\frac{2}{3}\right)^0 = 2(1) = 2$. In the same way, plug in -1, then: $y = 2\left(\frac{2}{3}\right)^{-1} = 2\left(\frac{3}{2}\right) = 3$. The only decay graph that passes through ordered pairs $(0,2)$ and $(-1,3)$ is choice C.

46) Choice B is correct

For this purpose, we need to find the first term a_1 and the common difference d of the arithmetic sequence. We have $a_4 = 15$ and $a_9 = 35$. Write the 4th and 9th terms as an explicit formula of an arithmetic sequence. Use the arithmetic sequence formula: $a_n = a_1 + d(n-1)$. So, $a_4 = a_1 + d(4-1) \rightarrow a_1 + 3d = 15$ and $a_9 = a_1 + d(9-1) \rightarrow a_1 + 8d = 35$. Solve the following equation system:

$$\begin{cases} a_1 + 3d = 15 \\ a_1 + 8d = 35 \end{cases}$$

By subtracting the second equation from the first equation, we have $(a_1 + 8d) - (a_1 + 3d) = 35 - 15$. Simplify, $a_1 + 8d - a_1 - 3d = 35 - 15 \rightarrow 5d = 20 \rightarrow d = 4$. Now, substitute $d = 4$ in the first equation: $a_1 + 3d = 15 \rightarrow a_1 + 3 \times 4 = 15 \rightarrow a_1 = 3$. Then, use this formula: $S_n = \frac{n}{2}(a_1 + a_n)$.

$$S_n = \frac{n}{2}(a_1 + a_n) \rightarrow S_n = \frac{n}{2}\left(a_1 + a_1 + d(n-1)\right) \rightarrow S_n = \frac{n}{2}\left(2a_1 + d(n-1)\right)$$

Finally, $S_{10} = \frac{10}{2}(2(3) + 4(10-1)) \rightarrow S_{10} = 5(6 + 36) \rightarrow S_{10} = 210$.

47) Choice A is correct

Solve for x: $2x - 5y = 10 \rightarrow x - \frac{5}{2}y = 5 \rightarrow x = \frac{5}{2}y + 5$

48) Choice A is correct

Simplify the numerator: $\frac{x + (5x)^2 + (3x)^3}{x} = \frac{x + 5^2x^2 + 3^3x^3}{x} = \frac{x + 25x^2 + 27x^3}{x}$

Pull an x out of each term in the numerator. $\frac{x(1 + 25x + 27x^2)}{x}$

The x in the numerator and the x in the denominator cancel:

$1 + 25x + 27x^2 = 27x^2 + 25x + 1$

49) Choice B is correct

The possible y values are between -4 and 3. Range: $-4 \leq y \leq 3$.

50) Choice D is correct

The initial deposit earns 2 percent interest compounded annually. Thus, at the end of year 1, the new value of the account is the initial deposit of $\$150$ plus 2 percent of the initial deposit:

$$\$150 + \frac{2}{100}(\$150) = \$150(1.02).$$

Since the interest is compounded annually, the value at the end of each succeeding year is the sum of the previous year's value plus 2 percent of the previous year's value. This is equivalent to multiplying the previous year's value by 1.02. Thus, after 2 years, the value will be $\$150(1.02)(1.02) = \$(150)(1.02)^2$; and after 3 years, the value will be $(150)(1.02)^3$; and after n years, the value will be $(150)(1.02)^n$. Therefore, in the formula for the value of Sara's account after n years $(150)(x)^n$, the value of x is 1.02.

Build Your Math Skills: Our Top Book Picks!

Download eBooks (in PDF format) Instantly!

Our Most Popular Books!

Download at

Download at

Download at

Download at

Download at

Download at

Our Most Popular Books!

Download at

Download

Download at

Download

Download at

Download

Download at

Download

Receive the PDF version of this book or get another FREE book!

Thank you for using our Book!

Do you LOVE this book?

Then, you can get the PDF version of this book or another book absolutely FREE!

Please email us at:

info@EffortlessMath.com

for details.

Author's Final Note

Congratulations on completing "High School Algebra I"! Your dedication and determination have brought you to the end, and I commend you for your effort.

With numerous study materials at your fingertips, it speaks volumes that you chose this guide to accompany you on your Algebra I journey. I truly appreciate your trust in this book as your academic ally.

Compiling this guide was an endeavor born out of my passion for making Algebra I accessible and comprehensible for all. Over the years, I've distilled my teaching experiences, student feedback, and extensive research into this comprehensive guide, all to provide you with the best possible resource for your studies.

For any questions, uncertainties, or feedback, please don't hesitate to reach out at reza@effortlessmath.com. Your insights are invaluable in refining future editions of this book. And, in the tradition of mathematics, should you identify any discrepancies or areas of improvement, please alert me so that they can be rectified promptly.

If this book has played a part in bolstering your understanding of Algebra I and contributed positively to your academic pursuits, I'd be overjoyed to hear from you. Kindly consider sharing your experiences by leaving a review on the book's Amazon page.

I closely monitor each review, seeking ways to elevate the learning experience for every reader. By leaving a review, you not only assist me but countless other Algebra students who will benefit from your insights.

Wishing you all the success in your future mathematical endeavors and beyond!

With gratitude,

Reza Nazari

Math teacher and author

Made in the USA
Middletown, DE
26 April 2025